Peace Be With You

Christ-Centered Bullying Solution

TEACHER'S MANUAL

by
Frank A. DiLallo
Thom Powers

Alliance for Catholic Education Press
at The University of Notre Dame

Notre Dame, Indiana

Alliance for Catholic Education Press
University of Notre Dame
107 Carole Sandner Hall
Notre Dame IN 46556
http://acepress.nd.edu

ISBN: 978-1-935788-02-7

Interior layout: Julie Wernick Dallavis
Interior images: Shelley Kornatz

Visit http://www.peace2usolutions.com for information on speaking, training, and workshops by Frank A. DiLallo.

This book was printed on acid-free paper.

Printed in the United States of America.

Table of Contents

Acknowledgments *v*
Foreword *vii*

Introduction 1
Scope of the Problem 5
What is Bullying? 6
Bullying as Group Dynamic 10
Introducing the Cast of Characters 11
Spiritual Perspective on Bullying 16
What Works in Bullying Prevention? 19
Bullying Prevention Programs 21

PHASE I: Christ is Our Model for Leadership
Phase I Summary 26
Ecumenical Impact and Spiritual Perspective 27
Activity One: Who Me? A Leader? 29
Christ Is Our Model for Leadership 30
Leader Words 33
Spiritual Perspective 33
Facilitator Script 35
Activity Two: Choose Your Flavor! 36
Eliminating Put Downs 37
Spiritual Perspective 39
Choose Your Flavor 39
Facilitator Script 41
Activity Three: Bully to Leader Role Plays 44
Role Play Scenario Guidelines 45
Role Play 1: What Goes Around Comes Around 46
Positive Behavioral Possibilities 48
Spiritual Perspective 49
Facilitator Script 50
Role Play 2: Odd Girl Out 55
Positive Behavioral Possibilities 56
Spiritual Perspective 56
Facilitator Script 57
Accountability 60
Activity Four: Two Stories 62
Spiritual Perspective 64
"Howard Gray" 65
"The Code of Silence" 66
Facilitator Script 67
Four Agreements 68
Teacher and Counselor Reflection 69

PHASE II: Dignity for All
Phase II Summary 72
Ecumenical Impact and Spiritual Perspective 73
Dignity for All 76
Emotional and Social Intelligence 78
Effective Interpersonal Communication Skill Development 80
Eight Pitfalls to Peer Mediation 81
Why a Circle? 81
Phase II Origins 82
Case Study: Circle of Boys 83
Phase II Advantages 85
Activity One: Phase I Review 86
Phase I Review 87
Facilitator Script 91
Activity Two: Positive Leader Words 94
Suggestions for Positive Leader Words and Leader Folder 95
Facilitator Script 96

Activity Three: Safety Check   97
     What Does It Mean to Be Safe   98
     Types of Safety   98
     Safety Diagram   100
     Safety Check Group Process   101
     Facilitator Script   103
Activity Four: Energizers/Ice Breakers   106
     Facilitator Script   108
Activity Five: Clear Talk   111
     Spiritual Perspective   118
     Clear Talk Scenarios   119
     CLEAR Listening   121
     Spiritual Perspective   122
     Clear Talk Facilitation Considerations   123
     Facilitator Script   130
Phase II Follow Up   138
Teacher and Counselor Reflection   139

PHASE III: Pure of Heart

Phase III Summary   142
     Ecumenical Impact and Spiritual Perspective   143
     Brief Background   146
Activity One: Life in Fast Forward   148
     What Is "Life in Fast Forward?"   149
     Technology and Cyberbullying   151
     Facilitator Script   152
Activity Two: Understanding Stress   153
     Definition and Implications of Stress   154
     Facilitator Script   159
     Stress Less Theatre Production   161
Activity Three: "The Gift"   162
     Cognitive Learning   163
     Negative Social Impact on Cognitive Learning   164
     Facilitator Script   166
Activity Four: Visual Exercises   167
     Facilitator Script   168
Activity Five: Relaxation Tips   171
     Relaxation Tip #1 - Stress Check   172
     Relaxation Tip #2 - Breath Check   174
     Relaxation Tip #3 - Tension Check   175
     Relaxation Tip #4 - Balance Check   176
     Facilitator Scripts   177
Activity Six: Short Meditation   185
     Facilitator Script   186
Activity Seven: Post-Meditation Stress Check   187
     Facilitator Script   188
Activity Eight: PeaceScape   189
     What Is a PeaceScape?   190
     Facilitator Script   191
Activity Nine: Put-Down Messages and Shift Formula   192
     Facilitator Script   193
Activity Ten: Crafting a Positive Affirmation   195
     Definition of Affirmations   196
     Guidelines for Crafting and Examples of Positive Affirmations   198
     Facilitator Script   200
Activity Eleven: Strength Bombardment & Buddy Up!   201
     Facilitator Script   202
Activity Twelve: Long Meditation   204
     Progressive Relaxation Exercises   205
     Facilitator Script   207
Teacher and Counselor Reflection   208

Appendix A: Peace2U Stress Less Series Audio CD Script   209
Appendix B: Internet Resources   221
Appendix C: Bibliography   229
About the Authors   241

Acknowledgments

Thanks to the many people who have helped me become who I am today and for your unwavering support of this work. To my wife Michelle, for her loving support and encouragement throughout the many long and grueling hours of research and writing. To Mom and Dad, for always being there. To my children Josh, Andrew, David, and Joy, for teaching me how to be a father, man, and human being. To my co-author Thom Powers and his loving wife Dianne, for believing in this work, walking together, and providing profound written spiritual wisdom making this book truly a Christian contribution to the field of bullying prevention. To my Uncle Gary and Aunt Susan, for all the great feedback and support. To Dr. Steve Cady, for his genius, inspiration, and generous help with the initial structural concepts of this book. To Fran Kick, for his initial review and feedback that opened the flood gates. To Gayle Burrer, for her interest and review of the model from her vast teaching experience and her assistance in setting up numerous trainings through the Social Work Department at Lourdes College. To friend and mentor Ric Stuecker, for "Reviving the Wonder" in me. To Tim Gallagher, for his clarity and wisdom. To Tim Story, for his friendship and "musical harmony" in my work and life. To Ari Sherwin, for his enthusiasm and guidance. To Jeff Zawodny, for his creativity and visual expertise. To Dr. Patti Agatston, for her generous time as a cyberbullying expert in critiquing the original manuscript. To Rose Anne Conrad and Ann Sardeson, for significant edits and editorial comments. To Joni Coci and Joette Rozanski, for the many hours spent on formatting and layout. To Jack Altenburger, for his 41 years in Catholic education, his trust and blessing in my ministry and confidence in this work as an important contribution to our diocese means more than he will ever know. To the CYSS Staff, for their support over the years and our collegial spirit. I continue to learn much from all of you. Thank you to Superintendent of Toledo Diocesan Catholic Schools, Mr. Chris Knight, for his support and recognition. To Bishop Leonard Blair and Fr. Mike Billian, for their trust and confidence in carrying out a bullying prevention ministry in our diocese. To the entire Diocese of Toledo and all diocesan principals, teachers, parents, and students, for trusting me in your schools and to be a part of your lives. This work could not have evolved without all of you. To Fr. Ron Nuzzi, Dr. Jim Frabutt, and Julie Dallavis with ACE Press at the University of Notre Dame for their invaluable feedback and the opportunity to publish this book. In memory of the beloved Sr. Miriam Ebel, for being such an inspiration and my "writing angel" from beginning to end.

-Frank A. DiLallo

I am filled with deep gratitude. The opportunity to take a friendship with Frank DiLallo and bring it to a new collaborative dimension has been truly a gift. Weaving our different academic traditions together and support for one another has brought out the best in each of us. To my wife Dianne, for her support, practical editing, and tremendous enduring patience, I am lovingly indebted. Likewise, my gratitude extends to our two married daughters, Patrice Powers-Barker and Krista Marie Athey, and their husbands, Jim and Richard, for encouragement, interest, and remarkable dialogues around the topic of bullying. May this work contribute to making lives more peaceful, supportive, and loving. To our three grandchildren, Taylor, Jordan, and Jackson, and all children: Peace be with you.

-Thom Powers

*On the evening of that first day of the week, when the doors were locked, where the disciples were, for fear of the Jews, Jesus came and stood in their midst and said to them, **"Peace be with you."***

*When he had said this, he showed them his hands and his side. The disciples rejoiced when they saw the Lord. Jesus said to them again, **"Peace be with you...."***

Thomas, called Didymus, one of the Twelve, was not with them when Jesus came. So the other disciples said to him, "We have seen the Lord."

But he said to them, "Unless I see the marks of the nails in his hands and put my finger into the nailmarks and put my hand into his side, I will not believe."

*Now a week later his disciples were again inside and Thomas was with them. Jesus came, although the doors were locked, and stood in their midst and said, **"Peace be with you."***

JOHN 20:19-26

Foreword

I remember the day all too well: Tuesday April 20, 1999. News broke out about the shootings at Columbine High School in Littleton, Colorado. Following the tragic news, I went into a dazed depression that lasted several months. What most likely sustained my state was the shame about feeling sad and overwhelmed by what happened, even though I was not present. I was ensnared in a cobweb of dark and frightening images gripped by what I could only imagine happened that day. I suffered from what could be described as "survivor guilt." What brought this alarming report so close to home were my experiences working in a high school. One year prior to the shootings, I closed an eight-year chapter as pastoral counselor for Central Catholic High School in Toledo, Ohio. During my tenure, I felt a meaningful connection with administrators, teachers, counselors, students, and parents in the school community. Trying to imagine such a horrific aftermath at our school and to people I grew to love and serve was unfathomable.

Many lessons were learned from this tragic incident, which undoubtedly left an indelible mark on our country and possibly the world. Columbine is a frightening and definable moment in our nation's history, forever altering any notion that schools are the immutable safe haven. The irreversible spectrum of wounds inflicted on students, faculty, staff, administrators, parents, and first responders from this carnage are undeniable; the enormity of its rippling effects are inconceivable. In its wake, present-day shock waves of bullying, cyberbullying, and bullicide incidents continue to pummel our American schools and communities. The good news is that since 1999, there has been an exponential increase in awareness on the topic of bullying and an evolving list of best practices on prevention and intervention strategies.

Lessons were also learned from my depression. One lesson that stands out the most is how we are truly "many parts, but all one body." Where we all fall asleep at the switch is when we deny our spiritual connectedness—the mystical body of Christ we all share—our humanness and our frailty. Why does it seem to take tragedies like Columbine or the magnitude of a 9/11 event to "awake from the slumber?" What does it take to find a loving place in our hearts to naturally be compassionate with our neighbor without it having to manifest from a crisis? To this day, my heart breaks for Littleton, Colorado, and all subsequent tragedies in which survivors carry wounds traced to bullying behaviors.

Another important lesson learned: depression can be cured by taking steps, even if they are only baby steps, toward a constructive action. After a period of prayerful reflection, my spiritual awakening was to create an audio CD on the topic of stress management and meditation, with the notion that there must be a correlation between stress and maladaptive behaviors, such as bullying. The Peace Project audio CD was released two months prior to 9/11. From this small contribution, I was guided by the Spirit to develop what you will discover in the contents of this manual.

Bullying hits close to home for all of us and we must do everything in our power to stop it. To do so, we must remain vigilant, compassionate, and hopeful. This book will guide you in taking the necessary action steps to stop bullying behaviors in your school, by creating and sustaining a safe and Christ-filled climate. With committed effort, prayerful dedication, and compassionate intention, the prescribed approach in this manual offers hope. May the Peace of Christ bless your school community as you embark on this important journey to compassionately address bullying, while creating a vibrant and thriving Christ-centered school.

Frank A. DiLallo
June 2010

Introduction

The *Peace Be with You* Teacher Manual and Student Workbook are specifically designed to be used in Christian schools as an integral complement to existing student formation. Program emphasis is on three essential themes that sequentially build critical life skills:

PHASE I: Christ is Our Model for Leadership (Social Responsibility)

PHASE II: Dignity for All (Interpersonal Skills)

PHASE III: Pure of Heart (Intrapersonal Skills)

There are countless private Christian schools around the world, including denominations such as Anglican, Catholic, Episcopal, and Lutheran. All Christian schools share a common thread of being uniquely Christ-centered. That is the good news. The bad news is that an unfortunate commonality also exists: none are immune to bullying. All students, whether enrolled in Christian or public schools, are subject to the same environmental and cultural conditions.

For the most part, all youth enjoy the same fast food restaurants, watch the same movies, indulge in the same video games, face the gamut of social peer pressures, are impacted by the exact same global concerns, deal with the same kaleidoscope of family issues, and have similar temptations. We are not going to change youth or the popular trends of the season. As educators in Christian schools, however, we are in a privileged position to counterbalance misguided behaviors with the strength of the Christian family. As the United States Conference of Catholic Bishops (USCCB) states:

> The Christian family is called to be a community of faith, hope and love in an environment of prayer. Aided by a number of other virtues, such as prudence, justice, fortitude, and temperance, the family that practices them begins to actualize its spiritual calling as a domestic church. When a family becomes a school of virtue and a community of love, it is an image of the loving communion of the Father, Son and Holy Spirit. It is then an icon of the Trinity. (2006, p. 377)

The Christian family community as an icon of the Trinity is the foundational model represented in this contextual framework. Jesus making a second appearance to include Thomas (John 20:24-26) is of major significance to this Trinitarian approach to bullying:

> At the center of the Gospel message is God's desire to share the communion of Trinitarian life with us. Jesus came to invite everyone to participate in the loving communion that Father, Son, and Holy Spirit have with each other. All of creation is meant to show us the Trinity's plan of love for us. Everything Jesus did pointed to this goal. (USCCB, 2006, p. 119)

As of this publication, no other Scripture-based initiative exists offering prescriptive anti-bullying guidance primarily to Christian schools. How Christian schools respond to bullying and disrespect is a defining ingredient setting them apart from the secular world. By staying alert and compassionately infusing Christ-centered prevention, intervention, and support strategies in student formation, Christian schools can transform the bullying epidemic. This Christ-centered bullying prevention approach is enhanced with Scripture, morality, theology, and spirituality, rooted in doctrinal statements and teachings.

Mission

We are called by Christ to follow His teachings of social justice, dignity for all, love for our neighbor, and purity of heart.

Elements of a Christ-Centered School

- Deeply rooted in the belief and teachings of Jesus Christ
- Committed to holistic efforts toward being a deeply reverent community
- Actively promotes dignity for all
- Leadership clearly occurs as influence, not as a power-over
- Honest, open, and transactional communication
- A high level of support is visible among peers
- Performance expectations are high for self and others
- School norms support academic excellence and maximize students' strengths
- Student conflicts are dealt with constructively and peacefully
- Student discipline is based on teachable moments and meaningful growth opportunities

Target Audience

Grades 4-8

How to Use This Book

The *Peace Be with You* Teacher Manual clearly outlines all three program phases with a purpose, learning objectives, and detailed lessons, including a facilitator script. At the end of each phase, you are encouraged to use the teacher reflections provided as a source of spiritual nourishment.

Read the entire manual in order to familiarize yourself with the program prior to implementation. During actual implementation of the program follow the phases in the order given and as close to the prescribed script as possible. Use the additional information and other resources provided to augment your understanding and use of the text.

The corresponding Student Workbook is a complement to this manual and is essential for the following reasons:

- Effectively helps your students integrate significant concepts and principles.
- Encourages students to become actively engaged in the process.
- References student worksheets that can be used as part of the primary lesson or as homework assignments.
- Expands the process beyond the classroom walls making it more than just a classroom curriculum.

Program Time Allotment

This program can be implemented at any time; however, the following schedule is considered optimal:

PHASE I

Lays the necessary groundwork establishing a common language important for program continuity and sustainability. Can be completed in 1-2 class periods and is best implemented in early fall.

- Manual: 4 guided classroom activities
- Workbook: 4 journal entries, 1 Leader Folder Activity and 19 student worksheets

PHASE II

Immerses teachers, school counselors, and students in a meaningful experiential learning session on community, as well as reconciliation and forgiveness. Teachers and school counselors are encouraged to use Phase II tools during community building time or during established classroom meetings throughout the school year. Successful integration is optimized when the tools are practiced beyond the initial Phase II experience. Best completed in a two-hour block of instruction time and implemented one week to no more than one month following Phase I completion.

- Manual: 5 guided classroom activities
- Workbook: 2 journal entries and 8 student worksheets.

PHASE III

Includes prayerful meditation tools to actively deepen students' relationship with Christ. Provides helpful prescriptive tips on how to slow down, reduce stress, and find a peaceful place inside.

- Manual: 12 guided classroom activities.
- Workbook: 3 journal entries and 20 student worksheets.

Staff Involvement

A school administrator along with the classroom teacher may decide to have an alternative person, such as the school counselor, facilitate the program. Teachers are strongly encouraged to be fully present during all activities for each phase, whether or not they are facilitating. Doing so affirmatively models the spirit of the program and demonstrates interest in the process. It is highly recommended that Grade 4-8 teachers, a school counselor, school nurse, school administrator, parent, and knowledgeable community member form a core team that meets regularly to support each other and the implementation of the program.

Teaching Style

In the Gospel of Luke, we read the story of the daughter of Jairus raised to life. In this Scripture passage, we find the temptation toward an incessant or desperate need to get to the desired outcome, rushing to get to the miracle. When we do this we will miss critically important aspects of the learning process. In this scripture Jesus models the steps to letting go and trusting God's presence in our lives:

> And a man named Jairus, an official of the synagogue, came forward. He fell at the feet of Jesus and begged him to come to his house, because he had an only daughter, about twelve years old, and she was dying. (Luke 8:41-42)

When the father received word that his daughter had died, he was told, "Do not trouble the teacher any longer." Jesus was so attuned to the moment for this father, He responded with comfort by saying: "Do not be afraid; just have faith and she will be saved" (Luke 8:49-50). Jesus could have ordered the man to return home, because He already knew the child would live. Instead, Jesus was present to the distraught father and accompanied him home.

At this point, Jesus allowed no one to go into the house with him "except Peter and John and James, and the child's father and mother" (Luke 8:51). Again, in the moment, Jesus was ultra sensitive to a twelve-year-old girl. Imagine how self conscious and embarrassed she would have been had she awoken to the stares of a household filled with adults. The Scripture continues: "All were weeping and mourning for her, when he said, 'Do not weep any longer, for she is not dead, but sleeping.' And they ridiculed him, because they knew that she was dead" (Luke 8:52).

From our human experience, how often has a parent been scared to death for a child's welfare and at the precise moment, realizing the child was safe, unleashed a barrage of questions? "Where were you? How could you? Why did you?" The parent's emotions of fear, love, and helplessness explode upon the child. Jesus was so aware of this, that he deflected the tension and had the parents laugh at him. The most sensitive piece was Jesus saying "she should be given something to eat" (Luke 8:55) after raising the girl from the dead. Nourishing the body, mind, and spirit is a sacred act for the living.

The lesson of this Scripture is first to be present and sensitive to the reality. We are called to be present to the activities in the classroom and school. Permit students to use their words and phraseologies as truths that need to be spoken. Students' truths are clues that will assist you in their spiritual formation. After sharing a common human experience about leadership, bullying, meditation, and just being a student, only then can we create the sacred. Timing is everything in introducing the sacred. First, honor the human, and then move to the sacred. Taking this approach throughout this text will make this program a rich and meaningful experience for students and for you as facilitator as well.

Importance of Prayer

Being a Christ-centered program, prayer is highly recommended to open each session. A spontaneous or recited prayer is appropriate. Consider concluding the session with a closing prayer or blessing, reminding students to exit the process with peace in mind.

Program Sustainability

When successfully infused and integrated into the school fabric, the *Peace Be with You* program will enhance the Christ-centered school climate and strengthen existing efforts in student formation.

Key elements for program sustainability include:

- Students, teachers, and support staff are present and engaged during the entire program.
- Students are treated as capable leaders in creating a Christ-centered school.
- Students are given an opportunity to safely practice interpersonal communication skills.
- Students are encouraged and supported in intrapersonal skill development.
- Support among students is encouraged, accepted, and expected at all times.
- Dignity for all persons is a constant throughout the program and beyond.
- Teachers and support staff take an active part in generating support for a positive peer norm.
- Fairness and equality are demonstrated at all times.
- Students are not left alone to work through bullying behaviors.

- Teachers and support staff take reports of bullying seriously and are responsive to bullying behaviors.
- Students feel safe reporting bullying behavior and are encouraged to do so.
- Teachers and support staff actively promote the skills inside and outside the classroom.
- Teachers and support staff consistently utilize the activities in each phase.
- Teachers make time for classroom meetings when students request to do Clear Talk with each other.
- Teachers and support staff utilize the Student Workbook in each phase of the program.
- Formative and corrective measures are consistent and meaningful around bullying and other disrespectful behaviors.
- Parents understand and are willing to implement the concepts and principles at home.

Materials Needed

- One Student Workbook for each student in the class
- One wooden stick (similar to a walking stick) approximately 4-5 feet long and 2-3 inches in diameter
- One folder per student to use as a leader folder
- One hula hoop
- Watch with a second hand or a stop watch
- Flip Chart and markers, blackboard, marker board, or Smart Board
- Peace2U Stress Less Series © one-time digital audio download (included) or audio CD (not included)
- Gentle background music (not included)
- CD player

Scope of the Problem

Bullying is one of the most pervasive and challenging problems facing American schools. Reports of students being bullies or victims vary anywhere from 15% to 30% (Rahal, 2010). In elementary schools worldwide, the prevalence of being bullied varies from 11.3% to 49.8% (O'Moore & Kirkham, 2001). Any statistical findings regarding the scope of bullying may be understated, however, due to underreporting of bullying incidents. In fact, the National Center for Education Statistics (2009) finds that students reported only 36% of bullying and 30% of cyberbullying incidents to adults or teachers.

Bullying seriously impacts psychosocial development and student learning. The National Association of School Psychologists reports that over 160,000 students stay home from school each day to avoid being bullied (Fried & Fried, 2003). Compared to non-bullied students, bullied students are four times more likely to skip school or extracurricular activities, out of fear of attack (NCES, 2005). According to Dake, Price, Telljohann, and Funk (2004),

> School bullying has been linked to individual problems such as depression, suicidal ideation, mental disorders, eating disorders, decreased self-esteem, sleeping problems, bedwetting, headaches, stomachaches, alcohol or tobacco use, fighting, weapon carrying, vandalism, stealing, and having trouble with the police. It has also been linked with interpersonal issues such as lack of social acceptance and difficulty in making friends....School adjustment (following rules, good performance on schoolwork) and school bonding (satisfaction at school, taking school seriously) were also found to be less likely to occur in students who were engaged in school bullying behaviors. (p. 373)

Bullying increases with each grade level during elementary school, with the highest rates occurring in early middle school (NCES, 2005). An inverse relationship exists between Grades 6-12. As grade levels increased, student reported bullying decreased: "Twenty four percent of 6th graders reported being bullied at school, compared to 7% of 12th graders" (NCES, 2005, p. 5). This finding suggests that with the increase in grade levels there is a decrease in reporting; however, this does not necessarily indicate a decrease in bullying.

School bullying has serious implications on teachers' abilities to teach, the school's academic mission, and the overall school climate. "With all of the negative issues associated with school bullying, it follows that schools would want to prevent such problems from occurring" (Dake et al., 2004, p. 373). This, however, is not the case. A primary factor perpetuating the bullying problem is how often adults—teachers, counselors, administrators, and parents—fail to stop it (Rahal, 2010). How adults respond to bullying is the key to change (Vail, 2009). In a study conducted by the LaMarsh Centre for Research on Violence and Conflict Resolution in Canada, students reported that teachers intervened often or almost always in bullying situations 23% of the time, while teachers reported they intervened 71% of the time (Coloroso, 2003). Some of the reasons adults fail to intervene in bullying situations may include:

- Educators underestimate the extent and effects of bullying.
- Indifference—nearly 25% of teachers report they do not take responsibility for intervening in bullying incidents.
- Lack of bully prevention training can cause indifference, underestimation, denial, and uncertainty about what to do.
- Students and adults have different levels of exposure to bullying.
- The surreptitious nature of the behavior.
- No clear plan or mechanisms in place to stop the problem (Feinberg, 2003; Rahal, 2010).

What Is Bullying?

The literature is replete with definitions surrounding the nature of bullying, including signs, symptoms, and etiology. After a comprehensive review of the literature, common threads consistently surface.

Bullying is:
- Any deliberate aggressive act by a person or group with the intent to inflict harm on another person.
- Typically repeated, although any one incident should not be ignored.
- An imbalance of physical strength or social power between aggressor and victim.
- An unjust use of physical strength or social power to dominate someone with less power.
- Gratifying for the aggressor.
- A deliberate act or threat that causes psychological distress and a sense of oppression for the target.
- Both overt and covert.
- Not bullying when it involves mutually dismissive kidding or horse play (Olweus, 1978, 1991, 1993, 1999; Rigby, 1996; Salmivalli, Kaukiainen, Kaistaniemi, & Lagerspetz, 1999; Slee, 1995).

Bullying can be classified into two broad categories:
- Direct (physical and verbal) aggression
- Indirect (psychological) aggression (Olweus, 1991, 1999; Salmivalli, Lagerspetz, Bjorkqvist, Osterman, & Kaukiainen, 1996)

Direct Physical

hitting, kicking, pinching, poking, biting, slapping, choking, intrusive sexual contact, damaging or destroying personal belongings, etc.

This is the most visible and more obvious form of bullying and "accounts for less than one-third of bullying incidents reported by children" (Coloroso, 2003, p. 16).

According to the research, direct or overt forms of bullying (physical aggression and verbal threats) are more prevalent in boys (Broidy et al., 2003; Sangwon, Seock-Ho, & Kamphaus, 2010). Two major determinants distinguishing boys from girls in this area are: (1) biological factors (e.g., higher levels of testosterone in boys over girls and higher levels of estrogen and oxytocin in girls over boys) and (2) psychosocial conditioning (e.g., boys are socialized to be overtly aggressive, dominant, emotionally restricted except for anger, while females are socialized to be more passive, pleasant, emotionally expressive except for anger; Campbell et al., 2010; Feder, Levant, & Dean, 2007; Susman & Pajer, 2004).

Research investigating direct physical bullying with girls is sparse (Adamshick, 2010). According to available literature, only two identified populations of girls are found to resort to direct physical bullying: African American girls (Crothers, Field, & Kolbert, 2005) and girls of lower socioeconomic status, due to family socialization practices (Taylor, Gilligan, & Sullivan, 1995).

Overall, the results of existing studies demonstrate low or no incidence of direct physical bullying among girls (e.g., Messer, Goodman, Rowe, Meltzer, & Maughan, 2006; Schaeffer et al., 2006). Interestingly, Moretti, Holland, and McKay (2001) found girls who use relational bullying to manipulate social situations, if provoked, could escalate into assaultive behavior—implying a correlation between direct physical bullying and indirect relational bullying for girls. Continued research is suggested to be more definitive in this area.

Direct Verbal

insults, name calling, racial slurs, taunting, sexual innuendo, threats, etc.

This is the most common form of bullying used by boys and girls and "accounts for 70% of reported bullying" (Coloroso, 2003, p. 15).

Indirect Psychological

gossip, spreading rumors, lies, exclusion, back biting, ignoring, cyberbullying, humiliation, use of relationship as a weapon, etc. (Rivers & Smith, 1994; Simmons, 2002; Whitted & Dupper, 2005; Wiseman, 2002).

In the last decade, commonly used terminology for indirect psychological aggression has included "relational aggression" (Crick & Grotpeter, 1995), or "relational bullying" and "social aggression" (Underwood, 2003), or "social bullying" (Simmons, 2002; Wiseman, 2002).

For the purposes of this text, we will use relational aggression to describe indirect forms of bullying. Relational aggression is considered a highly covert method of bullying—mostly enacted under adult radar—making it extremely difficult to detect, easy to deny, and adult intervention or sanctions nearly impossible (Simmons, 2002; Wiseman, 2002).

Relational aggression targets girls and boys on a continuum of social acceptance (Simmons, 2002; Wiseman, 2002). A high level of social intelligence—which increases with age and cognitive skill development—is positively correlated with the use of indirect aggression (Bjorkqvist, Osterman, & Kaukiainen, 1992; Rivers & Smith, 1994). According to Garandeau and Cillessen (2006), "Making aggression invisible involves use of subtle devices and requires good social cognitive skills on the part of the aggressor" (p. 619).

The perpetrator of relational aggression uses social manipulation to warp how others view an individual, isolating them physically, mentally, emotionally, and socially. This creates a psychological torment for the target, leaving him or her in a no-win situation. There is no forum for the target to challenge or refute the accusations since he or she is most likely socially outnumbered by the offending group. If he or she risks being upset by the opposing group behavior or complains to an authority figure, the torment is likely to escalate (Bjorkqvist, Osterman, & Lagerspetz, 1994; Simmons, 2002; Wiseman, 2002). Indirect forms of bullying are strongly considered pervasive among adolescent girls (Ahmad & Smith, 1994). Current literature and the popular media present a strong case that "mean girls" (e.g., Simmons, 2002; Wiseman, 2002), "female bullying" (Dellasega & Nixon, 2003) and "female aggression" (Crick & Grotpeter, 1995) tip the scales on perpetrating relational bullying.

This notion of girls using relational aggression more than boys, however, is inconsistent with other existing studies (Henington, Hughes, Cavell, & Thompson, 1998; Putallaz et al., 2007; Tomada & Schneider, 1997) reporting boys actually have higher prevalence rates in relational aggression than girls (Kim, Kim, & Kamphaus, 2010). A concern moving forward with research on this topic is current cultural lexicons typecasting both genders—with words such as "mean girls," or "boys will be boys"—casting negative dispersions that could possibly bias future empirical studies.

Although relational aggression occurs among both genders, Crick and Grotpeter (1995) found relationally aggressive acts to be more distressing for girls than for boys. Crick and Bigbee (1998) determined that relationally victimized children were most often girls. The psychological implications of relational aggression can cause serious short- and long-term harm to victims as well as aggressors, including anxiety, sadness, loneliness, depression, eating disorders, alcohol and drug problems, delinquency, sleeplessness, relational problems, and academic difficulties such as lower GPA and social inadequacy (Crick et al., 1996, 1999; Simmons, 2002; Wiseman, 2002).

Biology and Relational Aggression

A biological need for socially intimate bonds makes females more vulnerable than males to psychosocial distress—especially when exclusion and other forms of relational aggression are present. According to Brizendine (2006), "the breakup of a friendship, or just the thought of social isolation, is so stressful, especially among girl teens. Many brain circuits are geared to monitor closeness, and when closeness is threatened, the brain sounds the abandonment alarm loudly" (p. 41). Exclusion has been referred to as "social death" (Williams, Cheung & Choi, 2000, p. 750). When threatened, the male brain is hard wired to launch into physical activity (i.e., fight or flight). The female brain circuitry, on the other hand, is set up to connect with social relationships for protection. Cliques or "social huddling" are vital to females' very existence. When this social safety net is threatened, females can experience serious psychosocial distress (Brizendine, 2006).

Cyberbullying as Relational Aggression

Less than a decade ago, an additional section like this in a book on bullying would not have been applicable. However, with rapid technological advances, cyberbullying has become a very serious form of relational aggression and a pervasive problem for teens, families, and schools. Cyberbullying is "cruelty without walls." Teens can commit harmful online acts that invade homes, schools, and other locations locally and globally with very little effort. This cruelty has a lethal legacy: once the send button is hit, the harm cannot be undone. Electronic communications can have enormous implications and damaging consequences for both the sender and the receiver.

The National Crime Prevention Council defines cyberbullying as "when the Internet, cell phones, or other devices are used to send or post text or images intended to hurt or embarrass another person" (NCPC, 2010). Along with any benefits to the social networking explosion—including Internet sites such as Facebook, MySpace, Friendster, LiveJournal, Nexopia, Xuga,

Xanga, Imbee, Bebo, and hundreds more—a whole world of unlimited, unregulated opportunities for inflammatory cyber cruelty also exists.

Motivation of a Cyberbully

Parry Aftab (2006) is one of the foremost authorities in cyber law and describes four categories of cyberbullies: vengeful angels, the power-hungry, mean girls, and inadvertent cyberbullies.

Vengeful Angels. These cyberbullies do not see themselves as bullying others. They feel entirely justified, because they are righting wrongs, seeking justice for injustices inflicted on them or others. Their misguided efforts are mostly in retaliation for being victimized by cyberbullying and can also manifest from traditional bullying. Vengeful angels usually work alone, but may act with close friends who perceive themselves as being victimized by the "bad guy."

Power-Hungry. Similar to the traditional bully, this cyberbully is motivated by power and control, seeking to intimidate and exert authority over others. Typically, the power-hungry seek an audience, brag about their actions, and want a reaction. Interestingly, these cyberbullies are often the victim of traditional bullying and use their technology skills to release anger, retaliate, and appear bigger than they are in an effort to gain control over feelings of helplessness in the school environment. Cyberbullying is a way for them to act tough, because they are not tough in real life. They are empowered by the anonymity of technology, which allows them to avoid confronting their victims in person.

Mean Girls. Although boys engage in this type of cyberbullying, it is typically a group of girls who direct their actions toward another girl or girls. Their behavior is motivated by boredom and is mostly used for pleasure and entertainment value. There is a strong desire for an audience and for others to know who they are and that they have power. This type of cyberbullying thrives on group admiration, and without this dynamic the behavior usually subsides.

Inadvertent Cyberbullies. These cyberbullies are reacting to communication sent to them or something they have seen online. They react out of frustration or anger and do not think about the possible consequences of clicking the send button. They do not see themselves as cyberbullies and are surprised when they are accused of cyber abuse.

In focus group interviews with middle and high school students, Kowalski, Limber, and Agatston (2008) report motivations for cyberbullying to include "boredom, power, meanness, as retaliation for being bullied, for attention, looking cool and tough, and jealousy" (p. 59). Other motivating factors include the nature of cyberbullying, which is "safer than traditional bullying because it was anonymous and they were less likely to get caught and it was easier because it didn't involve face-to-face confrontations" (p. 59).

Kowalski and colleagues describe an additional causal factor in the popularity of this trend as the phenomenon of disinhibition. "The anonymity afforded by the Internet can lead people to pursue behaviors further than they might otherwise be willing to do. When they cannot be identified, people will often say and do things that they would not do if their identities were known" (p. 64). Willard (2006) clarifies that cyber assaults do not occur because of actual anonymity, but rather from perceived anonymity, as there are numerous ways to trace the origins of cyber violations.

There is current research to indicate that bullies use cyberbullying as an extension of traditional forms of bullying. Other evidence suggests an increase in the prevalence rates of being a bully/victim, due to the Internet and other forms of digital communications being a "safe" way for victims to retaliate (Aftab, 2006; Kowalski et al, 2008; Willard, 2006; Ybarra & Mitchell, 2004). More research is needed in this area. No matter how promising the current literature is on this topic, the field of cyberbullying is relatively new, and rapidly changing technology will make it difficult to pursue with pin point accuracy.

Bullying as Group Dynamic

Bullying is very rarely isolated aggression between the bully and victim. The literature describes bullying as a dynamic social interaction process, where most of the students are involved through playing different roles (Burns, Maycock, Cross, & Brown, 2008; Menesini, Codecasa, Benelli, & Cowie, 2003). Students are acutely aware of both direct and indirect forms of bullying and disrespect: "Most students in a classroom with bully/victim problems are involved in or affected by the problems" (Olweus, 2003, p. 16). Because bullying is a group dynamic, the only way to successfully address the problem is by involving the entire school community. Students are one of the essential keys to school climate change.

Even though bullying is considered a social interaction process, the behavior often flies under adult radar and is perpetuated by a code of silence or covert student contracts. Secrecy or "going underground" may possibly be a social ingredient, making bullying behaviors all the more thrilling to enact. Insidious in nature, covert contracts are like an invisible ever present gas ready to ignite into flames—making bullying a highly volatile and pervasive dynamic. Even though overt contracts or direct aggression is much more visible, these behaviors can also go undetected by adults. Although difficult to identify, adult intervention and exposure of bullying behaviors is critical wherever and whenever possible. A lack of response makes adults a part of the covert contract with students. Not knowing the exact nature of a bullying situation can be frustrating; however, with proper training adults will feel more confident in responding effectively.

Though complex, a simple visual will help identify three primary roles involved in bullying behaviors: the bully, the bullied (victim/target), and bystanders. This cast of characters is staged in a highly mysterious way, co-creating an alchemical triangular group dynamic called the "Bullying Triangle" (see Figure 1). This triangle is intentionally inverted—top heavy with the bully and bystanders—representing how relentlessly they can overwhelm their victim. The victim at the lone point is the outnumbered target of an unwelcome dilemma. The Olweus (2001) Bullying Prevention Program calls this dynamic "The Bullying Circle," which includes a more comprehensive list of the roles involved in the bullying dynamic.

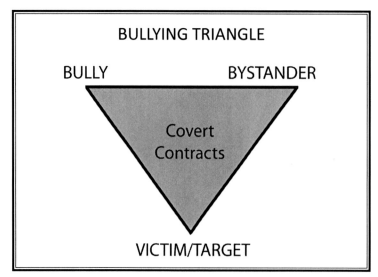

Figure 1

Introducing the Cast of Characters

The Bully

The bully can be either a male or female individual who is usually stronger physically or intellectually than other students and uses personal power to control those who have insufficient social and emotional skills or lack the ability to integrate into their peer group (Pellegrini & Long, 2002; Swearer & Espelage, 2004). The literature indicates that children who continually bully others tend to be physically stronger than average, are generally aggressive, manipulative, and low in empathy (Olweus, 1993; Sutton & Keogh, 2000). An aggressive person does not necessarily correlate with an angry person. Bullying is not about anger or about conflict, but rather about contempt: "a powerful feeling of dislike toward somebody considered to be worthless, inferior, or undeserving of respect" (Coloroso, 2003, p. 20).

The quality of family life is considered a contributing factor in the tendency for some children to engage in bullying their peers. Dysfunctional families and oppressive parenting have been implicated in promoting aggressive peer-to-peer behaviors (Rigby, 1996). According to researchers, those who bully were likely bullied themselves (Kumpulainen, Rasanen, & Henttonen, 1999; Swearer & Espelage, 2004). Other contributing factors include belief systems supportive of aggression and violence, feelings of depression, impulsivity, and a reduced sense of school belonging (Bosworth, Espelage, & Simon, 1999).

In a longitudinal study, Cillessen and Mayeux (2004) have shown the achievement of high status or perceived popularity precedes the use of aggression. In other words, bullies take advantage of their popularity by using social status and various forms of aggression to manipulate their peer group. A body of literature makes a link between aggression and a self-esteem deficiency in bullies. Salmivalli (2001) suggests

bullies have underlying insecurities even though they report high self-esteem. This suggestion is based in part by existing research on the relationship between aggression and narcissism, or "threatened egotism" (Bushman & Baumeister, 1998). According to Salmivalli and colleagues (1999), bullying is related to a defensive type of self-esteem, characterized by a refusal to believe anything negative about oneself.

In the book, *Living in the Age of Entitlement: The Narcissism Epidemic*, Twenge and Campbell (2009) share some compelling research to strongly suggest our American culture is cultivating narcissistic personalities. Their findings suggest educators are working hard to teach students how to feel "special," taking self-admiration and self-expression too far. "Narcissists brag about their achievements while blaming others for their shortcomings" (p. 19). Their more recent research suggests narcissism is not a cover for insecurity or a deficiency in self-esteem and cannot be cured with more self-admiration, which contradicts earlier cited literature.

Narcissism may be an unintended consequence of self-esteem building programs in schools. "Bullies need to learn respect for others. They already have too much respect for themselves" (Twenge & Campbell, 2009, p. 28). The latter would also reinforce the literature which suggests bullies have low empathy (Olweus, 1993; Sutton & Keogh, 2000). In an effort to redirect the current educational trend toward self-esteem building programs that emphasize individualism (i.e., I'm Special), assertiveness and extraversion, Twenge and Campbell (2009) strongly suggest measures that acknowledge connections and commonalities with others. Teaching students how to get along through educational programs that build empathy will benefit the individual, as well as the group. When students are educated and supported in understanding others' perspectives and feel compassion for the pain and suffering of others, egotism will dissipate (Twenge & Campbell).

Out of expedience, adults have a tendency to use quick labels to categorize students and assume the totality of their personalities into a small box. This is a pitfall that can lead to "writing a child off" rather than employing effective interventions. Labels can get reinforced from grade to grade and the student will only respond accordingly. Labels can be very damaging, casting negative aspersions on God's children.

The repetition of bullying behaviors can make us weary. Exasperated, our options become diminished as change seems impossible. With consistent boundaries, consequences, and formative support, all students—even the bullying student—is capable of change. Seeing the whole person as capable allows us to encourage and expect change in bullying behaviors. If change does not happen as quickly as desired, understand the most effective interventions are those that plant seeds that germinate in their own time—for a lifetime. Be patient!

The Victim/Target

According to Olweus (1978, 1993), there are two kinds of victims: (1) passive or submissive which represent 80-85% of all victims and (2) provocative or bully/victims who either actively instigate the bullying or overtly retaliate when bullied.

Non-provocative victims tend to be physically weak, slight in stature, introverted, unassertive, anxious, cautious, sensitive, have low self-esteem, are reticent to retaliate (Slee & Rigby, 1993), and are prone to blame their victimization on their own personality (Graham & Juvonen, 1998). Children with such characteristics as low self-esteem and self-blaming tendencies are unlikely to defend themselves against a bully and the rest of the peer group, thus making them convenient targets (Garandeau & Cillessen, 2006).

Provocative victims tend to be impulsive, aggressive, highly emotional, hot-tempered,

exhibit antisocial behavior, and may have very few if any friends (Espelage & Swearer, 2004; Olweus, 2001).

Interestingly, provocative victims are twice as likely to physically bully, but half as likely to verbally bully, when compared to the actual bully (Unnever, 2005).

The literature includes at least five stabilizing psychosocial factors for passive and provocative victims:

1. For both passive and provocative victims, most of their peers hold the responsibility for their plight (Juvonen & Graham, 2001; Owens, Slee, & Shute, 2001).
2. Peers may develop a negative view of either a passive or provocative victim to justify their hostile behavior toward the target (Garandeau & Cillessen, 2006).
3. Usually a provocative victim's temperament makes him or her more susceptible to bullying, rejection, and harassment (Pellegrini & Long, 2004).
4. Passive victims often perceive themselves as "deserving of what they get," because of the overwhelming group sentiment. This potentially can lead to isolation and even suicide (McNamara & McNamara, 1997; Olweus, 2001).
5. Passive victims tend to not retaliate and display more suffering, which may inadvertently reward bullying behavior and predispose the victim to constant harassment (Bernstein & Watson, 1997).

There is usually at least one victim and rarely more than two in each school class. Although there are multiple levels of peer conflict, there is typically one primary target of the victimization (Schuster, 1999). According to Garandeau and Cillessen (2006),

> this conveys the idea that there must be something about that particular individual that causes the victimization. The bullying seems warranted to witnesses, including school authorities. The victim is thought to have done

something wrong, or to possess some negative personality trait that encouraged the aggression; why otherwise would a whole group reject and victimize that person? (p. 620)

Furthermore, Garandeau and Cillessen (2006) argue a bully may knowingly target only one person for the following reasons:

- To make the aggression more inconspicuous, safer, and more efficient.
- If there were a group of victims, the targeted victim would feel less affected by the aggression.
- The aggression may seem justified to most witnesses if there is only one victim who appears responsible for the victimization.
- If there were a group of victims, they may support one another if they were attacked collectively.
- Several victims are in a better position to retaliate than a single victim without support, thus making the aggression less safe for the bully.

Bullying can lead to significant short- and long-term problems for victims. Such psychosocial implications may include anger, revenge in the form of extreme acts of hostility or aggression, self-pity, confusion, loneliness, physical and psychological distress, mild to severe depression, anxiety, somatic symptoms, and suicidal ideation (Kochenderfer-Ladd & Ladd, 2001; Nansel et al., 2001; Rigby, 2000, 2001, 2002). Victims may also be more prone to maladjustment difficulties reflected in school avoidance or absences, poor school performance, concentration, self-confidence, self-esteem, and prosocial skills (Knoff, 2007; Kochenderfer & Ladd, 1996).

In a longitudinal study, Paul and Cillessen (2007) explored predictors of physical, direct verbal, and indirect verbal forms of bullying victimization. The study examined the prevalence and longitudinal likelihood of bullying victimization in a sample of elementary school students. The study achieved a 95% participation rate across fourth ($n = 658$), fifth ($n = 638$), sixth ($n = 600$), and seventh ($n = 600$) grades. One aspect of the study was to determine if victimization was stable across the four consecutive school years, including the transition from elementary to middle school. The study found that of the students who were victims in Grade 4, 65% were also victims in Grade 5, 49% in Grade 6, and 34% in Grade 7. Of the Grade 5 victims, over 40% were also victims in Grade 6 and Grade 7. Finally, 48% of the victims in Grade 6 were also victims in Grade 7. The consistently high percentage of bullying victimization from Grades 4-7 indicates that in the absence of strategic bullying interventions, incidents of bullying are likely to persist for victims throughout their elementary and middle school years.

Another aspect of this study (Paul & Cillessen, 2007) examined elementary school variables that can be considered risk and protective factors of victimization in adolescence.

The risk factors included externalizing and internalizing behaviors for both boys and girls. Victims who externalize were found to have poor behavioral and emotional regulation, making them easy to antagonize. The deregulated reactions by victims reinforced the behaviors of peers who victimized them. This in turn led to more disruptive behaviors by victims, as a reaction to being victimized. The latter may help explain how disruptive behaviors may create a cause and effect in the victimization dynamic. This same dynamic seems to hold true for internalizing risk factors. Girls who exhibit anxious, withdrawn behavior and boys who exhibit loneliness lack a peer social network, which makes them vulnerable, defenseless, and easy targets for current and future bullying.

The protective factors found in the study (Paul & Cillessen, 2007) had both a social and academic component. For both genders, peer sociability—having friends and belonging to social groups—was a protective factor against adolescent victimization. The presence of prosocial skills is significant when dealing with social pressures of the peer system and having friends or belonging to social groups may serve as a buffer against victimization. Self-confidence from academic achievements may also make students less vulnerable to bullying. Paul and Cillessen (2007) suggest the way to break the cycle of bullying and victimization is by incorporating teambuilding and conflict management skill development in student groups to improve social skills.

The bullied individual is consistently labeled "victim" throughout the literature. Webster's Dictionary defines a victim as "one that is subjected to oppression, hardship, or mistreatment, one that is tricked or duped." Although applicable, the term implies an individual may be incapable of influencing change in their current predicament. Such a sympathetic view from adults surrounding what appears to be a hopeless situation could impair effective interventions. No one is deserving or responsible for any maltreatment. Victims should not, however, be absolved from taking responsibility or action to move out of firing range. With support, a person being targeted can acquire new behaviors and skills, becoming capable of mobilizing change in his or her psychosocial ecology. As a result, the term "victim" will be replaced with the term "target" throughout the remainder of this text.

The Bystander

According to Craig and Pepler (1995), in bullying episodes, 85% of students are aware of a bully's behavior. In fact most students are not only aware, but also witness the bullying (Craig, Pepler, & Atlas, 2000). Students who are indirectly or directly involved with the bully's behavior are called "bystanders." Bystanders are the third group of players in the Bullying Triangle: "They are the supporting cast who aid and abet the bully through acts of omission and commission" (Coloroso, 2003, p. 62). In the literature, bystanders play one of three primary roles: (1) passive bystander, (2) active bystander, and (3) defender (Salmivalli et al., 1996).

Passive bystanders. Passive bystanders remain silent witnesses or outsiders and avoid taking sides with either the bully or the target. Although passive bystanders may not take sides, their silence or inaction condones the behavior, nonverbally communicating tacit approval of the bully's behavior (Cowie, 2000). Passive bystanders may perceive themselves as uninvolved, neutral, and not responsible; however, the unintended consequence is that targets and other students perceive them as colluding with the bully. Researchers suggest passive bystanders are perceived to be more respectful and friendly to the bully than to the target, which may be a factor in prolonging bullying episodes (O'Connell, Pepler, & Craig, 1999; Salmivalli, 2010).

Active bystanders. Active bystanders join in and become "reinforcers" of the bullying behavior by laughing, cheering, or joining in physical or verbal aggression (Atlas & Pepler, 1998). Such behaviors create a social contagion that can quickly and easily undermine any prevention efforts. Because of this negative social contagion, active bystanders may also become bullies. Every attempt must be made to counter reinforcer behaviors by building empathy and encouraging defender behaviors.

Defender. A defender is a student who sticks up for the target. Defenders usually have strong anti-bullying attitudes, enjoy positive peer status, are perceived as popular by their peers, are well liked, are empathic, and have high self-efficacy (Salmivalli, 2010).

A relationship may exist between social status and a student's ability to be a successful defender. A defender with high social status is respected and followed, whereas a defender with low social status, who challenges the bully, may run the risk of becoming the next target (Salmivalli, 2010).

Although the majority of students say they disapprove of bullying and report intentions to support the target, actual defense of a target is very rare (Boulton, Trueman, & Flemington, 2002; Rigby & Johnson, 2006). Defenders intervene on behalf of the target in only 25% of cases (O'Connell et al., 1999). This is unfortunate, because other findings suggest targets who had one or more classmates defending them were less anxious, less depressed, and had higher self-esteem than targets without defenders.

The collective behaviors of bystanders reward the bully and keep the Bullying Triangle operational (Salmivalli, 2010). The perpetuation of the Bullying Triangle can be attributed to school climate and the existing social norms—favorable attitudes, beliefs, and behaviors—that support the physical, verbal, or relational aggression (Freeman & Mims, 2007). The presence of such norms may be highly influential in shaping and perpetuating overt and covert forms of aggression (Freeman & Mims, 2007). All prevention and intervention efforts should address existing social norms that are counterproductive to creating a Christ-centered school climate. Bystander participation in anti-bullying programs is considered necessary and valuable (Freeman & Mims, 2007; Rigby & Johnson, 2006; Salmivalli et al., 1999).

Bystander reactions—no matter how subtle or overt—impact the perceived sense of safety and affect the overall school climate. Research findings demonstrate a correlation between the presence of defender behaviors and a sense of safety in the school. There is also a correlation between the absence of defender behaviors and a low sense of safety in the school (Skiba, Poloni-Staudinger, Gallini, Simmons, & Feggins-Azziz, 2006; Stockdale, Hangadumbo, Duys, Larson, & Sarvela, 2002).

There are several findings in the literature on key elements that activate defender behaviors and increase the sense of school safety (Skiba et al., 2006; Stockdale et al., 2002):

- The school has a clear anti-bullying message and promotes a climate where bullying is not tolerated.
- The school has a clear and efficient reporting mechanism in place.
- Students convey attitudes that bullying is not tolerated in their school.
- Students feel connected to school and have a strong sense of belonging.
- Adult and student support for bystander interventions is available.
- When defender interventions are witnessed by other students, it creates positive behavioral reinforcement.

Spiritual Perspective on Bullying

The inverted Bully Triangle conveys a sinful dynamic—a disproportionate negative power focused upon another. From a spiritual perspective, bullying is a sin, defined as "an offense against reason, truth, and right conscience; it is failure in genuine love for God and neighbor caused by a perverse attachment to certain goods. It wounds the nature of man and injures human solidarity" (USCCB, 2006, p. 312).

At the core, this definition suggests that sin has serious implications not only for one, but for all. Intervening for a select few students may be perceived as an efficient strategy to rectifying bullying incidents; however, this approach dismisses the big picture. Even the silent bystander may have a moral obligation to the bullying dynamic and must be part of the change. Hope for any repair and human solidarity is contingent on the entire Christian school community being involved in making strides toward change and healing.

In *The Pastoral Constitution on the Church in the Modern World*, the Vatican II Council proclaimed:

Indeed, the Lord Jesus when He prayed to the Father, "that all may be one...as we are one" (John 17:21-11), opened up vistas closed to human reason. For He implied a certain likeness between the union of the Divine Persons, and in the union of God's sons in truth and charity. (Vatican II, 1966, p. 223)

"Righting" the inverted Bully Triangle creates a new life-giving, restorative dynamic through a Christ-centered approach (see Figure 2). This "new" triangle is the ancient symbol of the Trinity, and the foundational icon for this program's Christian approach to dealing with bullying. The Trinity Model includes all of the "players"—the bully, the target, and the bystanders—and empowers them to a higher calling. When all are welcome in Christ's love and compassion, the spirit of reconciliation, forgiveness, and communal healing are made possible. Only in this way can we begin to change the sinfulness of bullying.

The diagram depicts a clear visual of Christ being the model for leadership. Phase I: Christ Is Our Model for Leadership helps students come to a greater understanding of leadership rooted

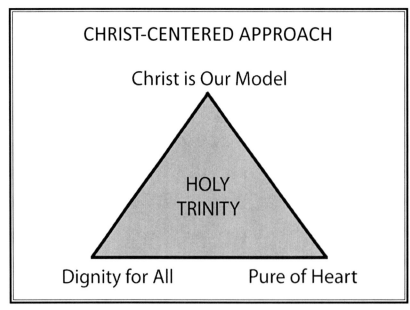

Figure 2

in Christ. Using this positive leadership—blessed by the gifts and fruits of the Spirit—students begin to understand their personhood as a gift and how their actions impact the larger community. Students enter into opportunities to practice reconciliation, forgiveness, and being pure of heart in their relationship God.

Phase II: Dignity for All delves into the compassionate component of our nature to heal and assist others in the healing process through reconciliation and forgiveness. It is vitally important to stress the word "all." When reference is made to the sinfulness of bullying, often this sinfulness is directed toward the bully alone. The Trinity models calls us to view bullying and sinfulness from a communal perspective. There are moral consequences to the actions of the bully, the active bystander, as well as the passive bystander, whose inaction encourages and reinforces the bully. The target may also experience moral consequences if his or her self-care is met with despair. In the Penitential Rite, we are all asked to recognize "what I have done and what I have failed to do," and through this confession one can be forgiven and find healing.

The Old Testament idea of "an eye for an eye," has been revised in the person of Jesus. It can be surmised that Jesus would have agreed with Gandhi when he said, "An eye for an eye and the whole world is blind." Mistakenly, we think that Jesus encouraged passivity when He said, "When someone strikes you on (your) right cheek, turn the other one to him as well" (Matthew 5:39). This Scripture passage calls us all to be non-violent; however, it does not suggest we become inactive in our self-care. The target is called to honor and protect the sacredness of his or her personhood. This same sense of dignity must be extended to the bully and the bystanders. Self respect helps us all to understand personal dignity, and to turn away from non life-giving actions. When dignity is vibrant within a communal environment, everyone benefits. Hope for any repair and human solidarity is contingent on the entire Christian school community being involved in making strides toward change and healing. Desmond Tutu (1999) writes:

> In one way or another, as a supporter, as a perpetrator, as a victim, or one who opposed the ghastly system, something happened to our humanity. All of us South Africans were less whole....Those who were privileged lost out as they became more uncaring, less compassionate, less humane, and therefore less human.... Our humanity is caught up in that of all others. We are human because we belong. We are made for community, for togetherness, for family, to exist in a delicate network of interdependence....We are sisters and brothers of one another whether we like it or not, and each one of us is a precious individual. (pp. 196-197)

The Good Samaritan Parable in Luke (10:25-37) gives us a perspective on the morality of how one responds to the plight of others.

> A man fell victim to robbers as he went down from Jerusalem to Jericho. They stripped and beat him and went off leaving him half-dead. A priest happened to be going down that road, but when he saw him, he passed by on the opposite side. Likewise a Levite came to the place, and when he saw him, he passed by on the opposite side. But a Samaritan traveler who came upon him was moved with compassion at the sight. (Luke 10:30-33)

Other Scripture translations refer to the man as Jewish. From a historical point of view, the Jews and Samaritans had strained, hostile relations. The Scripture continues:

> He approached the victim, poured oil and wine over his wounds and bandaged them. Then he lifted him up on his own animal, took him to an inn and cared for him. The next day he took out two silver coins and gave them to the innkeeper with the instruction, "Take care of him. If you spend more than what I have given you, I shall repay you on my way back." (Luke 10:34-35)

Psychological wounds from bullying behaviors last for a long time—sometimes a lifetime. There was no one in this Scripture story present to help the victim during the mugging. After the assault, there were two passive bystanders who independently and intentionally overlooked the target, leaving him to die. It was a social enemy who stepped in and "was moved with compassion at the sight" (Luke 10:33).

Imagine how the target felt when a person was kind enough to take time, care, and money to attend to him. Imagine the sense of worth and value the target felt by the actions of the Samaritan.

Bullying incidents may happen in one moment in time, but the negative effects are timeless. Defenders are sensitive to the wounds, even after the fact. At the end of this Scripture passage Jesus asks the scholar of the law,

"Which of these three, in your opinion, was neighbor to the robbers' victim?" He answered, "The one who treated him with mercy." Jesus said to him, "Go and do likewise." (Luke 10:36-37)

We are called to be defenders, to go and do likewise, treating others with mercy.

Phase III: Pure of Heart calls us to move beyond bullying behavior to a deeper relationship with The Trinity. Through meditation and prayer we are more open to the Spirit of God and empowered to the life we are called to live. Phase III contains many practical activities to reduce stress, which benefit the individual as well as the community. Through prayerful quiet and stillness, individuals can come to a deeper awareness of their own spiritual sacredness and spiritual connectedness to others.

What Works in Bullying Prevention?

The Health Resources and Services Administration (HRSA, 2006) identified ten best practices strategies in bullying prevention and intervention. Kowalski and colleagues (2008) highlight the HRSA best practices, summarized below.

1
Focus on the school environment.

A reduction in bullying requires change in the school climate and in social norms. The HRSA *Take a Stand, Lend a Hand* national campaign established that "It must become 'uncool' to bully, 'cool' to help out kids who are bullied and normative for staff and students to notice when a child is bullied or left out" (2006, para. 3). This will require total school involvement of adults, students, and parents.

2
Assess bullying at your school.

Through the use of an anonymous survey of students, staff, and parents, schools can break through indifference, underestimation, denial, and uncertainty around bullying behaviors. Having site specific data can help motivate adults and students to take action against bullying. A follow-up to the baseline assessment can also measure the progress of implemented prevention and intervention strategies.

3
Garner staff and parent support for bullying prevention.

Prevention efforts require that the majority of adults and parents take responsibility for and support the bullying prevention strategies once they are in place.

4
Form a group to coordinate the school's bullying prevention activities.

A core diverse group of committed school personnel and at least one parent should be established to coordinate bullying prevention efforts. They should meet regularly (once a week) to analyze survey assessments, establish and review bullying policies, plan anti-bullying activities, determine prevention strategies (i.e., classroom education, parent education, staff training, etc.), obtain feedback from staff, parents, and students about what is working and what is not working, and ensure all efforts continue over time through continuous motivation and encouragement of the entire school community.

5
Train school staff in bullying prevention.

All school personnel should be trained in bullying prevention and intervention best practices. Proper training will help everyone better understand the bullying dynamic, its harmful effects, and appropriate responses (i.e., intervention strategies and reporting mechanisms).

6
Establish and enforce school rules and policies related to bullying.

Simple, clear rules and expectations must be in place, specific (not implicit) to bullying behaviors. A "no bullying" policy should contain both corrective and formative intervention strategies.

7
Increase adult supervision in places where bullying occurs.

Bullying thrives in places where adults are not present. The coordinating group can ask school personnel to look at building floor plans to identify "hot spots" in and around the school campus, then develop strategies to increase supervision in these areas.

8
Focus some class time on bullying prevention.

Effective bullying prevention includes a classroom component. Just like the repetition of commercial advertisements, anti-bullying messages and themes should be infused in the classroom curriculum. Classroom meetings will help teachers tune into students' attitudes and behaviors around bullying. This is a time for students to honestly discuss concerns around bullying behaviors and how to improve on peer relationships by introducing meaningful social skills.

9
Intervene consistently and appropriately in bullying situations.

School rules and codes are only as good as the paper they are written on, unless there are consistent and appropriate interventions in place. Consistent enforcement establishes or will improve the credibility and safety of the school, whereas a lack of consistency has the opposite effect: a decrease in credibility and a decrease in sense of safety. All school personnel should be trained to intervene on the spot to stop bullying; delays cause mixed messages and confusion. Meetings may need to be held with bullies and targets separately to enforce corrective and formative actions. Parents of the students involved should be included whenever possible.

10
Continue these efforts over time.

As soon as school personnel let down their guard, bullying behaviors undoubtedly will be on the rise. A comprehensive anti-bullying approach has a beginning, but no end date. The school must weave bullying prevention efforts into its everyday fabric and continue these efforts over time.

Bullying Prevention Programs

This section will highlight four bully prevention programs including: (1) The Bullying Prevention Program (Olweus, Limber, & Mihalic, 1999); (2) Bully Proofing Your School (Garrity, Jens, Porter, Sager, & Short-Camilli, 2004b); (3) PeaceBuilders; and (4) Steps to Respect (Committee for Children, 2001). These programs were selected because they have at minimum some research evaluations and findings.

After a comprehensive review of the literature, there are a plethora of anti-bullying approaches and programs; however, none have the conclusive empirical evidence-based support or hold the international acclaim of The Olweus Bullying Prevention Program.

The Olweus Bullying Prevention Program

The most cited researcher and theorist on bullying is Norwegian professor, Dan Olweus. With over three decades of experience in the anti-bullying arena, Olweus has developed a "whole-school approach" to bullying prevention. The Olweus Bullying Prevention Program was found to reduce bullying by as much as 50% (Olweus, 1994) and is the only model program listed with the Center for the Study and Prevention of Violence [CSPV], *Blueprints for Violence Prevention* (2010a; Olweus et al., 1999a). "The Blueprints Initiative sets a gold standard for implementing exemplary, research-based violence and drug programs and for implementing these programs with fidelity to the models" (CSPV, 2010a).

The Olweus Bullying Prevention Program has four components to address school bullying: school, classroom, individual, and community (Kowalski et al., 2008).

School-Level Components:
- Establishment of a bullying prevention coordinating team to meet regularly and coordinate the program.
- Administration of a student bullying questionnaire for students in Grades 3 and above.
- Committee and staff training on bullying prevention. Ongoing staff discussion groups on bullying prevention.
- Development of school rules and discipline procedures surrounding bullying.
- A supervisory system that includes a special focus on bullying.
- Kick-off events to launch the program with students and parents.
- Parent involvement.

Classroom Components:
- Posting and enforcement of school-wide rules against bullying.
- Holding regular classroom meetings on topics of bullying and peer relations.
- Holding regular meetings with parents, if possible.

Individual Components:
- Supervision of students' activities.
- Effective on-the-spot interventions to address bullying.
- Follow-up meetings with students who are bullied and (separately) with students who bully.
- Meetings with parents of involved students.

Community Components:
- Involvement of community members on the Bullying Prevention Coordinating Committee.
- Development of partnerships with community members to support the school's program.
- Spreading anti-bullying messages and principles of best practice in the community.

Bully Proofing Your School (BPYS)

BPYS was developed by the Creating Caring Communities organization started in 1999 by William Porter, one of the mental health consultants to Columbine and the surrounding school districts in Colorado. The program is listed on the CSPV (2010) Safe Communities—Safe Schools Fact Sheet under "Favorable Program Descriptions." Research on BPYS at the elementary level was found to be promising, demonstrating positive impact on student attitudes toward bullying and reductions in bullying. However, research at the middle school level failed to yield conclusive results (Menard, Grotpeter, Gianola, & O'Neal, 2007).

BPYS is a system-wide, comprehensive prevention program focusing on school climate. The program is designed for adults and students to work together to create a safe and caring school community. BPYS has five key components which include staff training, student instruction, interventions with the bullies and targets, parent involvement, and developing a caring community (Demaray & Malecki, 2006).

Staff Training:
- Teaching staff are encouraged to form a team to provide support for each other around program implementation.
- Curricula on specific strategies and techniques to cope with and prevent bullying behavior available for Grades K-12.
- Resistance skills for targets.
- Prosocial skills for bullies.
- Defender skills for bystanders.

Student Instruction:
- Teacher implemented classroom instruction utilizing role-plays, modeling, class discussion, and classroom materials.
- Teaching victims friendship-building, self-esteem, and assertiveness skills.
- Strategies for students to use when bullied.
- Teaching bullies how to interact more appropriately by thinking, managing anger, and applying social problem solving skills.
- Teaching bystanders, often called the "caring majority," how to help and react in bullying situations (i.e., problem solving and increasing empathy for targets).
- Weekly "I caught you caring" sessions, recognizing students who engaged in kindness during the week.

Intervention:
- Individual interventions with the bullies and targets.
- Small support and informational groups for targets.
- Small support and informational groups for bullies.

Parent Involvement:
- Parent training
- Meetings with parents

Caring Community:
- All school personnel, students, parents, and select members of the greater community are involved in developing a caring community.
- All are encouraged to be engaged in a team approach to change the school climate.

PeaceBuilders

The Center for the Study and Prevention of Violence at the University of Colorado has established a "Matrix of Programs as Identified by various Federal and Private Agencies" (CSPV, 2010b). The PeaceBuilders program is listed on this matrix as *promising* with the U.S. Department of Education Safe Schools (2001), *favorable* with Mihalic and Aultman-Bettridge (2004) and *exemplary* with the Office of Juvenile Justice and Delinquency Prevention (OJJDP, 2007). Although the program indicates it is designed for Grades K-12, a literature search only found studies to include Grades K-5. A study by Flannery and colleagues (2003) "examined the initial behavior outcomes of PeaceBuilders, a universal school-based preventive intervention program focused on reducing aggressive behavior and increasing social competence" (p. 304). This study found the implementation of the Peacebuilders program reduced aggressive behavior and increased social competence.

PeaceBuilders is not an anti-bullying specific program, but more of a broad brush approach, addressing risk factors that predict violence—including bullying—as well as drug and tobacco use. The primary goal is to reduce youth violence. PeaceBuilders focuses on the increase and reinforcement of prosocial cues, which over time will increase students' social competence, resulting in a natural decline in the frequency and intensity of aggressive behaviors.

The program is not a time or subject limited curriculum, but rather a philosophy that is purposely infused into the daily school routine. Activities and strategies can be implemented on a daily basis by any teacher or staff member. "All of these strategies and activities are geared toward creating a positive climate and culture in the entire school, with an emphasis on reinforcement of positive behavior rather than simply the reduction of negative behavior" (Flannery et al., 2003, p. 294).

School:
- All school personnel and students are taught a common language, emphasizing six guiding principles: (1) Praise People; (2) Give-Up Put-Downs; (3) Seek Wise People; (4) Notice Hurts; (5) Right Wrongs; and (6) Help Others.
- Displays are visible throughout the school of prosocial cues and symbols to reinforce common language and positive behaviors.
- All school personnel encouraged to use "Praise Notes."
- Students sometimes sent to the principal's office for kind acts or good deeds, called "preferrals."
- Adults monitor "hot spots" (i.e., lunchrooms and hallways in between activities), while praising prosocial behavior.

- Site coaching
- Training and inservices

Classroom:
- Daily rituals are performed related to the common language and guiding principles for reinforcement.
- Students complete activities from a specially designed comic book in which they are the designated hero.
- Inclusion opportunities are created for special needs children (Flannery et al., 2003).

Home:
- Increase parenting skills
- Foster safe communities

Steps to Respect

In the "Matrix of Programs" (CSPV, 2010b), Steps to Respect is identified as *effective* by the Office of Juvenile Justice and Delinquency Prevention (OJJDP, 2007). This Grades 3-6 bullying prevention program was developed by the Committee for Children (2001). Based on the Olweus Model, the Steps to Respect curriculum teaches elementary children how to recognize, refuse, and report bullying. The program is designed to reduce bullying, as well as help students build more supportive relationships with one another. It is one of the few programs that emphasizes bystander involvement and the responsibility of all the members of the school community to decrease bullying (Coloroso, 2003).

A study on the Steps program was conducted out of the University of Washington, over a two-year period. The study examined the program in a local school district, with 360 students observed and 624 surveyed in six schools. In the *Journal of Educational Psychology*, Frey, Hirschstein, Edstrom, and Snell (2009) found the Steps to Respect program led to a 31% decline in bullying, a 70% decline in destructive bystander behavior, and a 36% decline in nonbullying aggressive behavior.

Through the use of curricula and other strategies, Steps to Respect teaches elementary students to recognize, refuse, and report bullying, be assertive, and build friendships. The program lessons are designed to help kids feel safe and supported by the adults around them so that they can build stronger bonds to school and focus on academic achievement. School-wide policies and training are used to support school personnel in building a safe environment free from bullying.

Student Instruction:
- Teaches friendship skills, empathy for targets, assertiveness, and coping skills.
- Coaches how to respond to bullying.
- Teaches how to report bullying.
- Offers emotional support to help create a caring and respectful school environment.

Staff Training:
- Promotes awareness of bullying.
- Teaches skills on how to respond (i.e., how to coach bullies and targets) after an incident report.
- Provides a student literature unit for program reinforcement.
- Provides parent handouts that correspond to student lessons and are to be sent out periodically.

Program Comparison

Many of our program components are consistent with those highlighted above. Namely, the *Peace Be with You* program helps schools create a safe and respectful school climate by changing norms and shifting attitudes that support bullying behaviors. The program promotes pro-social behaviors and skills, such as empathy, listening, community building, communication skills, relational skills, and internal asset building skills. Possible criticisms of the program may include:

- The curriculum is written for Grades 4-8 only.
- The Student Workbook relies on students to engage their parents in the process.
- The program does not have a community component to involve business partners.

What sets our program apart from those highlighted is that it is the only Scripture-based program of its kind. With the *Peace Be with You* Teacher Manual and Student Workbook, faith-based schools will not have to retrofit Scripture into this Christ-centered bullying prevention model. After a comprehensive search, to our knowledge, there is no other such bullying prevention program in existence. Also the program's communal classroom, which emphasizes reconciliation and forgiveness, is a unique approach that sets it apart from current programs.

Peace Be with You also addresses social responsibility in the context of positive student leadership and encourages students to explore their inner life through prayer and meditation, as well as through practical stress reduction approaches.

PHASE I

Christ Is Our Model for Leadership

PHASE I
Christ is Our Model for Leadership

"We are the mother of Christ when we carry Him in our heart and body by love and a pure and sincere conscience. And we give birth to Him through our holy works which ought to shine on others by our example."

ST. FRANCIS OF ASSISI

PURPOSE
To immerse students in structured opportunities to learn about social injustices and what Christ tells us about equality and justice for all

LEARNING OBJECTIVES
- Students will learn what it means to be Christ-like leaders.
- Students will learn how to become Christ-like leaders.
- Students will make a connection between Christ-like leadership and the Sacrament of Confirmation.
- Students will learn how Christ-like leadership influences school climate.
- Students will learn how to love their neighbor.

TEACHER MANUAL ACTIVITIES   4

CORRESPONDING STUDENT WORKBOOK PAGES
- Prayer   1
- Journal Entries   4
- Leader Folder Activity   1
- Student Worksheets   19
- Four Agreements Contract
- Quotation Pages   5

Prayer of Blessed John XXIII

Lord Jesus Christ,
Who are called Prince of Peace.
Who are yourself our peace and reconciliation,
Who so often said, "Peace to you,"
Grant us peace.

Make all men and women witnesses of truth, justice, and
    brotherly love.
Banish from their hearts whatever might endanger peace.
Enlighten our rulers that they may guarantee and defend the
    great gift of peace.
May all peoples of the earth become as brothers and sisters.
May longed-for peace blossom forth and reign over us all.
Amen.

Ecumenical Impact

> He said to them, "These are my words that I spoke to you while I was still with you, that everything written about me in the law of Moses and in the prophets and psalms must be fulfilled." Then he opened their minds to understand the scriptures. And he said to them, "Thus it is written that the Messiah would suffer and rise from the dead on the third day and that repentance, for the forgiveness of sins, would be preached in his name to all the nations, beginning from Jerusalem. You are witnesses of these things. And (behold) I am sending the promise of my Father upon you; but stay in the city until you are clothed with power from on high." (Luke 24:44-49)

Sending the power of the most high, the Holy Spirit, is the focal point in Phase I. We will re-examine the relationship between Christ as our model for leadership and the gifts of the Holy Spirit. We will redefine leadership and the Spirit's call to each of us in a leadership role.

This Scripture passage emphasizes the communal aspect of the Trinity working together. Jesus returns to the Father, so that the wishes of the Father are fulfilled and He can send the Holy Spirit to us. From a human phraseology, this is a remarkable support system. Each member of the Trinity is committed to the same purpose and honors each other's role.

Communal support becomes a teachable moment in Phase I for counselors and teachers using this program. As part of a school system, time is allocated for counselors and teachers to carry out their job descriptions, but time is not always allocated for renewal and rejuvenation with a core support team. A support system may give you air time to vent, but more importantly, this system should nurture and honor you. With such support, professional and personal growth is possible. Without it, teachers and counselors may experience burnout.

Modeling inclusiveness, the Committee on Ecumenical and Interreligious Affairs established by the United States bishops includes: "promoting in common with our brothers... joint witness to the Christian faith as well as cooperating in such areas as, e.g. education, morality, social and cultural matters, learning and the arts" (United States Catholic Conference, 1968, §K).

Speaking at a February 8, 2010, Vatican symposium, Cardinal Walter Kasper, president of the Pontifical Council for Promoting Church Unity said: "an ecumenism of basics that identifies, reinforces, and deepens [Christians'] common foundation" of faith and tenets of the creed (as cited in Wooden, 2010, para. 5).

In the spirit of the Bishop's Committee and the Vatican Office, together with the model of the Trinity, it follows that we invite our Christian brothers and sisters in education to jointly battle this social and cultural evil of bullying within our schools. One compatible Christian perspective comes from The Evangelical Lutheran Church in America (ELCA, 2010) in their bi-monthly resource, "Seeds for the Parish," which reads in part:

> What your congregation can do:
> - Provide opportunities to address issues of bullying from a Christian perspective...
> - Let the church be a place where young members know it is safe to talk about their role in the bullying cycle as the target, bystander, or even the aggressor...
> - Help parents and other church leaders spot warning signs of bullying and give them tips and tools for ending it. Ask the congregational council to model. (para. 10)

This textbook and the ELCA share a common concern. Together, as the Trinity models for us, we can model to the larger society a communal Christ-centered care for our students.

Spiritual Perspective

Scripture clearly reveals to us that our Lord Jesus Christ not only spoke of compassion and love for our neighbor but lived them when He "walked the walk." Our Catholic schools hold a consecrated purpose to actively evangelize by juxtaposing Christ's teaching with student behaviors and school expectations. The activities that follow were carefully and prayerfully designed to create opportunities for students to reflect on whether or not they are treating each other in a Christ-like manner. Christ is truly our model for leadership and must be our holy reference point for everything we say and do!

The whole of Christ's life was a continual teaching, His silence, His miracles, His gestures, His prayers, His love for people, His special affection for the lowly and the poor, His acceptance of the total sacrifice of the Cross for the redemption of the world, and His Resurrection are the actualization of His word and the fulfillment of Revelation. (USCCB, 2006, p. 85)

Activity One

Who Me? A Leader?

*"There are different kinds of spiritual gifts but the same Spirit;
there are different forms of service but the same Lord; there are different
workings but the same God who produces all of them in everyone.
To each individual the manifestation of the Spirit is given for some benefit."*

1 CORINTHIANS 12:4-7

PURPOSE

To empower all students to view themselves as leaders with the ability to positively influence the school climate

LEARNING OBJECTIVES

- Students will explore their perceptions of what it means to be a leader.
- Students will be challenged to create a new awareness of what the term leader means.
- Students will brainstorm words that describe what it means to be a positive leader.
- Students will generate leader words to establish ownership around positive leadership.
- Students will come to believe they are leaders.
- Students will understand how "followers" influence leadership.
- Students will create new norms, standards, and expectations for their own behavior.

CORRESPONDING
STUDENT WORKBOOK PAGES 6-12

- Journal Entry   1
- Student Leader Folder
- Student Worksheets   5

Journal Entry

Who Me? A Leader?

Reflect and journal what you learned from the first lesson on leadership.

6   **PHASE I**
Christ Is Our Model for Leadership.

Peace Be With You
WORKBOOK

Christ Is Our Model for Leadership

The notion of leadership, let alone effective leadership, can be a very abstract concept. Phase I contains some very simple yet essential and persuasive involvement activities to help students better understand what it means to be an effective leader. Each activity holds an opportunity to empower and inspire students to learn and grow as leaders—to help them understand how their leadership is a significant part of making the school one of the safest and most awesome places on the planet. Why settle for mediocrity?

In the first activity—Who Me? A Leader?—students are asked to, "Stand up if you are a leader." After the teacher asks this question it is common for students to begin talking and commenting. This is a healthy part of their discernment as leaders as they make a decision to stand or not to stand. Take mental note of who is standing, who is not standing, and who may have stood up and then sat down. There may even be

students that are on the edge of their seats and begin to stand, but slowly or quickly sit down.

The many reactions and responses you observe to this question are the many ways students grapple with the notion of themselves as leaders. In our experience, even those who stand up with confidence, when asked to share a word to describe what makes them a leader, have difficulty doing so. The dissonance this activity creates is intentional and essential for student leadership development. As students struggle, they are beginning to form new cognitions around the concept of leadership and how they fit into this schema. Do not be too quick to come to their rescue. Let students grapple with their current perceptions about what it means to be a leader.

Interview 5 to 10 students one at a time about their choice to stand or remain seated. You will not have time to interview every student, so randomly choose a few students to discuss their discernment. Mention that you noticed some students did not hesitate when asked

---

Student Leader Folder

Use a two-pocket folder to hold a collection of items that inspire you about leadership.

What to place in your Leader Folder:
• The list of leader words your class brainstormed together.

• Add new leader words to this list when you discover them.

• Journal about the leader words that best represent you and why.

• Journal about one leader word from the Leader Word List that you would like to develop more fully in yourself and why.

• Journal your own reflections about positive leadership.

• Journal concerns you have about current political or spiritual leaders. What would you do differently if you were in their position?

• Collect and add inspiring articles from magazines, newspapers, or Internet sources about leadership.

• Find and add quotes about positive leadership.

• Journal about your own personal leadership journey.

• Add anything else on leadership to your folder that you find interesting.

Worksheet 1

Whom Do I Admire?

Think of a person, real or fictitious, that you admire.
Reflect and write on the following questions:

Who is the person you chose? (Pick someone other than a parent)

_____

What positive characteristics, traits, or qualities do you admire in this person?

_____
_____
_____
_____

What does or did this person do that is so admirable?

_____
_____
_____
_____

What are some specific ways you strive to be more like this person?

_____
_____
_____
_____

If possible ask this person if you can interview him or her. Use Worksheet 4 on p. 11 as a guide for the interview.

this question, while other students did hesitate. Have students express their thought processes around the activity. Ask a student why he or she stood or didn't stand. Listen for key words that describe positive qualities and characteristics of leadership.

If a student says, "because I am on student council," take this a step further having the student describe why he or she was chosen for student council. Ask the student to name one personal quality, trait, or characteristic that describes him or her as a leader and how that enables actions of leadership. Typically, students perceive themselves as one of the following:

A. I'm not a leader.
B. I'm a follower not a leader.
C. I'm not a leader or a follower.
D. I'm a leader and a follower.
E. I'm a leader because I am a member of student council.
F. I'm a leader because I participate in a sport or sports.

In choices A, B, and C, students sometimes do not perceive themselves as leaders, because they misunderstand what it means to be a leader. They also misinterpret what it means to be a follower. Often the word "follower" has a negative connotation for students and even some adults. Although it is true that followers can be negative, just like negative leaders, it is also true that followers can be positive, just like positive leaders.

Positive leaders need positive followers, just like negative leaders need negative followers to support them in their efforts. Positive leaders and positive followers, just like negative leaders and negative followers, usually share a common vision or direction, but each brings different skill sets. Followers usually are not in the spotlight, but they work hard behind the scenes to ensure that the mission is accomplished. This makes a follower a leader of sorts, too.

Many students see themselves as followers. Who do they choose to follow? Is the leader they are following a positive or negative leader?

Worksheet 2

Tough Decisions

Scenario: A popular student has been bullying others by threatening to hurt them if they don't do what he or she wants them to do. You like this person but know what he or she is doing isn't respectful. Write your responses to the following questions:

What would your life be like if you followed this person?

_____
_____
_____
_____

What would your life be like if you stood up to this person and let him or her know what he or she is doing is wrong?

_____
_____
_____
_____

Describe how you would feel about yourself when you did the right thing.

_____
_____
_____
_____

List three people you could ask for help if you needed it:

1.
2.
3.

Worksheet 3

Parent Interview

Interview one of your parents or another relative.
Ask the following questions and record the responses:

Whom do you credit for influencing choices you have made in your life? Why?

_____
_____
_____

What did this person say or do that influenced your thinking and choices?

_____
_____
_____

What words of wisdom did he or she pass on that stick with you even today?

_____
_____
_____

What characteristics, traits, or qualities do you admire in this person?

_____
_____
_____

Which of these qualities do you believe you acquired from this person? How do you use these qualities to inspire others?

_____
_____
_____

Does the leader they choose to follow hold beliefs, values, and morals that are consistent with their own beliefs, values, and morals? Whomever they choose to follow is a choice and their choices do influence others. All students, in essence, are leaders through the consequences of their choices, whether positive or negative.

Students need to become more aware of how they are leaders in whom and how they choose to follow as well. This concept is important as they explore the notion of bullying behavior. Students must come to realize they have choices, whether they are positive or negative, and that these choices influence the classroom and school environment in very powerful ways.

Students who see themselves as choices A, B, or C typically believe leadership is based on position or title, that an individual has to earn the status of being called a leader. Adults and other students tend to elevate the students who choose choice E or F, ranking them in a higher leadership category than others based on the reputation of these groups rather than the individual student's actual leadership qualities.

Students who see themselves as choice C—I'm not a leader or a follower—see themselves as "neutral." This is not likely. To be neutral one would need to live in a bubble with no one around. Every interaction or seemingly non-interaction one has with other students has influence. There is no such thing as neutrality.

Overall student perception is mostly based on "more than/less than." If I am not popular ("more than"), I will likely be perceived or perceive myself as less than. We are conditioned in our culture to take on this posture with the way we idolize actors and actresses, professional athletes, and other high profile personalities. This ranking of a student or groups of students is debilitating and hampers students' ability to perceive themselves as leaders. Students do not realize that they influence the school climate just by being there. This lesson can help students understand that, even though they may not be involved in student government or extracurricular activities, they still can and do have the power to influence the school environment.

Positive Leader Interview

Thank you for your time today! What does it mean to be a positive leader?

_____
_____
_____

What important qualities make a great leader?

_____
_____
_____

Which of the qualities do you see in yourself?

_____
_____
_____

How do you think a person becomes a leader?

_____
_____
_____

Will you spend a few minutes a month mentoring me and helping me grow into a great leader? If not monthly, how often will work for you?

What would be a good day and time for you? What week is good in the month?

Circle One: **Monday Tuesday Wednesday Thursday Friday**

Time: Week   **1   2   3   4**

Thank you for the opportunity to meet with you about leadership today!
(*Make sure you extend a firm handshake!*)

Leader Reflection

Write a thoughtful reflection for a morning announcement
using what you learned from your interviews.

_____
_____
_____
_____
_____
_____
_____
_____
_____
_____
_____
_____
_____
_____
_____
_____
_____
_____

Share your reflection with your teacher or principal!

Helping all students see themselves as leaders is an important step toward coming to believe they have the power to create a safe and amazing school. This activity challenges all students to become more aware of what it means to be a positive leader and helps them come to believe they have the ability to be Christ-like leaders. The overall intention is to generate a condition whereby students become conscious of the power they have to influence the school climate. We want students to come to a deep understanding that everything they say and do has tremendous influence in the school and even the world. As students become more confident with this notion, they are in a good position to hold each other accountable by questioning disrespectful behavior and celebrating positive behavior.

In the last 3 to 5 minutes of Activity One students identify as many positive leader qualities, characteristics, or traits as possible. This exercise addresses multiple levels of processing:

- **Auditory**: Students hear the leader qualities as they are spoken.
- **Visual**: Students see the leader qualities written down on a flipchart as well as on a handout.
- **Kinesthetic**: Movement makes the exercise physically interactive.
- **Phonetic Code**: Students have an opportunity to listen to and verbalize the leader words during the "WordStorming" session.
- **Group**: Students brainstorm a collective list of positive leader characteristics together, which increases ownership and a common language of what leadership means to them.

Leader Words

Over 500 student-generated leader words have been compiled within a 5-year span from approximately 3,000 students in Grades 4-8. Figure 3 contains the top 32 leader words presented in order of frequency.

Part of the process in becoming positive leaders is connecting with positive qualities and characteristics of leadership. Students tune into this activity because the words chosen are student generated rather than adult imposed, making the leader words even more significant and relevant for them. This is a powerful and dynamic way to influence student perception and establish a positive norm around what it means to be a Christ-like leader in the school.

If a student attaches something negative to a leader word, just to be clever, pause the process and ask the class if this leader word is one they would include on their list. More often than not, the choice made by the class will overrule the negative. This is a wonderful glimpse of positive peer pressure at work. This activity lays the groundwork for a strong "collective voice" to grow as students speak up and out on what is and is not acceptable behavior. The student generated leader words can be used to set the bar on behavior. Any negative student behaviors are a contradiction to the positive leader words they have chosen.

Spiritual Perspective

In most Sacramental programs, young people between Grades 4-8 are presently candidates or have recently received the Sacrament of Confirmation. The gifts of the Holy Spirit seal and confirm the baptized in union with Christ. Confirmation calls them to greater participation in the worship and apostolic life of the Church. Often when we list leadership qualities we fail to connect the Sacramental gifts and graces of Confirmation. To link our leadership gift(s) and our sacramental life in concrete situations becomes a remarkable teaching tool. The traditional list of the gifts is based on Isaiah 11:1-2.

> But a shoot shall sprout from the stump of Jesse, and from his roots a bud shall blossom. The spirit of the LORD shall rest upon him: a spirit of wisdom and of understanding, A spirit of counsel and of strength, a spirit of knowledge and of fear of the LORD.

Leadership calls us to "act courageously on behalf of the teachings of Christ" and "to be brave in defending human life from conception to death, to be steadfast in seeking justice for the oppressed, and to be determined that the light of Christ's compassion and peace will shine everywhere on earth" (USCCB, 2006, p. 221).

Christ is our cornerstone as we are called to develop our leadership skills. Students need to be directed to this Christ-centered end and need modeling and encouragement to succeed. Scripture also invites us to look at leadership as service. It is important that our students understand that their leadership gifts may be revealed in many ways. After the Passover meal and the institution of the Eucharist,

> [Jesus] rose from supper and took off his outer garments. He took a towel and tied it around his waist. Then he poured water into a basin and began to wash the disciples' feet and dry them with the towel around his waist....So when he had washed their feet (and) put his garments back on and reclined at table again, he said to them, "Do you realize what I have done for you? You call me 'teacher' and 'master,' and rightly so, for indeed I am. If I, therefore, the master and teacher, have washed your feet, you ought to wash one another's feet. I have given you a model to follow, so that as I have done for you, you should also do. Amen, amen, I say to you, no slave is greater than his master nor any messenger greater than the one who sent him. If you understand this, blessed are you if you do it. (John 13:4-17)

Delve deeper into the topic of leadership with students!

- *Kick It In: Developing the Self-Motivation to Take the Lead, Volume 1 (Fran Kick, 2000)*
- *Inspiring Leadership in Teens: Group Activities to Foster Integrity, Responsibility, and Compassion (Ric Stuecker, 2010)*

Top 32 Leader Words

1.	Brave/Courageous	17.	Compassionate
2.	Sense of Humor	18.	Perseverance
3.	Trustworthy	19.	Positive
4.	Respectful	20.	Truthful
5.	Responsible	21.	Understanding
6.	Smart/Wisdom	22.	Organized
7.	Caring	23.	Flexibility
8.	Kind/Kindness	24.	Faithful
9.	Honest	25.	Friendly
10.	Helpful	26.	Creative
11.	Listener	27.	Role Model
12.	Loving/Lovable	28.	Pride
13.	Patience	29.	Forgiving
14.	Confidence	30.	Common Sense
15.	Cooperative	31.	Generous
16.	Loyal/Loyalty	32.	Pride

Figure 3

Facilitator Script
Who Me? A Leader?

TIME	PREPARATION & PROCESS	LOGISTICS
0:00	**Session Preparation**	
	• None	
	• Student Workbook, pp. 6-12	

Process

Say: *"Stand up if you are a leader!"*

Note. As the teacher says this, she or he should stand tall with toes pointing straight ahead and feet shoulder width apart. Remain silent and observe what students do.

(If necessary) *"No talking, please. This is a nonverbal or silent activity."*

Teachers are encouraged to have pictures or names of great leaders handy to post up on the wall or bulletin board.

| 1:00 | *"I am going to go around and ask (interview) a few of you about why you stood up or why you are seated."* | |

Note. Sometimes after saying you are going to interview a few students, some may sit down because they think they will be less likely to be interviewed and do not want to be put on the spot. Just notice this, but do not say anything to these students yet.

| 2:00 | *"Why did you stand up?"* and *"Why didn't you stand up?"* (Randomly pick students, alternating boys and girls) | |

Note. Listen carefully to the responses students share. Never devalue or put down what any student says. Thank them and then use whatever is said as an opportunity to emphasize or reframe into positive leadership.

| 3:00 | *"What quality, trait, or characteristic describes you as a leader?"* | Use a flipchart for writing leader words. If using the board have a student transcribe the words onto a sheet of paper. |
| 10:00 | *"Let's brainstorm as many qualities, traits, or characteristics of positive leadership as possible."* | |

"Look at all the great words you came up with together that describe positive leadership. Excellent job! Remember, these are just words. It's important for us to not just say the words or put them down on paper, but practice becoming what they mean."

| 15:00 | *"If you are willing to be a leader that practices being the leader words that you came up with, please stand up! Thank you for your commitment to practice being the best leader you can be every day!"* | Have all leader words typed on hardcopy from the flip chart or board and copies made for each student prior to Phase II Activity Two. |

Activity Two

Choose Your Flavor!

PURPOSE

To increase awareness around how attitude is a choice and how our choices create either a positive or negative ripple in the classroom, school, and in the world

LEARNING OBJECTIVES

- Students will increase awareness of how choices and attitude influence others.
- Students will be empowered to believe they can positively influence school climate.
- Students will increase ability to make the distinction between thoughts, feelings, and actions.
- Students will increase awareness of the pervasiveness of put-downs.
- Students will become sensitized to put-downs being a form of peer maltreatment.
- Students will increase awareness of how put-downs hinder student leadership.

CORRESPONDING STUDENT WORKBOOK PAGES 14-19

- Journal Entry   1
- Student Worksheets   5

Journal Entry

Choose Your Flavor

Journal about how our attitude influences other people.

_____
_____
_____
_____
_____
_____

Journal about how you influence others with your attitude.

_____
_____
_____
_____
_____
_____
_____

List three ways to change a negative attitude into a positive one:

   1.
   2.
   3.

List three ways you will be a "positive pebble in the school pond":

   1.
   2.
   3.

14 **PHASE I**
Christ Is Our Model for Leadership

Peace Be With You
WORKBOOK

Worksheet 1

Choose Your Flavor

Write about a time when you were put down.

_____
_____
_____

How do you feel about being treated this way?

_____
_____

How did you handle the situation?

_____
_____

How would you handle the put-down if you were faced with it today?

_____
_____
_____

What difference does it make with how we handle situations like this?

_____
_____
_____

List three positive things you can do to prevent being put down ever again:

   1.
   2.
   3.

Peace Be With You
WORKBOOK

PHASE I 15
Christ Is Our Model for Leadership

Eliminating Put-Downs

Attitude is everything! How students treat each other will send a positive or negative ripple throughout the school. A correlation exists between negative attitudes and put-downs. The word put-down is defined in the Merriam-Webster Dictionary as: "to degrade, disparage, belittle, disapprove, criticize, humiliate or squelch." One's attitude and everyday put-downs are infectious and can seriously contaminate efforts to move a community in a reverent direction. Put-downs contain all the ingredients of bullying behavior and when applied to our definition of bullying, put-downs are indeed bullying behavior.

To degrade, humiliate, or belittle another person—make them feel ridiculous, unimportant or less than—is an imbalance of power and certainly creates an unsafe and threatening environment. Teachers and students alike are undoubtedly aware of the glaring reality and frequency of put-downs. No one deserves to be put down. Put-downs are an unjust use of power. Often a target will retaliate in a way that is more severe than the actual bullying behavior. A bullying student can often be seen smiling or laughing following a target's reaction to a hurtful behavior; this could be considered satisfaction for the aggressor.

Students quickly learn that they can evoke specific reactions by initiating certain prescribed demeaning actions toward another student and even a teacher. Through trial and error students learn how to push "hot buttons" when they talk in class, yell out or at someone, make a particular gesture, poke, pinch, punch, grimace, call a person a derogatory name, or make fun of another about something to try to get a reaction. When students do get reactions they gain a sense of power and control knowing another person (student or teacher) reacts a certain way, most every time the action is directed at him or her.

Unfortunately it is often rare to find students complimenting each other for much

---

Worksheet 2
Choose Your Flavor
Write on the following:

A time when you put someone down.
_____
_____
_____

How did you feel after the put-down? After a short time? After a longer period of time?
_____
_____

How do you feel about treating another person this way?
_____
_____

Why did you put this person down? Were you trying to make yourself feel better? Were you trying to make the other person feel bad? Did this work?
_____
_____
_____

Did you increase or decrease your self-esteem by handling the situation this way? Why?
_____
_____

How could you have gotten what you wanted from the other student without putting him or her down?
_____
_____

How would you handle this situation today?
_____
_____

Worksheet 3
Choose Your Flavor
ACTION STEP:
Put up (compliment) as many classmates as you can today.

How do you feel when you are giving put-ups?
_____
_____

How do people respond when you put them up?
_____
_____

How do you feel after you see or hear the other person's response to your put-up?
_____
_____
_____

What would your school be like if everyone only gave put-ups to each other?
_____
_____
_____

How can you promote put-ups in your school?
_____
_____
_____

of anything. Put-downs are common and are both conscious and unconscious among youth, which creates a negative ripple in the school. Students' "knee jerk" reactions to just about everything are part and parcel of their underdeveloped brains. Students often act or react negatively in routine or habitual ways that do not reflect consideration for others. Guiding them to be more considerate and respectful is a continuous challenge. Even with developed brains, adults often struggle to remain positive and/or give compliments to others. It is not uncommon to be a part of everyday adult conversations filled with complaints or put-downs about one's work, spouse, the economy, the president, the Church, or in general what's wrong with the world.

Put-downs are an attempt to make ourselves feel like we have power and control over people, places, and situations where we may feel powerless and helpless. The truth of the matter is that students are testing their power to influence others and their environment. We are in a great position to help sensitize students to the positive and negative impact of their power and increase their awareness of overt and covert influences and how these operate in the school. Shedding light on this reality serves as an opportunity for students to reflect on their behaviors toward others. As educators, when we help students see bullying behavior as a violation of human rights to be taken seriously and not "mere" bullying, we can empower them to create a new reality of what it means to be a leader that can positively influence the school climate (Greene, 2006).

Put-downs are at minimum a gateway to bullying—a repetitious pattern of behavior of disrespectful peer maltreatment. Community-wide awareness of the destructiveness surrounding put-down behavior is necessary in order to create dissatisfaction with the current state. This dissatisfaction is essential in order to make a fundamental shift to "put-ups" or compliments, affirmations, and celebrations of what is right with each other, our school, and our world.

Worksheet 4

Choose Your Flavor

ACTION STEP:
Put up (compliment) one of your parents or another adult today.

How did you feel when you gave an adult a put-up?

How did he or she respond?

How did you feel after you saw the adult's response to your put-up?

Ask one of your parents or an adult to give you a put-up.

How did you feel when you received a put-up?

What would your family be like if you only gave each other put-ups?

Worksheet 5

Choose Your Flavor

Describe what your school would be like with only positive ripples.

What would your school look like if it was the most amazing school on the planet?

How would everyone be treating each other?

What would everyone be saying? What would everyone be doing?

Spiritual Perspective on Put-Downs

Speaking to a general audience on the humanity of Jesus, Pope John Paul II (1988) began with Scripture from Hebrews:

> For it is not as if we had a high priest who was incapable of feeling our weaknesses with us; but we have one who has been tempted in every way that we are, though he is without sin....The Word made flesh, flesh (*sarx*) indicates man precisely as a corporeal being (*sarkikos*), who comes into being through being born of a woman (cf. Gal 4:4). In his corporeal nature Jesus of Nazareth, like every man, experienced fatigue, hunger and thirst. His body was vulnerable, subject to suffering, and sensitive to physical pain. It was precisely in this flesh (*sarx*) that he was subjected to dreadful tortures and was eventually crucified. He was crucified, died and was buried. (para. 3)

Scripture references indicate that Jesus experienced the human condition of bullying, being jeered, mocked, and tormented. In the Gospel of John when Jesus was in the Temple celebrating the Feast of Dedication, he claimed to be the Son of God: "The Jews again picked up rocks to stone him" (John 10:31).

In Matthew 27:39-42, the crucified Christ is mocked.

> Those passing by reviled him, shaking their heads and saying, "You who would destroy the temple and rebuild it in three days, save yourself, if you are the Son of God, (and) come down from the cross!" Likewise the chief priests with the scribes and elders mocked him and said, "He saved others; he cannot save himself. So he is the king of Israel! Let him come down from the cross now, and we will believe in him."

Luke tells us: "Even the soldiers jeered at him. As they approached to offer him wine they called out, 'If you are King of the Jews, save yourself'" (Luke 23:36-37).

Bearing the physical and emotional wounds of life and death, the Gospel of John 20:19 tells us that Jesus stood with his Resurrection perfect body and proclaimed: "Peace be with you."

From bullying, put-downs, and shaming to healing and peace—this is the call of Christ to His followers.

Scripture from the New Testament aptly sums up what this program is about:

> So turn from youthful desires and pursue righteousness, faith, love, and peace, along with those who call on the Lord with purity of heart. Avoid foolish and ignorant debates, for you know that they breed quarrels. A slave of the Lord should not quarrel, but should be gentle with everyone, able to teach, tolerant, correcting opponents with kindness. It may be that God will grant them repentance that leads to knowledge of the truth, and that they may return to their senses out of the devil's snare, where they are entrapped by him, for his will. (2 Timothy 2:22-26)

Choose Your Flavor

Activity Two asks students to raise their hands if they have ever put someone down or have been put down by someone in the classroom. Introducing these questions is of significant importance for the following fundamental reasons:

- Students collectively witness the pervasiveness of putdowns. When the majority of students raise their hands, it reveals the sinful presence of put-downs that exist among them.
- Creating this unpleasant state is intentional and a desired outcome of this activity.
- This activity is not to shame students, but should create a level of dissatisfaction with the current reality.
- Dissonance or a level of tension is the necessary catalyst motivating change to the current state.
- Students must be empowered and inspired to end the mediocrity of put-downs and to be open to a much higher standard (Fritz, 1989).

Choose Your Flavor is designed to help students become aware of how they contribute to the negative ripple and, as a result, support bullying behavior. This is a defining moment for students to take appropriate responsibility for giving up put-downs, empowering them to make a fundamental shift toward influencing a positive ripple and a thriving school environment.

Below are some helpful ways to guide students toward positive choices and a positive attitude:

- Model positive choices
- Guide students to others—adults and students—who model positive choices
- Give students only positive options from which to choose
- Affirm students for positive choices they are making
- Capture student interest in an area that helps them focus and builds confidence
- Connect students with others—adults and students—that hold similar interests
- Establish clear boundaries and consequences regarding poor choices
- Consistently enforce clear and meaningful consequences for poor judgment
- Redirect poor decision making by giving only positive choice options

"Each time a person stands up for an ideal, or acts to improve the lot of others, or strikes out against injustice, he or she sends forth a tiny ripple of hope. And crossing each other from a million different centers of energy and daring, those ripples build a current that can sweep down the mightiest walls of oppression."

ROBERT KENNEDY

Facilitator Script
Choose Your Flavor!

TIME	PREPARATION & PROCESS	LOGISTICS

0:00 | **Session Preparation**
- None
- Student Workbook, pp. 14-19

Process

Say: *"Let's look at some things that get in the way of our being positive leaders!"*

"I will ask you some tough questions and all I expect from you is to be honest. Honesty is an important quality in a leader."

"Raise your hand if you've ever been put down."

Note. Notice how many hands are up. Most likely every hand is raised.

1:00 *"Thank you. Put your hands down."*

"Here's an even tougher question. Raise your hand if you've been put down by someone in this room?"

Note. Notice how many hands are up. Usually every hand is raised.

"Look around the room and notice all the hands up. You're not alone."

"Thank you for being honest. Put your hands down."

2:00 *"How does it feel to be put down?"*

Note. Allow students time to share. When a student says a word or phrase, repeat it back to them so the student and the class hear the "echo" of the experience and that you heard them.

Possible Responses: Hurt, depressed, alone, frustrated, sad, angry, like dirt, excluded, etc.

3:00 *"Raise your hand if you've ever put someone down."*

Note. Notice how many hands are up. Usually most, if not all, hands are raised.

"Thank you. Put your hands down."

"Now, the tougher question: Raise your hand if you've ever put down someone in this room."

"Look around the room and notice how many hands are up. You're not alone."

LOGISTICS column:

Teachers are encouraged to have pictures or slogans of positive messages posted around the classroom.

"Attitude is Everything!"

"It is our attitude at the beginning of a difficult undertaking which, more than anything else, will determine its successful outcome."

-WILLIAM JAMES

Choose Your Flavor!

TIME	PREPARATION & PROCESS	LOGISTICS

4:00 *"Why would anyone ever put someone down, knowing what it feels like being put down?"*

Notice what students say about why someone would put someone else down. Again, "echo" their responses. In particular, notice and recognize a student who admits that put-downs are a way of getting back, getting even, getting revenge, settling the score, etc. This is a very important concept to get out into the open.

"Is it normal and natural to want to get back, get even, or feel vengeful when we are put down?"

Expected Response: Yes!

5:00 *"Yes, this is a very normal feeling!"*

"Is it okay to do something to get even when you feel this way?"

Expected Response: No!

"You're right! Two wrongs do not make a right! It's not okay to go from the feeling to an action against someone."

"There were a lot of hands raised when I asked both of these tough questions. I really appreciate all of you modeling honesty and taking the risk to raise your hands."

"Now raise your hand if you want to be part of stopping all put-downs?"

6:00 *"I applaud you all for your willingness and courage to be a part of our effort to stop all put-downs!"*

Note. Notice any hands not raised. If not, ask the following question:

"(Student Name) Why wouldn't you want to be a part of this effort?"

Note. Give the student a chance to explain, thank him or her for sharing and use what is said as an opportunity to discuss with the class any fears or barriers to making this commitment with each other.

"There are probably at least 100 flavors of ice cream. Today we only have two flavors available: chocolate and vanilla."

7:00 *"Who would be the chocolate lovers? Who would be the vanilla lovers? Who raised their hand twice?"* Laugh out loud!

"If attitude came in two flavors, what would they be?"

Choose Your Flavor!

TIME	PREPARATION & PROCESS	LOGISTICS

Possible Responses: Good and bad, okay and not okay, right and wrong, helpful and not helpful, delicious and disgusting, positive and negative, etc.

"That's right! Positive and negative."

"Every day you have a choice of which flavor attitude you choose at school and in the classroom. Choose your flavor!"

8:00 *"You influence the school environment every moment of every day with the attitude you choose."*

"If the flavor you choose is negative, just like throwing a pebble in a pond, what kind of rippling effect will you make in the school?"

"That's right! Choosing a negative flavor of attitude affects everyone in a negative way."

"What kind of rippling effect do you want to make in this school?"

"The choice of flavor of attitude you make everyday is a way that you have the power to influence this school."

9:00 *"What kind of choice do you want to make as a leader in this school?"*

"Choose your flavor! But, choose the one that reflects the kind of school you want to be a part of. Choose wisely!"

"If you are willing to be a leader that chooses to have a positive ripple in our school, stand up!"

Note. If any student does not stand up, use this as an opportunity to have him or her share concerns and explain why committing to this step is difficult. This is not a time to shame or humiliate a student into compliance. By honoring a student's position you will actually be modeling compassionate leadership for all students.

Teachers are encouraged to post a picture of ripples in water.

Another option is to have students choose to be a positive ripple with a three-step commitment process:
1. **Raise your hand**
2. **Stand up**
3. **Take one step forward**

10:00 *"Look at all of you standing! Realize that you have the power to create an amazing school together. You can create a positive reality. Together we can create a 'Reality of Respect' by putting each other up and supporting each other!"*

"Everybody talks about wanting to change things and help and fix, but ultimately all you can do is fix yourself. And that's a lot. Because if you can fix yourself, it has a rippling effect."

-ROB REINER

Activity Three

Bully to Leader Role Plays

PURPOSE
Students actively participate in two role play scenarios that depict common gender specific bullying behaviors and practice Positive Behavioral Rehearsal to integrate positive choices with positive outcomes.

LEARNING OBJECTIVES
- Students will increase awareness of the roles in the "bullying triangle" through two scenarios.
- Students will understand that no one wins with bullying behaviors.
- Students will understand no one person is better or less than another.
- Students will neutralize bullying triangle roles by learning how to break the code of silence.
- Students will identify what it takes to create a "win/win/win" with each other.
- Students will understand that everyone is responsible for bullying behavior.
- Students will discover what it means to be accountable for their behavior.
- Students will work toward eliminating divisions such as classism, sexism, racism, and rankism and a culture that determines who is and who isn't popular and that ascribes power to the more popular students.

CORRESPONDING STUDENT WORKBOOK PAGES 21-24
- Journal Entry   1
- Student Worksheets   3

MATERIALS NEEDED
Sturdy chair
Optional bed sheet or blanket

Bully to Leader   *Journal Entry*

Journal how your understanding of being a leader has changed since the first session.

_____
_____
_____
_____
_____
_____
_____
_____
_____
_____
_____
_____
_____
_____
_____
_____

Three things I learned about myself as a leader:

1.

2.

3.

Peace Be With You   **PHASE I**   21
WORKBOOK   *Christ Is Our Model for Leadership*

Role Play Scenario Guidelines

The use of scenarios—role plays or skits—engages students in the learning process. The scenarios are used to create a language and help define the roles played out in the bullying dynamic. The key to this activity is keeping the intended goals and outcomes in focus. Always be certain that all students are safe during and after the activity.

Do not end a role play scenario with unfinished business. Always end a role play scenario positively, emphasizing the intended lessons.

Remember the script for these scenarios evolved over years of discovering what works and what doesn't work. Following the script allows you to conduct both scenarios in a safe and successful manner. Resist the temptation to ad lib the script the first time you do this with students. If, however, after a time or two you feel confident the direction you are heading will further enhance student awareness around the intended outcomes, feel free to expand the scripted process.

As new bullying dynamics enter the social arena, more updated information can be added to the scripts (i.e., sexting and cyberbullying).

The intention of the scenarios is to expose the dynamic of bullying and increase student awareness. This exposure sensitizes students to the real-time bullying dynamics they are either directly or indirectly involved with both in and out of the school environment. Educating students on a common language which defines the roles in the Bullying Triangle empowers them to collectively view this dynamic as countercultural. Positive Behavioral Rehearsal also equips students with alternative choices, building confidence in their ability to change behaviors. Transparency levels the playing field and is critical in shifting this dynamic from the present covert norms to an open, honest, and positive school climate (See Figure 4).

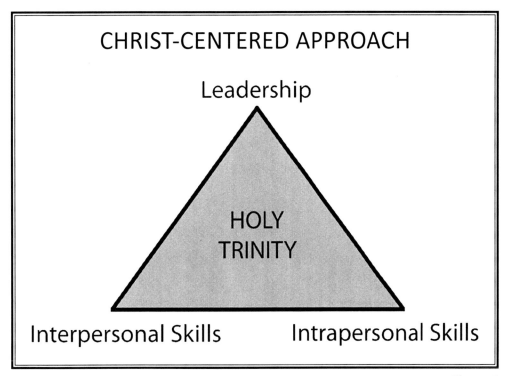

Figure 4

Role Play I:
What Goes Around Comes Around

This first scenario is a classic male version of bullying behavior titled, "What Goes Around Comes Around." Girls can play this game, too! Both role plays overlap and are not exclusive to any one gender, but each scenario is typical of how the specific gender engages in bullying behavior.

Have six boys come to the front of the room. Make sure you have enough room for movement and placement of the roles the boys will be playing. Have one sturdy chair in front of the room facing the side of the class. Huddle the boys and briefly let them know the theme of this scenario. Ask one of the boys to volunteer to be the *Bully*, one to be the *Target*, two to be *Active Bystanders*, and the two remaining to be *Passive Bystanders*. Tell the Bully that he is going to be standing on top of the chair and putting down the Target kneeling in front of him. Tell the Active Bystanders that they are going to encourage the bullying behavior by going along with what the Bully is doing. Ask the Passive Bystanders to go to one side of the room and just watch.

Have the sturdy chair in position and ask the Bully to stand on top of the chair. Ask the Target to kneel down in front of the chair. Ask the Active Bystanders to stand behind the Bully and the Passive Bystanders to stand on the other side of the room. Make sure the boys and the rest of the class hear that the only rule is that they cannot touch another student during the role play.

Announce to the entire class that the name of this role play is "What Goes Around Comes Around." Instruct the students in the scenario to begin and wait to see what happens. If the boys look confused or are hesitant at first, give the Bully a line or two and some gestures to get started such as, "You are such a loser" and "You'll never be as good as me!" Use your index finger and gesture downward toward the Target. Allow the role play to go for about one minute then say, "Stop."

Worksheet 1

Bully to Leader Role Plays

Write about what you learned from one of the two role plays:
"What Goes Around Comes Around" or "Odd Girl Out"

Here are some hints to help you get started:
- The "Passive Bystanders" are the most likely to help stop the bullying triangle.
- Everyone is responsible for bullying.
- Exclusion is hurtful and is a way of saying that we are better than someone else.
- How we treat others affects not only others but ourselves, too.
- What is the "code of silence" and how does it make the bullying problem worse?
- Having the courage to speak up is hard, but is what it takes to make a safe and amazing school.
- No one is better than anyone else. We are all equal.
- Other things not listed here that you might have learned from the role plays.

_____
_____
_____
_____
_____
_____
_____
_____
_____
_____
_____
_____
_____

Worksheet 2

Bully to Leader Role Plays

Write about the person you identified with most in the first or second role play.

What role do you identify with? Why?
_____
_____

What did you learn about yourself being in this role in real life?
_____
_____

Do you like being in this role in real life?
_____
_____

What choices do you have to help yourself get out of this role?
_____
_____

What choices will build your self-esteem?
_____
_____

List three people who will support you in making good choices:
1.
2.
3.

Interview the *Bully* and ask him how he feels right now. Listen for statements like, "I feel big...better than...stronger than...superior... powerful...like I am king of the mountain...bigger than life." These are some probable responses that would be expected from a bully. Ask the class who is on the chair. They will undoubtedly answer that the person on the chair is the Bully.

Next, interview the *Active Bystanders* asking them how they feel supporting the Bully. Listen for statements like "I feel stronger being on his side....I am glad I am on his side and not where the target is....I feel sorry for the target, but I like it better over here....If I stick up for the target I might get treated the same way....I want to do what is popular even though it may not be right." These are some probable responses that might be expected from active bystanders. Ask the class which two cast members are supporting the Bully. The class may not be familiar with the term "bystander." Probable answers are posse, accomplice, gang, etc. This is an opportunity to educate the class on the term and definition of an active bystander.

Worksheet 3

Bully to Leader Skit

Write a skit about disrespect or bullying behavior
that ends with a positive outcome. Keep safety in mind!

List your characters here:

_____
_____
_____

Write your script here:

_____
_____
_____
_____
_____
_____
_____
_____
_____
_____
_____
_____
_____
_____
_____

Share your script with your teacher, who will most likely allow you to perform your skit in front of the class if there is enough class time and if your skit has a meaningful lesson to teach your classmates.

24 **PHASE I**
Christ Is Our Model for Leadership

Peace Be With You
WORKBOOK

Next interview the *Target*. Ask him how he feels being down there on the floor. Listen for statements like "I feel little, less than, weak, inferior, unworthy, like dirt, powerless, a loser....I want to get back....I want to hurt him." These are probable responses that would be expected from the Target. If the student does not say anything like, "I want to get him back or I want to hurt him," ask him what he would like to do to the Bully for treating him this way. This usually encourages one of these kinds of statements. Ask the class who this cast member is on his knees. They will usually respond that this is the "Victim." Agree with them and let them know that you prefer the term, "Target," because a target usually has choices and a victim doesn't. Ask the class, "What are some of the choices targets have in bullying situations?" Some probable answers are "Fight back....Say stop....Report it to a trusted adult, teacher, counselor, or parent."

When the Target says he wants to hurt the Bully or get him back, flip the script asking the Bully and Target to reverse roles. Have the Bully step down from the chair and get on his knees in the Target position. Have the Target step onto the chair in the Bully position. Look at the class and say, "What goes around comes around!" Allow the role play to continue for a minute or so with the boys in their new roles. Often the former Targets are more convincing and even more harsh than the former Bully.

Interview the *new Bully* and ask him how he feels in his new role. Listen for statements like "I feel better now....I am making this right....I am getting even....I feel stronger, more powerful....I'm the superior one now....I'm on top." Interview the *new Target* and ask him how he feels. Listen for statements like "I don't like it down here....I want to get back up there....I want to hurt him." These are some of the kinds of statements that would be expected from the Bully and Target with the script flipped.

Interview the *Passive Bystanders* asking them how they felt watching the bullying behavior and why they didn't do anything to stop it or help the Target. Listen for statements like

"I didn't do anything so it's not my fault….I feel sorry for the Target but he deserves it….I can't help the Target because he and the Active Bystanders will treat me the same way….I don't want to tell a teacher because nothing will happen or I will really get it once the Bully finds out." These are some probable responses that would be expected from the Passive Bystanders.

Every response or statement made during the role play by the Bully, Target, and Active or Passive Bystanders is a potential teachable moment. Use any of the cast members' responses to help define, discuss, and explain the bullying triangle and emphasize the "lose/lose/lose" lesson of this dynamic. This can be accomplished by asking the class questions like, "Who is the winner in a Bully Triangle?"

There are no winners in the Bully Triangle. It isn't even a win/lose. The Bullying Triangle is always a lose/lose/lose! Putting someone down, trying to get even, and bystanders either actively or passively supporting this behavior can never amount to a winning situation. Who is at fault? Each role is at fault. Each role plays a significant part in keeping this behavior going. Who is responsible for ending it? Each role is responsible for ending the behavior.

The Bully, Target, and Active Bystanders may have trouble seeing any choices other than the ones they are already making. The possible choices they do have may seem more like dilemmas, because of actual or perceived risk. For instance, an Active Bystander may think if he sides with the Target, he may become a target too or be ostracized from the group in some way or the same way the Target is being ostracized. Most likely, the Passive Bystanders are the best ones to do something about the situation. Note that all students watching the role play in the class also have become passive bystanders.

Immediately follow up this role play with what is called Positive Behavioral Rehearsal. This is an opportunity for the boys to practice doing the right thing by reworking the scenario, creating a positive win/win/win outcome. By ending the exercise positively, we are more likely to reinforce expected behavior. The entire class helps by adding lines or other helpful ideas. This involves the entire class by getting them to work together to figure out more acceptable norms for handling these situations.

Positive Behavioral Rehearsal Possibilities

- An *Active Bystander* might say to the Bully, "I don't think this is a good idea to treat him this way. Let's find something better to do."

- A *Passive Bystander* intervenes by saying something to the Bully and Active Bystanders. If the Passive Bystanders can't think of anything to say, offer one or all of the following statements: "Stop this!…How would you like it if you were treated this way?… This is not the way we treat each other in our school….Are you really making yourself feel better or improving your life by treating (Target) this way?" Whatever statement the Passive Bystander chooses is most likely the statement he feels most comfortable with and is confident will work.

- Have the *Target* display courage by standing up and saying something to defend himself. If he can't think of anything to say, ask the class what the Target could say that would be helpful in this situation. If necessary, offer one or all of the following statements: "Stop! I am not going to be a part of this any more….I don't deserve this kind of treatment….Why don't you find something better to do." Of course, it is always an option for the Target to not say anything at all and just walk away.

When students come up with their own resistance statements, they create a collective language or new norm that works to empower each other in taking a stand together against bullying behavior.

After doing the Positive Behavioral Rehearsals, have the boys who originally played the roles of Bully and Target stand in front of each other and ask the class again, "Who is better?" It is important to emphasize that there is really no such thing as better than or less than, even though our culture makes it appear this way. No one is better than or less than because of the color of their skin, the size or shape of their body, the kind of clothes or shoes they wear, how much money they have or don't have, the kind of car they drive or the house they live in, whether they wear glasses or not, have braces or not, play sports or not, etc. We are all equal. No one is better than anyone else or less than anyone else, even when we act like we are. We need to practice treating each other as equals and as we would like to be treated. We have more to gain by putting each other up and being supportive.

Before you send the boys back to the classroom audience, remind them and the class the first part of the exercise was just a role play. The second part, which is the Positive Behavioral Rehearsal is what is expected in this school. Thank them for volunteering to play their roles in front of the class. Let them know that you admire them for their courage to participate by having the class applaud them for their good work.

Spiritual Perspective

The boys' role play and Positive Behavioral Rehearsal bring to mind the Scripture story of the adulterous woman in John which reads:

> [The Scribes and Pharisees] said to him, "Teacher, this woman was caught in the very act of committing adultery. Now in the law, Moses commanded us to stone such women. So what do you say?" They said this to test him, so that they could have some charge to bring against him. Jesus bent down and began to write on the ground with his finger. But when they continued asking him, he straightened up and said to them, "Let the one among you who is without sin be the first to throw a stone at her." Again he bent down and wrote on the ground. And in response, they went away one by one, beginning with the elders. So he was left alone with the woman before him. Then Jesus straightened up and said to her, "Woman, where are they? Has no one condemned you?" She replied, "No one, sir." Then Jesus said, "Neither do

I condemn you. Go, (and) from now on do not sin any more." (John 8:4-11)

Using the phraseology of the Bullying Triangle with this Scripture passage, we are able to objectively see a new intervention option. We have the Scribes and Pharisees who want to trick Jesus and stone a woman for her sinfulness. They use their righteous position supported by the Law for stoning. In Matthew 1:19, Mary the mother of Jesus, is with child, and Joseph, "since he was a righteous man, yet unwilling to expose her to shame, decided to divorce her quietly." The Scribes had options, like Joseph, yet they chose to be bullies with their rigid righteousness.

The woman is the target. It is imaginable the people present could have been easily stirred into group frenzy by the Scribes and Pharisees to stone the woman, becoming active bystanders. Jesus was a bystander as well and became actively engaged in teaching when the problem was presented to him. Jesus' courageous words asked the question, who is sinless among you? His act of writing in the sand without engaging in argument defused the bullying.

Jesus was straightforward and firm with the Scribes, but in a very respectful way. Most importantly, when Jesus addressed the woman alone, He respected her dignity as a person and invited her to grow by sinning no more. The power of one person intervening in a bullying incident can create positive rippling effects.

Read the Scripture story, John 8:1-11. Ask students to identify:

- The bully(s): *the Scribes and Pharisees*
- The target: *the woman*
- The bystanders and what were they doing? *Trying to find a way to justify stoning the woman.*
- Do you think the Scribes and Pharisees could have gotten the crowd to stone the woman? *Yes!*
- What role did Jesus play? *Active bystander whose simple question—"Who is sinless among you?"—got the bullying or potential bullying to stop.*

What Goes Around Comes Around

TIME	PREPARATION & PROCESS	LOGISTICS
0:00	**Session Preparation**	Stand on the chair prior to the role play to test it for sturdiness.

Session Preparation
- Have a sturdy, non-collapsible chair at the front of the room. Read the methodology carefully before attempting this role play.
- The classroom environment and seating can remain as usual for this activity. Make sure there is enough space at the front of the classroom so students can maneuver for the role plays.
- Two simple scenarios are played out by students in this session that reveal bullying behavior. It is important to juxtapose the two role plays by doing the Positive Behavioral rehearsal as a follow up to reinforce the desired behavior.
- Student Workbook, pp. 21-24

Logistics: Stand on the chair prior to the role play to test it for sturdiness.

Place the chair at the front of the class with one end facing either side of the room.

Process

Say: *"We will role play two very real situations without anyone being hurt. Remember, these are just role plays to help us learn a more positive way of relating with each other."*

"I need six boys to come to the front to help with this role play." Pick six boys from hands that are raised.

Logistics: Emphasize that this is just a role play! Establish a no contact and no swearing agreement.

1:00 Note. At this point huddle the boys. Ask for one of them to play the part of the *Bully*, one the *Target*, two the *Active Bystanders,* and two the *Passive Bystanders*. Tell the *Bully* he is going to be on the chair and bullying the *Target*.

Role Play 1 Set Up
Bully stands on the chair. Target kneels on the floor in front of the chair facing the Bully. Two Active Bystanders stand behind the Bully and encourage the Bully's behavior. Two Passive Bystanders are not directly involved, standing in the periphery of the room where they can clearly see what is going on.

"Class, the name of this role play is 'What Goes Around Comes Around.' Boys, you may begin."

3:00 Note. Let the role play continue for about one minute or less.

"Stop."

Note. Interview the *Bully* first.

"How are you feeling being up there?" Echo his responses.

4:00 *"I can see you are feeling pretty full of yourself."* Echo his responses.

"How do you feel about having these guys behind you cheering you on and supporting what you are doing?" Echo his responses.

What Goes Around Comes Around

TIME	PREPARATION & PROCESS	LOGISTICS

"*This seems to make it okay doesn't it?*" Echo his responses.

"*Class, notice how the Bully gets blinded by his own sense of self. He does not even consider that he is hurting someone else—not even himself by his bullying behavior.*"

5:00 "*This is kind of like having an addiction, similar to using alcohol, tobacco, and other drugs. A person gets 'high' from the power and control and does it over and over again in spite of the consequences.*"

"*The Bully thinks he's winning, but it is just fools gold—looks like gold, feels like gold, but it is not worth anything.*"

"*How are you (Target) feeling about being down there?*" Echo the Target's responses.

"*I can see this is a pretty depressing place to be and I hear you want to change this by getting back or even in someway.*"

"*Class, is it normal for someone to want to get back at another person for being put down like this?*"

Expected Response: Yes!

6:00 "*Yes, but is it okay to act on this feeling?*"

Expected Response: No!

"*Would getting back make it right?*"

Expected Response: No!

"*For the purposes of this role play, let's say (Target) does something to get back at (Bully) so we 'flip the script.'*"

Note. Place the *Bully* in the *Target* position and the *Target* in the *Bully* position.

"*What goes around comes around. You may begin.*"

7:00 *Note.* Let this play out for about one minute or less.

"*Stop. How does it feel for you to be up here now?*"

9:00 Possible Responses: "I feel stronger, better, more powerful, invincible, etc."

"*I can see you like it as much, if not more, than (previous Bully).*"

What Goes Around Comes Around

TIME	PREPARATION & PROCESS	LOGISTICS

10:00 (To the new Target): *"How does it feel to be down here instead of on the chair?"* Echo his responses.

"Is there a part of you that wants to get back at (Bully)?"

Usual response: Yes!

"Class, do you think this will ever end between (Bully) and (Target)?"

Expected Response: No!

11:00 *"I think you are right! No, this will never end, what goes around comes around, unless something different happens between them, or the Bystanders do something different."*

Optional: When the time is right, you could have a large flat bed sheet available and have two students hold it up in front of the Bully Triangle. Use this as an opportunity to demonstrate the "code of silence" that shrouds all involved and keeps them from speaking up.

(To Active Bystanders): *"How are you feeling about cheering on the Bully?"* Echo their responses.

Note. There will be a variety of responses to this question, so "go with the flow." Some examples of what could be said in response are: "Good to be on the winning team," "We feel powerful," "We feel strong," "This is fun."

12:00 *"I hear you like being on the 'winning side' and you are feeling pretty full of yourselves, too!"*

The sheet being held up is like an "invisible cloak" or shroud that gets draped over these situations, perpetuating the problem.

"Class, who is winning in this bullying triangle?"

Usually the class says, "Nobody is winning," but sometimes they say the Bully is winning. Below are two response options.

Option One: *"Class, you're right, nobody wins in the bullying triangle. This is not a win/lose; it is a lose/lose/lose. Any time a person puts someone else down to make themselves feel better, it is a lose/lose/lose."*

Option Two: *"I understand how you might think the Bully is winning, but win/lose or lose/lose is not okay in relationships, only win/win."*

"Who is better? The Bully or the Target?"

Possible Responses: The bully. No one. Emphasize no one wins no matter what their response.

13:00 *"You're right! No one person is better than another and no one is less than another. We are all equal even though it doesn't seem like it in our world sometimes. When we make ourselves out to be better than someone else, we create divisions between each other."*

What Goes Around Comes Around

TIME	PREPARATION & PROCESS	LOGISTICS

(To Passive Bystanders): *"How are you two feeling as you watch this going on?"* Echo their responses.

Possible responses: We don't like it, but it's not our fault or responsibility....He's a loser anyway....There is nothing we can do....If we do anything, the Bully and the Active Bystanders will turn on us.

"Class, who's responsible for the bullying triangle?"

Possible Responses: The Bully...The Bystanders...The Target. Emphasize everyone is responsible for bullying behavior.

"You're right! Everyone! Not one person is at fault, because everyone in these roles is doing something or not doing something to keep this going."

Note. At this point it is a good opportunity to have students say what each role each could do differently to support a win/win outcome. Students will have a variety of responses to all of the questions below. Below the questions are a variety of possible student responses you can echo with them.

14:00 *"What could the Bully do differently?"* Echo their responses.

Possible Responses: The Bully could realize that he is using someone else (Target) for his own satisfaction, but it's at the Targets expense which is a lose/lose. The Bully could find some other way to feel better about himself. The Bully could do something to include the Target to make the situation a win/win.

"Is it likely that the Bully will come up with these options to make this situation a win/win? Probably not."

"What can the Target do for himself?"

Possible Responses: He can stand up for himself by saying "stop" to the Bully. He can walk away. He could tell a trusted adult if the Bully doesn't stop.

"No one can make you feel inferior without your permission."
-ELEANOR ROOSEVELT

15:00 *"What could the Active Bystanders do?"*

Possible Responses: They could realize they are hurting someone else by supporting the Bully. They could speak out against the Bully, by saying it's not right for us to treat (Target) this way. They could say something to a trusted adult if it doesn't stop. They could stop cheering the Bully on for what he is doing.

"If you see something wrong and don't do what's right it is the worst of cowardice."
-ANONYMOUS

"What could the Passive Bystanders do?"

Possible Responses: They could step in to help the Target. They could say "stop!" They could ask the Bully and Active Bystanders if what they are doing is a win/win. They could tell them that we don't treat each other like that here at our school. If it doesn't stop they could also tell a trusted adult.

Begin Positive Behavioral Rehearsal at this point in the role play.

What Goes Around Comes Around

TIME	PREPARATION & PROCESS	LOGISTICS

16:00 *"Class, you did a great job coming up with very positive ideas for turning the bullying triangle around!"*

"Now let's see what happens when we redo the role play by trying out your ideas."

"I would like each role at the same time to act out one of the ideas. For example, the Bully realizes he is not helping himself by using the Target, so he stops; the Target walks away from the situation; the Active Bystanders can say to the Bully it's not okay to treat people this way in our school; and the Passive Bystanders go to a trusted teacher in the room and report the behavior."

17:00 *"You may begin."*

Note. Allow the Positive Behavioral Rehearsal to continue for about a minute. Because this is the kind of behavior we want to reinforce, if you would like to go longer please do so.

"Please stop. What do you notice happening when you tried out one of your ideas?" Echo their responses.

Possible Responses: The bullying triangle goes away....We created a win/win/win....We all feel stronger/better without making someone else feel bad. Students in the audience may say they feel safer as a result.

"You are right! When each of us does our part to do the right thing by not fanning the flames to the bullying triangle, the flame goes out! A new spark gets ignited; one that makes us all feel stronger and better about ourselves."

20:00 *"Let's applaud the boys for having the courage to show us how to create a win/win/win with each other! Thank you, boys!"*

Role Play 2: Odd Girl Out

This second scenario, titled "Odd Girl Out," is a classic female version of bullying behavior in the form of relational aggression. Although relational aggression is a form of bullying that boys can engage in as well, it is more commonly observed in females. Because boys can play this game, it is good to mention that this behavior is not exclusive, but more commonly occurs among girls. This scenario could possibly be adapted as a cyberbullying situation rather than the face-to-face situation given. It may be modified to fit into a discussion about cyberbullying.

Have 8-10 girls come to the front of the room. Make sure there is enough room for movement and placement of the roles the girls will be playing. Ask the girls for a volunteer to play the Odd Girl Out. Most all of them will volunteer; choose anyone. Have the girl playing the Odd Girl Out stand on one side of the room. Have the rest of the girls stand far apart from her on the opposite side of the room. Huddle with the group of girls and let them know that they are role playing planning a party and are not including the Odd Girl Out. They are to mention her and the reason they won't include her in the party. Give the girls a minute to discuss what they are going to say.

Announce to the entire class that the name of this role play is "Odd Girl Out." Instruct the students in the role play to begin and wait to see what happens. Usually the girls will begin to laugh. Some of the statements that the group could be expected to make about the Odd Girl Out are: "She's ugly, fat, smells, wears glasses, has braces, doesn't wash or comb her hair, wears dumb clothes, isn't one of us, isn't popular, thinks she's better than we are, is a loser, etc."

Ask the group of girls how it feels to exclude the Odd Girl Out from the group. Listen for statements such as: "We feel powerful....We have the control....We feel stronger being in the popular group....It feels better than it must feel over there (pointing at the odd girl out)....I feel like I belong."

There might be one or a few of the girls who say they feel guilty going along with the group. This is good! Acknowledge this feeling, but hold them off temporarily. During this first part have them emphasize the imbalance of power (i.e., the group is popular, in control, uses the odd girl out for its own gain, etc.).

Now ask the *Odd Girl Out* how she feels about being excluded by the group of girls. Listen for statements such as: "I feel all alone... like I want to crawl under a rock...unwanted... unloved...like I'm not worth anything...depressed and like I want to get back at them." These are all probable responses that would be expected from the Odd Girl Out.

Turn to the *Group* and ask them if they hear how the Odd Girl Out is feeling. They will undoubtedly acknowledge what she is feeling. Ask them how they feel about causing this terrible feeling in the Odd Girl Out.

The expected response is a statement around feeling guilty. If one of the girls doesn't say she felt guilty about going along with the group, ask the group if anyone felt guilty for treating the Odd Girl Out this way.

Ask each girl with her hand up why she ignored her feelings of guilt and went along with the group. Listen for statements such as: "I was afraid I would get treated the same way." "I was too afraid to say anything different." "If I defended the Odd Girl Out I was afraid I would risk being unpopular." This is a good example of how the need to belong is often more powerful than doing the right thing. The need to belong is important and powerful, but isn't acceptable when a group's power is used to exclude or oppress another person. This is a lose/lose/lose situation.

Immediately follow up the Odd Girl Out scenario with a Positive Behavioral Rehearsal. This ends the exercise with the positive behavior expected. A critical part of the process is to ask the girls to show how they can do the right thing by including others. Have them share their ideas for inclusion. Ask the girls to show the class at least one of these ideas by redoing this scenario, making it a win/win/win for everyone.

Positive Behavioral Rehearsal Possibilities

• The group of girls could walk over to the Odd Girl Out and invite her to attend the party.

• The group of girls could apologize for excluding the Odd Girl Out and promise to include her beginning with this party.

• One or more of the girls in the group who felt guilty about excluding the Odd Girl Out could speak up and say: "This isn't okay to exclude (Odd Girl Out), we need to consider her feelings by inviting her to the party."

• The Odd Girl Out could take a risk and say something to the group about how she feels excluded and those in the group who felt guilty about going along could back her up.

• A bystander (boy or girl) from the student audience could speak up and say she noticed the girls excluding (Odd Girl Out) and would like them to consider how she might feel.

Before you send the girls back to the classroom audience, remind them and the class the first part of the exercise was just a role play. The second part, which is the Positive Behavioral Rehearsal is what is expected in the school. Thank them for volunteering to play their roles in front of the class. Let them know that you admire them for their courage to participate by having the class applaud them for their good work.

Spiritual Perspective

The Odd Girl Out role play focuses on the experience of bullying and exclusion. In the Scripture story of Zacchaeus in Luke 19:1-10, we have tremendous insight about Jesus again being an active bystander and modeling inclusion. Scripture says that the crowd was thick and Zacchaeus was physically challenged by being too short; he could not see Jesus. Zacchaeus was excluded from the group.

Often a dynamic is created that results in an inconsiderateness of an individual person who unintentionally gets excluded by the group or crowd. In the case of Zacchaeus, the crowd may have dismissed him not only because of his size, but because he was considered a social outcast. Nonetheless, Zacchaeus was the target of exclusion. However, Zacchaeus was not a helpless target.

> He ran ahead and climbed a sycamore tree to catch a glimpse of Jesus who was to pass that way. When he reached the place, Jesus looked up and said to him, "Zacchaeus, come down quickly, for today I must stay at your house." And he came down quickly and received him with joy. When they all saw this, they began to grumble, saying, "He has gone to stay at the house of a sinner." (Luke 19:4-7)

Jesus is an active bystander seeking out the excluded Zacchaeus at the expense of the bullying, complaining crowd. The powerful message of inclusion that Jesus demonstrates is not come into my space and circle, rather, "I must stay at your house" and enter your sacred domain. Jesus teaches His message by raising the bar from inclusion to preferential treatment.

Read the Scripture story from Luke 19:1-10 to students.

• Who is the excluded person in this story? *Zacchaeus*

• Does anyone in the crowd pay any attention to Zacchaeus? *No*

• Did he remain helpless? *No*

• What does Zacchaeus do to help himself? *He ran ahead and climbed a sycamore tree to catch a glimpse of Jesus who was to pass that way.*

• So, as a target of exclusion, did Zacchaeus actively take care of himself? *Yes*

• What role would we label Jesus in this story? *Active bystander*

• What did Jesus do? *He spoke to Zacchaeus and said: "Come down from the tree. Hurry, because I must stay at your house today."*

• How does Jesus "go the extra mile" to include Zacchaeus? *Instead of inviting Zacchaeus into the crowd, Jesus made him feel extra special and went to him and his house.*

Odd Girl Out

TIME	PROCESS

0:00   **Say:** *"The next role play is a classic girl's version of how bullying behavior is played out. I will pick ten girls to volunteer for this role play."*

Pick 10 girls from those with hands raised to come to the front of class.

Note. Have the girls huddle and ask who would like to play the *Odd Girl Out*. Pick one with her hand up and ask her to go to the other side of the front of the room. Tell the other nine girls they are planning a party, but they are excluding Odd Girl Out for various reasons. The teacher can let the girls come up with their own reasons for excluding the odd girl out or give them some predetermined words or phrases.

1:00   *"Now presenting, 'Odd Girl Out.'"*

Note. Let the girls role play the scenario for a minute or so, then stop and interview the group first.

2:00   (To the Group): *"How does it feel to plan this party together?"*

Possible Responses: Really cool...fun...we're awesome!

"Girls, if this were real, what do you think the motivation is in planning a party and excluding someone like this?" **or** *"Why does this happen in real life?"* Echo their responses.

Possible Responses: We feel popular...in control...strong...like we belong.

Note. Just like with the boys' role play, there are a variety of responses to this question. Listen for words expressing power, control over who's in and who's not, popularity, fun, laughter, the sense of belonging.

3:00   (To the Odd Girl Out): *"How do you feel right now?"*

Possible Responses: I feel all alone...excluded...lonely...sad...depressed...worthless...like I want to crawl under a rock... unwanted...unloved...angry and I want to get back at them. Echo the responses.

"Class, is this how someone who is excluded might feel?"

Expected response: Yes!

"I think you're right. Thank you (Odd Girl Out) for letting us know how awful and painful it is to be in this position."

4:00   *"I can see this is a pretty depressing place to be and I hear a part of you wants to change this by getting back or even in someway."*

"Class, is it normal for someone to want to get back at another person for being put down like this?"

Expected Response: Yes!

"Is it okay to act on this feeling?"

Expected Response: No!

Odd Girl Out

TIME	PROCESS

5:00   *"Girls, how do you feel after listening to (Odd Girl Out) share her feelings?"*

Possible Responses: Terrible...guilty...ashamed...awful.

"Class, is this how people who exclude others should feel?"

Expected response: Yes!

"Girls, does excluding another person create a win/win/win?"

Expected response: No!

"A lose/lose/lose?"

Expected response: Yes!

"Just like the boys' role play, this is a lose/lose/lose. Whenever we try to make ourselves feel good (popular) and someone else pays a price, we can never get to a win/win/win by excluding anyone."

6:00   *"Girls, are any of you better than (Odd Girl Out)?"*

Expected response: No!

"When we exclude someone isn't this the same as saying we are better than or the other person is less than we are?"

Expected response: Yes!

7:00   *"Did any of you who felt even a little bit guilty about excluding (Odd Girl Out) from the group?"*

Expected response: Yes!

Note. One or more of the girls usually raises a hand, which is certainly a good thing.

"Why didn't you speak up about this being wrong to the other girls?" Echo their responses.

Note. There will be a variety of answers to this question. Some expected responses are below. Echo all of them.

8:00   Expected responses: Because I was afraid they would turn on me and treat me that way....I felt better going along with the group....I believe I have to do what is popular....I was just going along with it.

"We all need to fit in or belong. To exclude someone is a very cruel and powerful weapon and can be very damaging."

"Let's be more aware of when and how we might exclude someone and have the courage to be inclusive and considerate of everyone."

"Just like with the Bully, the Target, and the Bystanders in the boys' role play, a group of girls might not realize what they are doing or may not have the strength to get out of the situation."

Odd Girl Out

TIME	PROCESS
9:00	*"What could the girls in the group do when they realize that this is wrong?"* Echo the responses.
	Possible Responses: Take a risk by speaking up to the group about it being wrong....Say something to a trusted adult....Spend time befriending the Odd Girl Out.
	"Great job coming up with very positive ideas for turning exclusion into inclusion!"
	"Now let's see what happens when we redo the role play by trying out your ideas."
10:00	*Note.* Have the girls pick one of the ideas to include the Odd Girl Out.
	"What happened when you tried out that idea?" Have students share what they observed.
11:00	*Note.* Check in with the Odd Girl Out to see if this idea helped her feel included. If not, ask her for suggestions as to what would help. Take the time to do a Positive Behavioral Rehearsal around her suggestion.
	"Let's applaud the girls for their role play and the courage to make it right with (Odd Girl Out)."

"Loneliness and the feeling being unwanted is the most terrible poverty."

MOTHER TERESA

Accountability

In Phase I students are empowered to recognize the power and influence they have with each other, with their school, and beyond—the ripple they all make, be it positive or negative. This phase also takes a close look at the problem and establishes that we all play a part in an inverted bullying triangle, no matter what the vantage point.

Accountability means I take personal responsibility and own my actions/behaviors for the part I play in the drama. This is the first big step toward transforming bullying behaviors. Bullies must have the courage to become more empathic and sensitized to how their behavior impacts others, often with serious long-term consequences. Active and Passive Bystanders must find the courage and strength to shift their actions and inactions, going against the grain to become defenders of what is truly just. Targets must see that this complex dynamic cannot happen without them and it will not shift unless they, too, find the courage to advocate for themselves by getting support and gaining new skills and resources to move out of the target role.

Professionals must see and support all the characters in the inverted bullying triangle as capable of change and transformation and righting the triangle. Professionals are capable of inspiring and helping students believe they have the power to make changes in the current reality and see them as capable of transforming their school into the school of their dreams.

In Phase II, students begin to see they are accountable and responsible to the larger community. This step begins in Peace Circles by increasing awareness and practice of the obligation to help not only oneself but others transform the inverted triangle. Clear Talk and CLEAR Listening are communication tools that help students learn how to hold themselves and others accountable for their behaviors. In Phase

---

Worksheet 4

Accountability

Write about what it means to be accountable for my behavior.

_____
_____

How will I hold myself accountable for my behavior?

_____
_____
_____

What specific things will I do to show I am accountable for my behavior? (*Hint:* Admit it when you have not treated a person with respect. Let the person know what respectful behaviors you will show in the future.)

_____
_____
_____
_____

How can I hold others accountable for their behavior? (*Hint:* Let others know when they have not treated you or someone else with respect. Tell them you expect them to show you or others respect in the future.)

_____
_____
_____
_____
_____

List three people who will help you hold yourself or others accountable:

1.
2.
3.

26   **PHASE I**
      Christ Is Our Model for Leadership   *Peace Be With You*
                                                              W O R K B O O K

Worksheet 5

Historic Event

Write about a time in history when a group of people did what was popular, but not what was right. *Examples:* the Holocaust, Apartheid, Genocide, etc. Describe what it would take to make a situation like this "right."

_____
_____
_____
_____
_____
_____
_____

How does it feel as you write about an event in history that has had a negative ripple in the world?

_____
_____
_____

What are you doing to create a positive ripple in the world?

_____
_____
_____

List three people who will support you in making a positive ripple in the world:

1.
2.
3.

Peace Be With You
W O R K B O O K   **PHASE I**   27
                                   Christ Is Our Model for Leadership

III, students practice going inside and being accountable to God for their behaviors.

Page 25 in the Student Workbook contains some powerful quotes on accountability. Have students read these quotes aloud and discuss them as a class for five minutes. Following the discussion have students fill out Worksheet 4, titled "Accountability" on page 26 in their Student Workbooks, for 5-10 minutes. Have students do a pair and share on the worksheet for 2 minutes each and then ask for volunteer pairs to share with the entire class. If little class time is available, have students read page 25 and fill out page 26 as homework, and the next day ask for volunteers to share what they learned about accountability.

Have students complete Worksheet 5, "Historic Event," on page 27 in their workbook either in class or as homework. The purpose of this activity is to give students a macroperspective of how doing what is popular isn't always what is "right," and in fact can have devastating consequences. Follow up with classroom discussion (10-15 minutes) on a microlevel, helping students make the connection that what they do might be popular, but if anyone is hurt physically, mentally, emotionally, or spiritually in the process, it is not just and cannot create a positive ripple. Pay close attention to what students are sharing with regard to how they are creating a positive ripple in the school and in the world. Respond and clarify for students accordingly.

Activity Four

Two Stories

PURPOSE

Use storytelling as a medium to increase sensitivity and awareness of the harmful impact disrespect and bullying can have on the person and the school environment.

LEARNING OBJECTIVES

- Students will increase sensitivity and compassion through the use of two true stories about bullying.
- Students will distinguish the difference between short-term "feel good" gain and long-term consequences of the bullying dynamic.
- Students will recognize that "unfinished business" exists in current peer relationships.
- Students will create positive tension around wanting to "clear" unfinished business.
- Students will build confidence and school safety through peer support and encouragement.

CORRESPONDING STUDENT WORKBOOK PAGES 29-34

- Journal Entry   1
- Student Worksheets   4
- Four Agreements

<table>
<tr><td>

Worksheet 1

Howard Gray Story

Write your reaction to the "Howard Gray" story.

_____

_____

_____

_____

_____

_____

_____

How many years after seventh grade did the author write this story?

_____

_____

What might the author have been feeling when he wrote this story?

_____

_____

How can you "right" a "wrong" against another person or group?

_____

_____

_____

_____

_____

_____

Peace Be With You
WORKBOOK
Christ Is Our Model for Leadership   **PHASE I** 29

</td><td>

Journal Entry

Visioning Your Future

Journal what you think your life will be like in 20 years if you use positive leadership skills now.

_____

_____

_____

_____

_____

_____

_____

_____

_____

_____

_____

_____

_____

_____

_____

_____

_____

30 **PHASE I**
Christ Is Our Model for Leadership   *Peace Be With You*
WORKBOOK

</td></tr>
</table>

Two Stories

Most teachers understand the power of stories to help students make an emotional connection to the lesson. Research shows that students who make an emotional connection to the lesson are better able to retain the lesson and its meaning. Two real stories are provided for you to read to students. You are encouraged to read them with passion and sincerity.

A third story regarding disrespect or bullying may be your own. By telling your own story, your authenticity will increase the credibility of the lesson and students' ability to recognize that how we treat each other can have a damaging long-term impact. What we say and do to each other doesn't just go away when we move on to the next grade or middle school or high school. How we are treated by and how we treat others stays with us for a lifetime.

The two stories in this lesson are true. The first story, "Howard Gray," is by Lee Domann and is actually a song. Domann wrote this song 20 years after he mistreated Howard, a seventh-grade classmate. Domann recorded the song with the hope that Howard would hear it some day. In the lyrics, Domann expresses remorse and asks for forgiveness for how he and others treated Howard. The upside of this powerful song is that Howard did hear it and has since forgiven him. You can read more on this story at http://www.leedomann.com/howard_gray.html.

The second story, "The Code of Silence," is a poem written in November 2007. This is also a true story and occurred when one of the authors (Frank) was in seventh grade, some 37 years ago. The poem is about how seventh-grade classmates, Eric (an active bystander), Tommy (the target), and Frankie (the bully) are caught up in a bullying triangle. The author has only recently told family and friends about the incident and does not know if Tom or Eric have discussed it with anyone. This is how powerful the "code of silence"—a covert contract—is in bullying behavior and the long-term implications it can have for everyone involved.

Code of Silence Story

Write your reaction to the "Code of Silence" story.

_____
_____
_____
_____
_____
_____
_____
_____
_____

Do you think Frankie (the bully) showed strength or weakness in this story? How about Eric? How about Tommy? Why?

_____
_____
_____
_____
_____

Who is responsible for bullying? Frankie? Eric? Tommy? Why?

_____
_____
_____

Code of Silence Rewrite

Rewrite the "Code of Silence" story in a way that would make it a win/win and have a positive rippling effect in the school.

_____
_____
_____
_____
_____
_____
_____
_____
_____

Write about what you would say to Frankie, Tommy, and Eric if you had a chance to meet with them.

_____
_____
_____
_____
_____
_____
_____
_____

The author is still saddened, even after all these years, by his part in this chaotic and wrongful scene in which he physically assaulted Tommy. If he had a magic wand, he would have waved it long ago to make this scene go away. But this is not a possibility. His story doesn't have a happy ending like Lee Domann's. He doesn't know where Tommy is to this day. The author hopes Tommy has forgiven him and prays that he is doing well in spite of the wrongful treatment inflicted on him by everyone in the class.

Although this story doesn't have a happy ending, the incident not having a successful resolution is partly what fuels the author's passion to work with youth and speak out against bullying behavior. He hopes to prevent students, bullies, targets, or bystanders from feeling the shame and regret he continues to feel for having treated another human being this way. He dedicates his work and this mission to Tommy, Eric, and others who get caught in the harrowing snare of the Bully Triangle. His experience with Tom and Eric has taught him volumes and has launched his personal mission to proactively end bullying with compassion. By increasing the level of compassion among students, we will also increase the likelihood that bullying behavior will be significantly reduced.

All of our stories must be told in order to increase compassion. If these stories go untold, they become the "code of silence," an invisible cloak that perpetuates the problem long after the initial behavior. Students need to become more aware of the reality and cost of this bullying. The stories can and do help students come to realize there is a long-term impact as well as consequences for all involved: target, bully, and bystanders.

The "Howard Gray" story and "The Code of Silence" are shared to sensitize students to how bullying behavior affects everyone, not only for the moment, but for many years to come. Thank you for your willingness to share these stories and your own.

Spiritual Perspective

We can gain a new perspective about carrying our wounds when we read the Gospel of John 20:19-31. Christ carried His wounds into resurrection. In the words of Father Joseph Nassal, CPPS, in his book, *Premeditated Mercy*:

> God kept the wounds of crucifixion visible on the body of Christ so that we may touch them. These are the openings, if you will, that allow us to enter the body of Christ. We keep the wounds open so we can get into each other's lives. These wounds are our doorway into each other's experiences, the way we can crawl under each other's skin rather than allowing those we find most difficult to love to make our skin crawl....[It is] from this place within the other's soul, we stand under that one's suffering which was unknown to us before, and we begin to understand that a prerequisite for premeditated mercy is compassion: to handle each other, even our enemies, with care. (Nassal, 2000, pp. 38-40)

Worksheet 4

Your Story

Write your own poem or story about bullying
from the viewpoint of the bully, target, or bystander.

_____
_____
_____
_____
_____
_____
_____
_____
_____
_____
_____
_____
_____
_____
_____
_____
_____
_____
_____
_____

Ask your teacher if you can read your poem or story to the class.

Peace Be With You
WORKBOOK

PHASE I   **33**
Christ Is Our Model for Leadership

Howard Gray
Music and Lyrics by Lee Domann

Most everyone I knew put the whole Gray family down.
They were the poorest family in that little Kansas town.

Howard always looked too big for his funny, ragged clothes,
The kids all laughed at him, and Jimmy Jones would thumb his nose.

Howard sat across from me in seventh grade at school,
I didn't like it much but Mama taught the Golden Rule.

So when the spitballs flew at him, I never would join in,
I guess that was the reason Howard thought I was his friend.
And after things would quiet down, sometimes I'd turn and see
The grateful eyes of Howard Gray lookin' back at me.

Howard Gray, oh Howard Gray,
Somehow they got their kicks out of treating you that way.
Deep down I kinda liked you, but I was too afraid
To be a friend to you, Howard Gray.

One day after lunch I went to comb my hair and I saw
That they had Howard pinned against the locker in the hall.
They were pokin' fun about the big hole in his shirt,
They had his left arm twisted back behind him 'til it hurt.

To this day I can't explain, and I won't try to guess
Just how it was I wound up laughin' harder than the rest.
I laughed until I cried, but through my tears I still could see
The tear-stained eyes of Howard Gray lookin' back at me.

Howard Gray, oh Howard Gray,
I can't believe I joined them all treatin' you that way.
I wanted to apologize, but I was too afraid
Of what they'd think about me, Howard Gray.

From that moment on, after I'd made fun of him,
He never looked my way, he never smiled at me again.
Not much longer after that his family moved away,
And that is the last I ever saw or heard of Howard Gray.

That was twenty years ago and I still haven't found
Just why we'll kick a brother or a sister when they're down.
I know it may sound crazy, but now and then I dream
About the eyes of Howard Gray lookin' back at me.

Howard Gray, oh Howard Gray,
I've never quite forgiven us for treatin' you that way.
And I hope that maybe somehow, you'll hear this song some day
And you'll know that I am sorry, Howard Gray.

We'll probably never meet again, all I can do is pray,
May you and God forgive us, Howard Gray.

The Code of Silence
by Frank A. DiLallo

Just an ordinary day not much different from all the rest
Eric, Tommy and Frankie in 7th grade taking a different kind of test
Tommy's tall, thin and picked on by most of the class
Eric short, stout, lots of hot air and a voice full of brass
Frankie's tall, strong less brain and more brawn
Always trying to prove he's better than, making everyone his pawn

Three boys in the restroom at Guy Middle School
Eric standing in the corner playing it so calm, so cool
With his arms folded and leaning back against the cold block wall
Frankie and Tommy standing in front of an unfriendly bathroom stall
Suddenly the tension mounts and Eric shouts in a loud sarcastic tone
"We should hit Tommy and do whatever we can to make him moan!"

Shouting even louder, "We don't like Tommy, we don't like his kind!"
The tension is high and like a puppet possessed, Frankie lost his mind
He began to hit Tommy in the upper left arm; he hit him with all his might
Tommy stood stiff trying not to flinch, not even an inch, to show no fright
Eric got louder and louder, "hit him harder!" he yelled, counting every blow
Just like a movie director this active bystander was surely running the show
"We don't like odd numbers," Eric counted along with hit number five
"We don't like even numbers," taunting and provoking to keep this insanity alive

Tommy didn't do anything, he never fought back, he never even muttered a word
Why is it he didn't do something to stand up for himself, how strange, how absurd?
Somehow some way this frightful bullying triangle came to a screeching halt
Three boys in a restroom, just an ordinary day, who would you say is at fault?
Three boys casually walking out of this nightmare and back to class just shows
The code of silence, not telling, makes a negative ripple, even if no one else knows
Bully, bystander and target will forever keep this shadowy secret and shame
They will never forget the damage done; they will always feel the pain

Many, many years have gone by and you would think this would all just go away
But every decision we make and how we treat another is always here to stay
Every hurtful action, every hurtful word, leaves a lasting imprint on others
Why not treat everyone with respect, with dignity, like equal sisters and brothers?

Just like an etching in granite, what kind of impression do you want to make?
We only have but one life to live so treat yourself and others well for God's sake
Everyone deserves our very best no matter what their beliefs or color of their face
Treat others with kindness, love and respect, because we are all one in this human race.

Two Stories

TIME	PREPARATION & PROCESS

Session Preparation

0:00 Read the two stories prior to sharing them with the class
Have the two stories ready to read to the class.
Stories are found on pp. 65-66.
Student Workbook, pp. 29-33

Process

Say: *"Let's listen to two stories about bullying. As I read each story, pick out the important points you hear and write them down on a piece of paper."*

1:00 *"The first story is really a song, written by Lee Domann and is called 'Howard Gray.'"*

Note. Read the lyrics with passion and conviction. Below are some specific questions regarding the Howard Gray story. Feel free to go beyond these questions in order to facilitate classroom discussion in a way that fits with student reactions to what they heard.

4:00 *"How do you think Lee Domann was feeling when he wrote this song?"*

Expected responses: Sad...sorry...ashamed...guilty...regretful...bad...terrible. Echo their responses.

"Why do you think he wrote this song?" Echo their responses.

"How long after seventh grade did he write the song?"

5:00 Correct response: 20 years

"What does it tell you that a grown man would write something like this after 20 years?"

6:00 Possible response: This doesn't go away when you're an adult....This stuff lasts a long time. Echo their responses.

Note. Read the poem with passion and conviction! Below are some specific questions regarding the poem Code of Silence. Feel free to go beyond these questions in order to facilitate classroom discussion in a way that fits with student reactions to what they heard.

8:00 *"What is similar about the two stories?"* Echo their responses.

"What are some similar feelings these two authors have, that made them want to write about these situations?"

11:00 Possible responses: Both feel sad...sorry...ashamed...guilty...regret...bad...terrible. Echo their responses.

"What could Tommy have done differently in this story?" Echo their responses.

"What could Eric have done differently in this story?" Echo their responses.

"What could Frankie have done differently in this story?" Echo their responses.

12:00 *"Who is at fault in this story?"* Echo their responses.

Four Agreements

Four Agreements is a simple yet important contractual commitment students make with facilitators, family, administration, peers, and the entire school community.

The agreements can be used in corrective and formative measures with students when broken. When students do adhere to the agreements on a consistent basis, it is cause for reward or celebration. Rewards can be as simple as verbal acknowledgements or extended privileges.

Instructions:
1. Have students take their workbooks home to read and sign with their parent(s).
2. Establish a date for students to complete this task. The agreements should be signed soon after Phase I and preferably prior to the Phase II start date.
3. Teacher and principal then sign each student's Four Agreements form, preferably in a ceremonial signing so that the adults can acknowledge each student's commitment to the Four Agreements.

Four Agreements

1. I agree to not bully anyone (including adults).

2. I agree to include anyone who is left out.

3. I agree to help myself and others (including adults) get closer to a 10.

4. I agree to SPEAK UP with two adults—one at school and one at home—whenever I see anyone not being treated like a 10.

Student Signature _____ Date _____
Parent Signature _____ Date _____
Teacher Signature _____ Date _____
Principal Signature _____ Date _____

- Take this contract home.
- Read this contract over with a parent.
- Sign this contract with a parent.
- Show this signed contract to your teacher and principal to sign.

Christ Is Our Model for Leadership

Teacher and Counselor Reflection

Your vocation is honorable and of lasting proportions. Working with young people is both gift and challenge. Congratulations! You have completed Phase I of the program. We invite you to recall the words used at your Baptism into our faith community. Each of you is anointed priest, prophet, and king or queen. Baptism calls every member of the Church to participate in Christ's role as priest, prophet, and royalty. We do this in the context of our daily lives within our families, in our schools as teachers and counselors, and our communities. The everyday gifts of ourselves to love and care for one another, our families, coworkers, students, and friends is our priestly offering joined to the sacrifice of Christ in the Eucharist. By words, deeds, and professional talents—faithful to the Gospel message of Jesus—we live out our prophetic role. By seeking to build the common good of society, especially within our academic community, on the basis of moral principles, we live out our royalty. In the role of teacher or facilitator of this program, you are invited into the communal healing ministries of Christ. Your personhood, presence, and professionalism is Christ present.

Throughout this text there are student worksheets that challenge students to reflect and share to make the experience more meaningful. We invite you to also do a reflection at the end of each phase.

After self-critiquing how the session transpired, take some quiet time and reflect on your Baptismal role as priest, prophet, and a person of royalty. Setting aside the ego, honor your sacred work of leadership and care for the Mystical Body of Christ within your academic community. Take time after each session to still yourself.

Reflect on the vulnerability of the young people and their eagerness to fully understand that they are all called to leadership. Reflect how this leadership piece affects each student and the rippling effect, like the pebble in the water, it will have in homes, families, classrooms, with friends, and the greater community—even the world!

Soak in the holiness of your leadership and healing ministry. Journal about the shifts, growth, and healing pieces that are taking place within the sacred space you create. Reflect on shifts that are happening within you and the way you view each student.

Peace be with you!

PHASE II

Dignity for All

PHASE II
Dignity for All

"'Hear, O Israel! The Lord our God is Lord alone! You shall love the Lord your God with all your heart, with all your soul, with all your mind, and with all your strength.' The second is this: 'You shall love your neighbor as yourself.'"

MARK 12:29-30

PURPOSE
Students are immersed in a communal process of reconciliation to experience the work of the Holy Spirit in an effort to reconcile injustices and move compassionately toward forgiveness, healing, and personal growth.

LEARNING OBJECTIVES
- Students will discover the power of building community.
- Students will learn an "Injury to One is an Injury to All."
- Students will learn restorative justice through Clear Talk.
- Students will learn compassion and forgiveness in real time.
- Students will deepen their understanding of the Sacrament of Reconciliation.

TEACHER MANUAL ACTIVITIES   5

CORRESPONDING STUDENT WORKBOOK PAGES
- Prayer   1
- Journal Entries   2
- Student Worksheets   8
- Quotation Pages   2

"If we have no peace, it is because we have forgotten that we belong to each other."

MOTHER TERESA

Prayer of St. Francis of Assisi

Lord, make me an instrument of your peace;
  where there is hatred, let me sow love;
  where there is injury, pardon;
  where there is doubt, faith;
  where there is despair, hope;
  where there is darkness, light;
  where there is sadness, joy.

O divine Master,
  grant that I may not so much seek to be consoled as to console;
  to be understood, as to understand;
  to be loved, as to love;
  for it is in giving that we receive,
  it is in pardoning that we are pardoned,
  and it is in dying that we are born to Eternal Life.

Amen.

Ecumenical Impact

If we say, "We are without sin," we deceive ourselves, and the truth is not in us. If we acknowledge our sins, he is faithful and just and will forgive our sins and cleanse us from every wrongdoing. (1 John 1:8-9)

In Phase II, the Trinity is our model for creating a sacred honoring space for all students as they step into the center circle. Taking this step to begin making peace, is a critical benchmark for students. The sacred circle becomes the setting to make public the sinfulness of bullying. This Trinitarian model calls us to be lovingly supportive and non-judgmental and to nurture lifelong changes. The sacred circle helps to safely bring out bullying behaviors so we can better see and understand the dynamic. This process is not about merely "making the bullying go away." The invitation is to see the actions—the wounds created by the bully and bystanders with the target—as well as the far-reaching effects of bullying, so that counselors and teachers can go to a deeper level of communal healing.

A global perspective is shared by St. James Ethics Center of the Anglican Church of Sydney Australia in their publication titled, *Living Ethics*. Author Maree Faulkner (2009) writes:

Determining an ethical stance must be difficult for young people in a society where "making fun" of other people could be seen as a national pastime. The repeated images of sporting "heroes" and politicians haranguing each other, erstwhile team-mates ganging up to "vote each other off the island" and canned laughter responding when a camera captures a person (often a child) being humiliated or hurt must cloud the boundaries of acceptable behaviour. (para. 2)

Faulkner notes that "some adults believe that bullying is a natural passage of youth, that it makes kids tougher and that they'll be better adults if they're bullied." The Australian Anglican community supports the Kandersteg Declaration (2007), which states that "every child and youth has a right to be respected and safe.

Bullying is a violation of this basic right." This text provides support to create a stronger force against bullying within our schools, our homes, and our communities.

Spiritual Perspective

"God created man and woman in his image as his creatures called to love and serve him and to care for all creation" (USCCB, 2006, p. 73). Because of our common origin, we enter into human solidarity and charity, treating each other with dignity. Sin wounds our relationship with God and others and our human dignity. Faith reveals to us the destructive force of sin in our lives and the world. Sin "wounds the nature of man and injures human solidarity" (USCCB, p. 312). Reconciliation not only calls us to repent, it calls us to "repair the damages our actions have caused" (USCCB, p. 240).

Phase II immerses students in an opportunity to make a connection with many difficult spiritual concepts—to shift from talking about these concepts to truly experiencing them with each other in a communal process. This program offers a way to explore and discover what it means to be in a community where there is dignity for all.

In the Second Vatican Council document, *The Pastoral Constitution on the Church in the Modern World*, the Council Fathers wrote:

God did not create man as a solitary, for from the beginning "male and female He created them" (Genesis 1:27). Their companionship produces the primary form of interpersonal communion. For by his innermost nature man is a social being, and unless he relates himself to others he can neither live nor develop his potential. (1966, §12)

The following Scripture passage models the Trinity present to one another at a sacred moment in the public life of Jesus.

I [John the Baptist] am baptizing you with water, for repentance, but the one who is coming after me is mightier than I. I am not worthy to carry his sandals. He will baptize you with the Holy Spirit and fire. His winnowing fan is in his hand. He will clear his threshing floor and gather his wheat into his barn, but the chaff he will burn with unquenchable fire." Then Jesus came from Galilee to John at the Jordan to be baptized by him. John tried to prevent him, saying, "I need to be baptized by you, and yet you are coming to me?" Jesus said to him in reply, "Allow it now, for thus it is fitting for us to fulfill all righteousness." Then he allowed him. After Jesus was baptized, he came up from the water and behold, the heavens were opened (for him), and he saw the Spirit of God descending like a dove (and) coming upon him. And a voice came from the heavens, saying, "This is my beloved Son, with whom I am well pleased." (Matthew 3:11-17)

The dove, a time-honored symbol of the Holy Spirit, and the voice of God the Father hovering over Jesus, become the sacred space of loving support.

Creating sacred space that will manifest dignity for all becomes the initial responsibility of the counselor or teacher. Often we become so focused in doing—creating the space, studying lessons, classroom management—that we forget the real sacredness of our role. In the Scripture account of Matthew 17:1-5, Peter offers to create sacred space with three tents and something profound happens:

> After six days Jesus took Peter, James, and John his brother, and led them up a high mountain by themselves. And he was transfigured before them; his face shone like the sun and his clothes became white as light. And behold, Moses and Elijah appeared to them, conversing with him. Then Peter said to Jesus in reply, "Lord, it is good that we are here. If you wish, I will make three tents here, one for you, one for Moses, and one for Elijah." While he was still speaking, behold, a bright cloud cast a shadow over them, then from the cloud came a voice that said, "This is my beloved Son, with whom I am well pleased; listen to him."

In Luke 22:7-16, the preparation by the disciples created sacred space for the Last Supper to be celebrated.

When the day of the Feast of Unleavened Bread arrived, the day for sacrificing the Passover lamb, he sent out Peter and John, instructing them, "Go and make preparations for us to eat the Passover." They asked him, "Where do you want us to make the preparations?" And he answered them, "When you go into the city, a man will meet you carrying a jar of water. Follow him into the house that he enters and say to the master of the house, 'The teacher says to you, "Where is the guest room where I may eat the Passover with my disciples?"' He will show you a large upper room that is furnished. Make the preparations there." Then they went off and found everything exactly as he had told them, and there they prepared the Passover. When the hour came, he took his place at table with the apostles. He said to them, "I have eagerly desired to eat this Passover with you before I suffer, for, I tell you, I shall not eat it (again) until there is fulfillment in the kingdom of God."

Counselors and teachers are creating an environment for the sacred to happen. Work in a Christian school is not just a job; it is a calling to work with the Trinity to create a holy space of peace, respect, and healing. Take time to reflect on how you create sacred space as an important part of your ministry.

Creating sacred space is essential to help facilitate the work of reconciliation. Reconciliation requires a change of heart, that is, a conversion, confessing and asking for forgiveness. It is important to understand the concept of sin in relation to making peace and the process of Clear Talk.

> Confession liberates us from sins that trouble our hearts and makes it possible to be reconciled to God and others. We are asked to look into our souls and, with an honest and unblinking gaze, identify our sins. This opens our minds and hearts to God, moves us towards communion with the Church, and offers us a new future. (USCCB, 2006, p. 238)

> Absolution takes away sin, but does not remedy all the disorders sin has caused. (Catholic Church, 2010, §1459)

It is obvious that we need to repair certain damages that our sins have caused, such as restoring the reputation of someone we have injured, returning money that we have stolen, or rectifying an injustice.

The Clear Talk process in this phase is an opportunity to begin to heal our relationships. A student voluntarily enters the sacred circle, committing to a five-step process with another student, inviting the person to reconcile and repair any damage done between them. The sequence of the steps is spiritually significant.

In Step 1: "Thank You," students must be clear that to thank another student who is willing to be in the circle, goes beyond good manners. "Thank you" in this context means, "I enter the circle with an attitude of gratitude and see the Christ in you."

In Step 2: "Data," a sinful offense has occurred. The student who initiated entry into the circle clearly states the nature of the offense. For the bully to state what the action is and take responsibility for violating the target is a critical step. When this happens it is a glorious moment and the bully should be acknowledged for courage. For a target to state in this step how he or she was "wronged," is also a big step in taking a stand, possibly for the first time. When this happens the target should also be praised for courage.

In Step 3: "Feelings," the student initiating entry shares what he or she feels about having committed the offense or about being the offended party. It is important to understand the moral aspect of feelings. The Markkula Center for Applied Ethics at Santa Clara University (http://www.scu.edu/ethics) states it most concisely: "Ethics is not the same as feelings. Feelings provide important information for our ethical choices."

Feelings in and of themselves are amoral; the actions that we carry out contain the morality. The belief that anger, jealousy, hatred, sadness, and the like are bad feelings is incorrect. Anger is not immoral! What is done with the anger contains the morality. Even Jesus got angry. In Mark 11:15-19, Jesus was angry with the conduct in the Temple:

He began to drive out those selling and buying there. He overturned the tables of the money changers and the seats of those who were selling doves. He did not permit anyone to carry anything through the temple area.

We are reminded of Jesus and his sadness in John 11:35 when he comes to the town where his friend Lazarus is buried: "Jesus asked: 'Where have you laid him?' They said to him, 'Sir, come and see.' And Jesus wept."

In Step 4: "My/Your behavior said.....?" the student states the implications of the behavior on self and others, which is an important step in being held accountable for actions and holding others accountable for their actions.

In Step 5: "Wants," a student states what he or she wants to see happen in order to repair the damage done and to restore the relationship to a place of dignity and respect. A student may apologize and ask for forgiveness. It is important to note that the concept of forgiveness can be misunderstood. Giving or receiving forgiveness does not release another of their responsibility; forgiveness is an act of self-freedom.

Forgiveness is meaningfully described in the life and words of Father Michael Lapsley. Lapsley, an Anglican priest, joined the African National Congress (ANC) in 1976 and became one of their chaplains. Later he was exiled by the South African Government. While living in exile in Zimbabwe he discovered he was on the South African Government hit list. In April 1990, he received a letter bomb in the mail. He lost both hands and an eye.

Quite early on after the bomb I realized that if I was filled with hatred and desire for revenge I'd be a victim forever. If we have something done to us, we are victims. If we physically survive, we are survivors. Sadly, many people never travel any further than this. I did travel further, going from victim to survivor, to victor. To become a victor is to move from being an object of history to become a subject once more. That is not to say that I will not always grieve what I've lost, because I will permanently bear the marks of disfigurement. Yet I believe I've gained through this experience. I realize that I can be more of a priest with no hands than with two hands. (Lapsley, 2010, para. 5)

After being physically wounded, Lapsley discovered the importance of healing. He came to the realization that being filled with pity, anger, and revenge would keep him a victim forever. Granting forgiveness is about healing, both self-healing and communal healing.

The purpose and learning objectives of Phase II focuses on the bullying dynamic which "wounds the nature of man and injures human solidarity" (USCCB, 2006, p. 312). By naming, addressing, and seeking resolution and repair of relational damages, this process becomes a sacramental tool for healing. It is a reclaiming of ourselves and our full potential as individuals and as a society.

Dignity for All

Phase I gives students a common language and empowers them to "do the right thing" and to be a part of the solution rather than part of the problem. Phase II is an opportunity to practice doing the right thing, putting into action the common language, while learning critical life skills such as community building, relationship building, effective communication, and listening skills.

As we have established, bullying is a group dynamic. Therefore, it is imperative that bullying behaviors be viewed and addressed as a group dynamic. This certainly does not mean this approach should be employed to the exclusion of any necessary individual interventions. However, cultural change takes place with personal responsibility, dignity for all, and everyone working together toward a safe and thriving school climate as a Christian community.

Students safely disclose actual bullying incidences in real time in a communal process. In this real-life context, prosocial skills are integrated more effectively, compared to contrived conditions. In a non-punitive approach, all Phase II activities and processes conducted in a communal setting will:

- Build student confidence
- Build student trust
- Create a renewed sense of belonging
- Give students increased confidence and permission to report bullying behaviors
- Make bullying behaviors more transparent
- Create a level of accountability among students
- Create a new norm that supports a safe and respectful school climate
- Provide opportunities for reconciliation and forgiveness

Some adults may feel uncomfortable and challenged by the level of vulnerability and open disclosure encouraged during the Phase II process. Discomfort may stem in part from a lack of safety and structure and an uncertainty around what to do when students disclose. The sequential order of activities in this phase are specifically designed to build personal and classroom safety. Through a series of community building activities, students' trust is elevated, creating a safe space for them to practice within the structure of the model. The greater the safety created in the circle, the greater the level of transparency is present to help shift any existing norms that support bullying behaviors. Facilitators are encouraged to welcome self-disclosures and vulnerability among students within the structure and safety of the process.

Phase II can be described as a modified version of the Restorative Justice model. The U.S. Department of Justice (2007) defines the seven guiding principles of restorative justice as follows:

1. Crime is an offense against human relationships.
2. Victims and the community are central to justice processes.
3. The first priority of justice processes is to assist victims.
4. The second priority is to restore the community, to the degree possible.
5. The offender has personal responsibility to victims and to the community for crimes committed.

6. Stakeholders share responsibilities for restorative justice through partnerships for action.
7. The offender will develop improved competency and understanding as a result of the restorative justice experience.

Bullying is an offense against human relationships and the communal process in Phase II is an effort to restore the community. If implemented properly the following are intended outcomes:

- All students, including targets, will feel empowered and safe.
- All students will feel valued and experience a stronger sense of belonging in the classroom and school community.
- All students experience first-hand the healing power of reconciliation and forgiveness.
- Targets can eventually forgive their offenders.
- Active and Passive Bystanders will make a fundamental shift to become Defenders.
- Defender behaviors will be the norm, having a greater level importance in the school community.
- Bullies will increase empathy, acknowledge wrong doing, and improve their prosocial behaviors.
- All the players in the Bullying Triangle have an opportunity to restore their relationships. If not during the Phase II learning session, at some point when ready during the school year.

During Phase II, students will learn and practice restoring their relationships through a five-step process that incorporates reconciliation and forgiveness. Reconciliation is an extension of compassion and care to reaffirm and restore the relationship between the bully and the target through a "mutual understanding." This mutual understanding means the bully makes a commitment to refrain from offending behaviors and moves forward, treating the target with dignity and respect (Ahmed

& Braithwaite, 2006). Including the bystanders in the communal process increases the likelihood of accountability for the bully and safety for the target. The latter increases the likelihood of this process directly reducing bullying behavior and the growth of supportive peer relationships. Desmond Tutu (1999) regards forgiveness as the most powerful weapon to end the cycle of violence.

Phase II creates a positive social contagion where students can safely practice and integrate prosocial behaviors. Prosocial behavior refers to "voluntary actions that are intended to help or benefit another individual or group of individuals" (Eisenberg & Mussen, 1989, p. 3). Prosocial behaviors are altruistic in nature, whereby an individual gains satisfaction from "doing what is right," for the common good. A foundational approach to promoting prosocial behaviors are rooted in the concepts of emotional intelligence (EI) and social intelligence (SI). Phase II activities are designed to build students' emotional and social intelligences. EI is one's ability to be aware of and to self-regulate personal emotions, as well as the ability to empathize with the emotions of others. SI is the ability to deal interpersonally with others through effective communication and interact well with others in social settings.

In an article titled, *The Preeminent Intelligence–Social IQ*, educational researcher Raymond H. Hartjen asserts intelligence is enhanced by expanded opportunities for social interaction. Hartjen (2004) states:

> Traditional classrooms do not permit the interaction of complex social behavior. Instead children in traditional settings are treated as learners who must be infused with more and more complex forms of information. One need only look at the "Standards" that have been created by each of the subject specialties to become aware of the vast amounts of factual knowledge that a student should have acquired by various stages of their progress through school. (p. 19)

Hartjen further asserts that when students enter the job market they are handicapped to the point of being incapable of surviving on their own. Hartjen continues,

> When industry and local businesses condemn education for not properly educating our students they fail to recognize the true source of the problem. They always make reference to the students' academic inadequacies when in fact what the students are lacking are social confidences, self reliance, thinking skills, and personal resourcefulness. (p. 29)

He argues that students must have continuous opportunities for interpersonal experiences every day, if they are to survive in the real world. Through these interpersonal experiences, students will have a good sense of self and the confidence—along with the necessary skills—to do well throughout life. EI and SI are critically important in reducing bullying behavior and giving students the necessary skills for a lifetime.

Emotional and Social Intelligence

In his groundbreaking book, *Emotional Intelligence Why It Can Matter More Than IQ*, Daniel Goleman (1994) defines EI as a spectrum of competencies that drive leadership performance. The four main constructs of EI are:

1. **Self-Awareness:** the ability to read one's emotions and recognize their impact while using gut feelings to guide decisions
2. **Social Awareness:** the ability to sense, understand, and react to others' emotions while comprehending social networks
3. **Self-Management:** involves controlling one's emotions and impulses and adapting to changing circumstances
4. **Relationship Management:** the ability to inspire, influence, and develop others while managing conflict

Phase II promotes emotional intelligence by providing a simple five-step process that safely encourages students to experientially learn and practice communicating feelings. When thoughts and emotions are in check and balanced, behavior is likely to be appropriate. Utilizing the five-step process throughout the year provides a communication structure to help students maintain this balance.

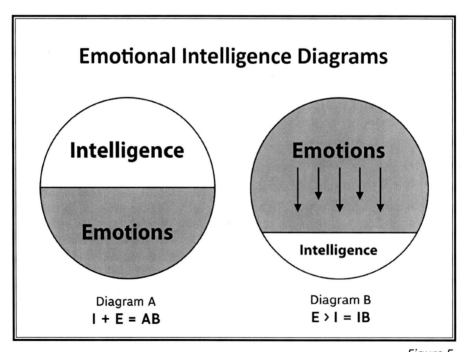

Figure 5.

Figure 5 contains two emotional intelligence diagrams. In Diagram A, intelligence (I) is balanced with emotions (E) when a person thinks before acting and makes good decisions. With emotions in check, a person is considerate of self and others and exhibits Appropriate Behavior (AB).

When emotions are not in check or dominate our ability to think through situations clearly, we are more apt to make poor decisions and project our overwhelming feelings on to others. This can lead to inappropriate behavior (IB) in the form of poor decision making and increased likelihood of inconsiderate actions toward self and others, as illustrated in Diagram B.

In a more recent book titled, *Social Intelligence: The New Science of Human Relationships*, Goleman (2006) recognizes an intricate weave between our social interactions and our emotions. He states:

> The major functions of the social brain—interaction synchrony, the types of empathy, social cognition, interaction skills, and concern for others—all suggest strands of social intelligence. The evolutionary perspective challenges us to think afresh about the place of social intelligence in the taxonomy of human abilities—and recognize that "intelligence" can include non-cognitive abilities. (Howard Gardner notably made this case in his groundbreaking work on multiple intelligences). (p. 329)

Goleman (2006) organizes SI into two broad categories:

1. **Social awareness** is what we sense about others and refers to a spectrum that runs from instantaneously sensing another's inner state, to understanding his or her feelings and thoughts, to "getting" complicated social situations. Social awareness includes:
   - **Primary empathy**: Feeling with others; sensing non-verbal emotional signals.
   - **Attunement**: Listening with full receptivity; attuning to a person.
   - **Empathic accuracy**: Understanding

another person's thoughts, feelings, and intentions.
   - **Social cognition**: Knowing how the social world works.

2. **Social facility** is simply sensing how another feels, or knowing what he or she thinks or intends, and does not guarantee fruitful interactions. Social facility builds on social awareness to allow smooth, effective interactions. The spectrum of social facility includes:
   - **Synchrony**: Interacting smoothly at the nonverbal level.
   - **Self-presentation**: Presenting one's self effectively.
   - **Influence**: Shaping the outcome of social interactions.
   - **Concern**: Caring about others' needs and acting accordingly.

Phase II contains the key elements of social awareness and social facility, safely creating an opportunity for student practice in a "laboratory experience" which actively builds social intelligence (SI).

Phase II is an opportunity for students to learn powerful interpersonal skills to create change in the school climate. At times the process can be intense, requiring special attention and concentration on the part of the facilitators. Respect and a "positive leader" theme must be conducted and maintained throughout the process. Students could possibly display strong emotions during some processes.

If a student makes oneself vulnerable, it must be clear that this student and all students are to be respected not only during the process, but outside of the process as well. The rule "what's said here stays here" must be clearly established. Personal information disclosed during the process is to be held sacred and should not be used to harm another in any way.

Put-downs are not to be tolerated during any part of the program especially during all processes in Phase II. Patiently conveying that bullying and disrespect will not be tolerated establishes a clear norm for a safe school climate. Ignoring or overlooking a put-down contradicts the overall purpose of the program and an overall safe school climate. If a put-down occurs during Phase II, it is an immediate opportunity for meaningful "real-time" processing, utilizing the prescribed protocol.

Students and even adults do not feel safe being themselves in a climate of disrespect and bullying because the risk is too great. There is a natural propensity to protect one's self from the threat of harm, perceived or real. Although this is understandable, even normal at times, it is also sad to think that many students are revealing only a tiny fraction of the person they really are. This undoubtedly shows up in academic and social underachievement.

Effective Interpersonal Communication Skill Development

Basic interpersonal skills are undeveloped in youth and many adults. As mentioned earlier, with the majority of emphasis on academic standards, opportunities to cultivate emotional and social intelligence are deficient and downplayed. This is evidenced by the growing global concern around bullying and cyberbullying behavior. Increasing academic intelligence does not necessarily increase emotional intelligence. The technological age we live in makes interpersonal communication skill development even more significant and relevant now and for the future.

Effective skill development in interpersonal communication must include experiential practice in the following:

- **Active Listening**: more than just being quiet until I can have my turn identifying and reflecting feelings—empathy
- **Paraphrasing**: mirroring the speaker by summarizing and restating what the listener heard
- **Using Closed and Open Ended Questions**: when and how to use them properly

- **Using "I" Statements**: taking responsibility for actions as opposed to blaming "you" statements
- **Reading Non-Verbal Cues**: such as eye contact, body language open or closed, hands open or closed, facial gestures, etc.

One of the authors conducted mediation trainings with middle and high school students for many years. There are many concepts borrowed from the mediation process that are woven into the Clear Talk model. Having a step-by-step process allows students to facilitate disputants from a starting point, establishing the ground rules and boundaries to establish safety through the conflict to outcomes of possible realistic solutions. Staying within the parameters of a prescribed step-by-step procedure makes the process less chaotic and safer for disputants and mediators. The structure also helps students learn essential skills much more quickly as it is easier for the brain to follow and assimilate a sequential pattern. Monthly and even weekly practice and feedback sessions—giving and receiving feedback—are invaluable in helping students hone their skills and work toward mastery.

If we expect ourselves to take on the whole problem all at once, we can easily feel overwhelmed by the enormity of a problem. How do you climb a mountain? One step at a time! How do you eat an elephant? One bite at a time! Learning a step-by-step, problem-solving procedure is an important life lesson. It is much more manageable to take on a challenge in smaller increments. As students facilitate challenging conflicts within a sequential structure, it translates into doing the same kind of problem solving for them.

Working with hundreds of student mediators at the middle and high school level was a wonderful learning experience for the authors. Many lessons were learned on how to help students learn key interpersonal skills. There were also many lessons learned about the pitfalls to student mediation.

Eight Pitfalls to Peer Mediation

1. Only a small cadre of students is chosen to become peer mediators.
2. Having all students go through Peer Mediation training is effective, but highly inefficient. A whole school mediation approach may be more realistic in a smaller school.
3. Students may not get an opportunity to practice the skills in a real-time student mediation.
4. Students who do have an opportunity to conduct mediation do so in isolation.
5. The only ones truly benefiting from a student-led mediation are the two disputants and two mediators, which has minimal impact on social climate.
6. Students not trained are essentially excluded from the process.
7. Students not involved—the majority of the student population—in real-time mediation are not privy to any outcomes. As a result, everyone except the four students involved in the mediation process are "in the dark" about successful resolutions or transformations that occur.
8. Student mediators are asked to maintain or sign a contract with a confidentiality clause which actually reinforces and perpetuates the notion of covert contracts.

Important Note

Phase I, as well as Activities One through Four in Phase II, are critically important precursors to the Clear Talk process. Omitting any of the following activities and going directly to Clear Talk is highly discouraged. Students are best prepared and open to Clear Talk when you follow the sequence and flow of Phase II.

When doing Clear Talk, know it can be an exciting and powerful process, but always remember that Clear Talk is not counseling, even if a school counselor facilitates the process. Clear Talk should not be used in lieu of discipline for policy violations regarding bullying.

Enforcing your discipline policy and conducting Clear Talk are critical corrective and formative steps to creating a safe and thriving school. Although the five-step process can be successfully navigated by students, the process should always have a supportive adult present.

All activities in Phase II are to be conducted in a circle. Facilitators are encouraged to participate in all the activities, unless there is a physical reason for not doing so. Students who have injuries or risk injury during the physical activities also should remain seated and not directly participate for safety and health reasons. During the Clear Talk process, one of the co-facilitators is encouraged to be in the center of the circle at all times with all students entering the circle to do Clear Talk. An adult in the circle will help students feel safe, keep the process safe, and demonstrate a sincere interest in students having a successful experience.

Facilitators are encouraged to support and help students stay focused on the five-step sequence and prevent any student from going to a "blaming stance" during the process. If a student is not able to refrain from blame or take the other student seriously, calmly stop the process. Do not shame either student. Just let them know that you will give them a chance to resume a new Clear Talk process when they can do so in a spirit of gratitude, seeing the Christ in each other.

Trust yourself, trust the process, and trust that your students can do this!

Why a Circle?

We are social animals and have a biological need for human interaction. Human interaction increases opportunities for social and emotional learning. People of any age or culture can be observed daily sitting or standing across from one another either in pairs or in groups. If there are more than two people the configuration usually takes on a circular arrangement. Notice how students literally get into social circles in hallways, during recess, and in the cafeteria.

In a traditional "desk in rows" seating arrangement, students see the backs of heads. This does not allow for the interactive face-to-face learning a circle can offer. A circle is an effective way to optimize social and emotional learning. As mentioned earlier, social interactions enhance learning. With a circle everyone in the classroom is visible to each other, making even subtle, nonverbal communication possible. In our technological world, face-to-face opportunities are essential. Our face communicates volumes of important information, and technology robs us of this vital social interaction. Many gloat over what the iPad can do. Isn't it amazing what is communicated and processed verbally and nonverbally from such a small circumference like the human face? The circle invites and encourages everyone to get involved. Even if a student is shy or says nothing verbally, he or she still affects the group outcome and is vicariously impacted by the human interaction occurring throughout the process. The possibilities are infinite!

In the classroom, there are advantages and disadvantages to every style of classroom seating arrangement, whether it consists of desk rows, table rows, activity zones or stations, clusters, pairs, a semi-circle, or a circle. To go into detail about the pros and cons of each is beyond the scope of this book. For the Phase II process, students are to sit in a circle with the center free from obstructions. The dynamic of the circle creates an open and collaborative social and emotional learning environment. The activities designed for this phase provide the necessary structure if there is concern about the circle not being the usual seating arrangement.

The Celtic Trinity symbol within Christian art is an interwoven circle representing the intimate relationship of the Holy Trinity gazing love toward each other. Our assembly circle is creating a sacred safe space where we remember the pains caused and received. This sacred assembly circle empowers us to practice reconciliation. Actions within this sacred space will touch the courageous student who first steps within circle. It will touch all who are invited in to begin the healing. Finally, the rest of the group, who hold the sacred space are touched deeply by the actions. The Bully Triangle is transformed into a new healing configuration.

Creating sacred space with a circle externally invites us to create sacred space internally. Father Joseph Nassal, CPPS (2009) writes:

> How do we create a space where remembrance and reconciliation can be practiced? We find a clue in the ancient word atonement, which some have dissected into three words "at-one-ment." The word recognizes that all our relationships are grounded in the truth that God is holy.... The holiness of God is etched upon our souls because we are made in God's image and likeness. We create space for mercy by realizing that God's Spirit dwells within us. In the temple of our heart, we make space for God's holiness to be active by practicing certain spiritual exercises that strengthen our resistance to evil, our resolve to forgive and our ability to make peace. (p. 34)

Phase II Origins

Early on when one of the authors was consulted about bullying, the concerns from principals were frequently regarding male students. Having been influenced by Michael Gurian's extensive work on the psychology of boys and being the father of three sons, the author decided to use presentations and educational groups with boys as an interventional strategy.

This work focused around the notion that social responsibility, effective student leadership, and the five-step process Clear Talk could possibly make a difference in bullying behavior with boys. Most of the presentations and groups conducted over a 2-3 year period were made up of boys, with only a half dozen or so with boys and girls.

The author's initial thinking was to segregate the boys from the girls, because they are hard wired to learn differently and also to "act out" differently.

Case Study: Circle of Boys

A middle school principal contacted one of the authors about having serious problems with several boys in her seventh grade class. A number of the boys were picking on two overweight boys in the same class. The offending boys were directing daily derogatory and highly demeaning remarks at the two targeted boys, as well as tweaking—pinching and twisting—their nipples. Most of the peer abuse occurred in the boys' restroom at school.

The parents of each boy in the seventh-grade class were notified and appropriate disciplinary action was taken with the offending boys. One of the responses in my consultation with the school principal was to commence a "boys' group" with the female school counselor co-facilitating the process. All the parents supported the group except for the mother of one of the targeted boys. This particular mother was concerned her son would be subjected to more of the same treatment from the boys during the process. Although it would have been preferable to include the boy in the group, parental rights were upheld, and he was excused from participating in the group.

The group of 20 boys went through a six-week process that contained much of what is currently the three-phase bully program. The response from the boys and the parents was overwhelmingly positive. The female counselor who co-facilitated often commented how amazed she was with the responsiveness and openness of the boys throughout the process. She also noted that there was a marked decrease in the peer maltreatment during school time.

Although there were numerous highlights during the six weeks, the most amazing session was the last. Toward the end of the group time, the boys were asked to do a "check out," which is a very simple closure activity. During this activity each student shares one significant highlight about the group experience. When finished each of the boys was to say "I'm complete." This meant he worked hard throughout the process

and had done his personal best to get back in integrity with others in the group and felt a sense of accomplishment and pride in doing so.

The group sessions went so well that the author didn't anticipate any problems with all the boys checking out with flying colors. About half of the boys in the circle had checked out when three of the boys seemed to impulsively interrupt the process. The author felt confused and a bit annoyed by this apparent anarchy, since time was running out. The immediate inclination was to exercise "facilitator privilege" (i.e., pull rank) and not allow the three boys to speak, especially out of turn, about whatever they were about to say. Everyone had worked hard—facilitators included—and were very deserving of the final check out.

The author asked the boys what was going on. The three boys said almost in unison that they could not finish the check out, because it wouldn't be honest for them to say "I'm complete." The author asked them to say more about this. The boys asserted that "we can't say we're complete, because we have to clear with Trevor to be complete." The boys had obviously learned something from the process about leadership. The boys demonstrated in that very moment the virtues the author wanted to instill.

The group witnessed the honesty and integrity demonstrated by the three boys. They courageously took responsibility for their actions by wanting to pursue resolution with Trevor. The boys knew they couldn't honestly say "I'm complete" without reconciling and asking for forgiveness from Trevor. There was a demonstration of compassion for Trevor by being thoughtful and mindful enough to want to include him. What a wonderful and amazing contrast from the behavior that caused the group to be set up in the first place.

By taking a risk to disclose their truth, something else magical happened. They taught the other boys something about stepping into their leadership. This contagion inspired a positive rippling effect in which the entire group wanted to do Clear Talk with Trevor, too. The author could not have consciously designed a better comprehensive "final exam."

The three boys could have very easily ignored this step and "just got it over with" and said "I'm complete." Instead they were living examples of leadership by taking the initiative to speak up about doing the right thing. This was a huge risk for them to take as they overcame overwhelming obstacles: negative peer pressure from the group and the parent's refusal to allow Trevor in the group. These boys were determined not to let anything get in the way of taking this very necessary step.

The immediate challenge and biggest obstacle at this juncture was how to help them check out with an "I'm complete" in the process. The facilitator put it back on the group to explore ways they might propose getting back in integrity with Trevor, even though his mother refused to allow him to participate. After several options were tossed around, the option reaching consensus was to have the school counselor ask Trevor's mom if she would allow Trevor to come to the group so they could apologize to him. While the counselor pursued their request, the author prepared the boys for likely disappointment and an alternative plan if the mother continued to refuse contact.

The counselor returned and said the mother would permit the boys to do Clear Talk with Trevor, under one condition: they do so one at a time in her presence. The boys agreed. One at a time they used the five-step process with Trevor. A talking stick is used in the process and the boys decided to take the stick with them as a supportive totem from the group. Each boy returned from his quest with an expression of utter joy beaming from his face. It was as if the weight of the world was lifted off their shoulders. The group would ask their peer as he reentered the group if Trevor "got it." This meant that Trevor heard their apology and they were able to get in integrity with him by taking responsibility for wounding him and asking for forgiveness. There was no doubt the mission was accomplished. All the boys could now check out

of the group by saying "I'm complete" honestly and with total integrity. There were undoubtedly many successful outcomes throughout this entire group process. The boys had a chance to bond and learn about such virtues as honesty, integrity, compassion, accountability, and responsibility.

This was the last boys' group the author facilitated because of "the rest of the story." Although powerful and meaningful, the boys' group caused a negative ripple with female students who felt excluded from the process. School feedback, self evaluation of the situation, and looking at the bigger picture, helped the author to realize the process was similar to posting a "no girls allowed" sign on the clubhouse door.

Excluding the girls from the process disenfranchised them. The girls were very aware of and deeply affected by the peer maltreatment that transpired among the boys. The author unwittingly created a covert contract with the boys by excluding the girls.

A gender specific group ignores the reality and possible insights—overt and covert—the opposite gender and the community as a whole have to offer. It also excludes an entire gender from being a significant part of many essential learning outcomes. Any shifts the boys made during the process were not actualized by the girls; they had no opportunity to directly witness, contribute, or gain from the transformative process of their counterparts. In turn, the boys had no opportunity to directly benefit from the girls either.

The boys probably would not have had the same bonding experience or successful outcomes had the girls been included in the process. However, conducting gender specific groups is synonymous with isolating and excluding the other gender specific group, perpetuating covert contracts and in time overshadowing any of the perceived benefits. The girls' valuable and caring insights are critically important to a communal experience that is hungry for reconciliation and forgiveness. This experience demonstrates how schools are a community and change can only happen in a communal way.

In conclusion, segregating the boys from the girls is not an effective approach to reducing the incidence of bullying behavior and creating a Christ-centered school. In order to have the greatest impact on school climate, both genders must be included in the process. Conducting gender specific groups has many benefits and may be a viable approach in other venues, such as treatment. In the school setting, gender specific groups have at least two serious implications:

1. Gender specific groups produce isolation and exclusivity; and
2. Bullying and disrespect are predicated on exclusivity and isolation.

Phase II Advantages

Phase II contains numerous advantages over traditional student-led mediation and gender specific groups. Phase II is an inclusive and integrated process that should only be conducted with coed groups. These advantages include:

- Includes and integrates the entire class
- Increases gender sensitivity
- Increases the learning outcomes utilizing a systems approach
- Reduces covert contracts
- Enhances and integrates learning by utilizing real-time peer relationship situations
- Builds conflict resolution and problem-solving skill sets through active or passive participation
- Allows everyone, including teachers to be privy to the shifts and outcomes
- Increases the level of responsibility through whole class participation
- Increases the level of accountability through whole class participation
- Gives teachers an opportunity to affirm demonstrated virtues and reinforce meaningful life skills
- Creates a successful platform for effectively increasing social and emotional learning
- Offers real-time "train the trainer" for students, teachers, and support staff for effective program implementation and sustainability.

Activity One

Phase I Review

"To each individual the manifestation of the Spirit is given for some benefit. To one is given through the Spirit the expression of wisdom; to another the expression of knowledge according to the same Spirit; to another faith by the same Spirit; to another gifts of healing by the one Spirit; to another mighty deeds; to another prophecy; to another discernment of spirits; to another varieties of tongues; to another interpretation of tongues. But one and the same Spirit produces all of these, distributing them individually to each person as he wishes."

1 CORINTHIANS 12:7-11

PURPOSE

- *To enhance student learning and integration of key concepts from Phase I*
- *To review and test student comprehension of Phase I*
- *To reinforce Phase I key concepts for optimal Phase II results*

Phase I Review

The review of a previous lesson in any subject is essential for the integration of student learning. This review, in particular, surfaces key concepts from Phase I, setting the stage for the Phase II process. Each of the key concepts listed below is significant and is to be initiated by the facilitator during the review process, especially if students do not initiate the concepts themselves. This will help keep students aware of these important concepts. When you consider the Bullying Triangle, all students are actively or passively involved in some form of bullying behavior. A critical element to this program is to make a shift toward transparency, keeping light on all bullying and disrespectful behaviors. Students must continue to acknowledge that this behavior exists, the current reality of the behavior as it exists among them, and the reason the class is doing this program in order to shift to the desired outcomes.

If students accept bullying and disrespect as the norm, they will not be compelled to make necessary changes. This activity intentionally causes students to come to a collective dissatisfaction with the way things currently are in order to motivate change. Often bullying and disrespect occur unconsciously and out of habit. It is likely that students do not realize that the possibility exists for anything better than the way things currently are. A significant aspect of this process is for students to understand the "norm" is not normal; most often it is substandard to what is possible. We want students to come to understand that disrespectful and bullying behavior is an extremely unsafe and unhealthy way to treat each other with many short- and long-term implications. Until students become sensitized to this reality and connect with a sense of dissatisfaction around the current reality, they will not feel empowered to be a part of the solution.

Phase I and Phase II are important because they give students hope, empowering them with the notion that they possess the knowledge and the capability to make the necessary changes to this collective dissatisfaction. The list of leader qualities and characteristics students generate in Phase I is actually the beginning of a collective student vision for what is possible. In Activity One, students are asked to help themselves and others in the room make the changes necessary for all to feel safe and trust that respect is possible.

The following are seven key concepts that are critical to the Phase II process. Allow students an opportunity to bring these concepts up on their own and add any of the concepts missed.

1
All students have the capacity to be leaders and the potential to positively or negatively influence the school.

There is no such thing as a "bad kid!" In fact, every student holds a key to unlock great things, not only in school, but in the world. Phase I is specifically designed to help students come to believe they have the power (in cooperation with others) to positively impact the school environment. Creating a safe and even amazing school can be a reality when students connect with a positive "flavor of attitude." Every day students are faced with a very simple choice. Asking the rhetorical question—"What kind of ripple do you want to make in our school, positive or negative?"—will help students come to one and only one conclusion. All students have the capacity to be leaders and have the potential to positively or negatively influence the school. Guide them to ways in which they can make positive ripples!

The tag line "choose your flavor of attitude" can be used by teachers and students as an effective communication tool. If I see someone misbehaving or treating another in a way that is counter to the culture we are attempting to create, I can simply ask the question, "What kind of ripple do you want to make in our school?" or "What kind of ripple do you think you are making in our school by behaving this way?" These questions alone are a form of intervention that will ideally cause students to pause and reflect on their behaviors and make adjustments. Of course, hearing the tag line once may not cause individuals to change their behavior, but if they hear it multiple times from multiple sources, it is bound to have an impact. Conversely, the tag line can be used to affirm and reinforce positive choices students are making: "I see the positive ripple(s) you are making in our school....Way to go, I see you positively influencing our school by choosing a positive-flavored attitude today!"

Students express feeling disempowered and can easily come to believe they do not possess the capacity to impact positive changes in the school environment. As a result, students leading in negative ways can be red-flagged as discouraged students. They can often be heard blaming others, including teachers, the principal, or other students for why they "can't stand" or "hate" this school. Many students do not see themselves as capable and therefore lack the ability to own how they can change their negative current reality.

As educators we can blame the student and his or her family for the way the student is. Of course, this will not help the student come to a place of positive leadership. Students who display less than desired behaviors are very capable of becoming positive influences in spite of themselves or their family's dysfunction. Resiliency research clearly conveys how individuals triumph over the most difficult of odds. Let's not sell any of our students short. Challenge them and inspire them to greatness; inspire them to be more of the person they positively are!

2
Students create a "collective reality" of leadership by brainstorming qualities and characteristics.

Students often bring up in the review the positive leader words they listed together in Phase I. This simple yet powerful interactive exercise generates positive feelings among students. Brainstorming qualities and characteristics of leadership helps students create a "collective reality" by encouraging ownership around what it means to be a leader. This is a good time to hand out the list of leader words generated from the Phase I exercise. Affirm the students for creating this list and doing such a great job of working together. Have each student in the circle say one word starting at the top of the list. Let them know the words they came up with are very powerful and important. The Phase II process will be an opportunity for them to practice many of the qualities on their list.

The list of student generated positive leader qualities and characteristics from Phase I are a wonderful bar or standard to set in and out of school. These words should be compiled and typed in a hard copy ready to be handed out during Phase II. Typing the positive leader words can be a student project to encourage additional ownership. As you hand out the leader word list to students, honor them for how well they worked together to create the list.

3
Hand identification of who has been put down, disrespected, or bullied or has put down someone else in the room.

A show of hands is a non-threatening way for everyone in the room to become acutely aware of the current culture that exists in the school. This simple exercise is a powerful exposé of put-downs, revealing the truth that put-downs only generate disrespect and instigate bullying behavior. The major objective of this exercise is to increase tension and a collective dissatisfaction among students. This tension creates a natural propensity to seek resolution. With positive conditions in place, students are motivated to elevate their normative substandard conduct.

This demonstration should be redone during the review section in Phase II in order to increase the tension and dissatisfaction among the students in the room. Students never say they are proud to have their hand up or proud to see their entire class with hands up because of put-downs. This is actually encouraging! We want students to feel dissatisfied with this and desire something better, to strive for a higher standard that reaches closer to their true potential. The series of questions below will help facilitators elevate the level of dissatisfaction among students.

4
The possibility exists to create a Christ-centered school when reverence and dignity for the person are the cultural norm.

The antithesis of this statement is true as well: it is totally impossible for us to create the desired norm if disrespect and bullying are the current cultural norm.

Students are asked to raise their hand as a nonverbal confession if they have put down or been put down by another student, bringing the culture of disrespect into the light. A few simple yet important questions can be asked in order to create dissonance around the current climate of disrespect students create with each other. Because of Phase II time constraints, it may be best to have students answer the questions as an assignment. If you do decide to use the questions for class discussion, do not use them in a way that humiliates or demeans, but rather with the intention to empower and challenge students to envision a new reality with each other.

- What are your thoughts and feelings as you see yourself and others with hands up because of being put down or having put down someone?
- What is it like to be a part of the mistreatment of others in this way?
- How possible is it to create an amazing school if disrespect is a common way to treat one another?

- How do put-downs influence our school environment?
- How do you personally influence our school environment by putting down others?
- How do put-downs targeted at you influence your attitude?
- How does it feel when you see others being put down or disrespected in any way?

5
Choose your flavor of attitude: Positive or Negative "What kind of ripple do you want to make in your school?"

Students often remember the "flavor of attitude" analogy used in Phase I. Understanding the rippling effect a pebble makes in a pond connects them to how a negative or positive action impacts the whole school in some way. This question can be used and/or posted as a part of the community language created by this program. Students really want to do the right thing. I have never had a student say he or she wanted to be a negative ripple in the pond. Remember, a "negative student" can be red-flagged as a discouraged and disempowered student. The following questions are another way to emphasize the previous key concept:

- What kind of ripple is created by treating others with put-downs?
- What kind of ripple is created when we watch others being put down and don't do anything about it?
- What kind of ripple is created by treating others with put-ups?
- What kind of ripple do you personally choose?
- What kind of ripple do you envision creating together for our school?

6.
Briefly review the lessons learned from the skits and role plays.

- Name the roles played in the bullying triangle: *Bully, Target, Active* and *Passive Bystanders.*

- Who is responsible for changing the bullying situation? *Everyone.*
- Who wins in a bullying triangle? *No one.*
- Is it normal to feel like you want to get back after someone hurts you or puts you down? *Yes.*
- Is it okay to do anything to get back at someone? *No.*
- Is anyone ever better than anyone else? *No.*
- Why not? *We are all created equal.*
- What was the lesson in the girls' role play "Odd Girl Out"? *Including and not excluding others is the right thing to do.*

7.
Howard Gray and Code of Silence Stories—Talking Points

- Why do you think Lee Domann wrote the Howard Gray song?
- How do you think he felt when he wrote it?
- What did Lee want to be different about his relationship with Howard?

- How long after seventh grade did Lee write the Howard Gray song?
- Encourage students to learn more about Lee and Howard (http://www.leedomann.com/howard_gray.html)
- How do you think the characters in the "Code of Silence" story felt?
- The character Frankie is actually the author of this story. How do you think he felt when he wrote it?
- Emphasize that disrespect and bullying behavior doesn't just go away. In fact, it lasts for many years. For Lee it was more than 20 years and for Frankie it was more than 30 years.
- Emphasize that this phase is a way to "clear" any wrongs so no student has to go one more day, let alone 5, 10, 15, or 20 plus years down the road regretting having treated another student in a negative way. This process gives students the power to "right" any "wrong" that may exist between them.

Phase I Review

TIME	PREPARATION & PROCESS	LOGISTICS

0:00   **Session Preparation**

- Be familiar with the Key Concepts in Phase I
- Arrange chairs in a circle with no obstructions in the center.
- All Phase II activities are to be conducted in a circle.
- Students should use the restroom prior to the start of the session. There should be no scheduled breaks.

(Logistics) Make note cards or a working document to reference the Key Concepts.

Process

Say: *"Let's start off with some review of what we learned from our previous lesson."*

"What 'stuck' for you from our first lesson: Christ is Our Model for Leadership?"

(Logistics) Use student recall from Phase I as a spring board to discussion. Use the lesson plan questions for any missed key concepts.

2:00   *Note.* Use one of the two options in the logistics window.

Phase I Key Review Concepts:
1. All students have the capacity to be leaders and the potential to positively or negatively influence the school.

"What did you learn about what it means to be a leader?"

"How does each of you have influence in our school?"

(Logistics) Option 1: Divide students into teams. Have each team take one of the concepts.

Option 2: Place each concept on a wall sign and have students move and discuss.

3:00   *"What kind of leadership is needed to keep everyone safe and create an amazing school together?"*

2. Together students create a "collective reality" of leadership by brainstorming qualities/characteristics.

"Here is the list of leader words you did such a great job brainstorming together."

Note. Begin Activity Two only when all the key concepts are reviewed.

4:00   **3. Hand identification of who has been put down, disrespected, or bullied or has put down someone in the room.**

"Raise your hand if you have been put down by someone in this room."

"Look around the room and notice all the hands up."

"Raise your hand if you have ever put someone down in this room."

"Look around the room and notice all the hands up."

Phase I Review

TIME	PREPARATION & PROCESS	LOGISTICS

5:00   *"Today is an opportunity for us to change this and I'll show you how in a little bit. I want to ask you a few questions first."*

Note. Ask all or a select few of the following questions depending on time.

- *What thoughts and feelings come up as you see yourself and others with hands up because of being put down or having put down someone?*
- *What is it like to be a part of mistreating others in this way?*
- *How possible is it to create an amazing school if disrespect is a common way to treat one another?*
- *How do put-downs influence our school environment?*
- *How do you personally influence our school environment by putting down others?*

6:00
- *How do put-downs targeted at you influence your attitude?*
- *How does it feel when you see others being put down or disrespected in any way?*
- *What kind of ripple is created by treating others with put-downs?*
- *What kind of ripple is created when we watch others being put down and don't do anything about it?*
- *What kind of ripple is created by treating others with put-ups?*
- *What kind of ripple do you personally choose?*
- *What kind of ripple do you envision creating together for our school?*

4. The possibility exists to create a safe and amazing school when respect is the cultural norm.

"Do you think it is possible for us to create a safe school together?"

"What will it take to do this?"

7:00   *"Do you think it is possible to create an amazing school together?"*

"What will it take to do this?"

"What would a safe and amazing school look like?"

8:00   *"How would everyone be treated?"*

5. Choose your flavor of attitude: positive or negative. What kind of ripple do you want to make in your school?

"What two flavors of attitude are there?"

"What kind of ripple do you want to make in this school?"

Phase I Review

TIME	PREPARATION & PROCESS	LOGISTICS

"Choose your flavor!"

9:00   **6. Briefly review the lessons learned from the skits/role plays.**

"What are the roles in the bullying triangle? Bully, Target (victim), Active and Passive Bystander?"

"What did you learn about the Bullying Triangle?"

"Who is responsible for the Bullying Triangle? Everyone!"

"What responsibility will you take to keep Bullying Triangles from happening here at our school?"

10:00   **7. Howard Gray and Code of Silence Stories and talking points.**

"What do you remember about the two stories told in the Phase One lesson?"

"How did the writer (Lee Domann) feel about treating Howard Gray the way he did?"

"How many years after what had happened did Lee Domann write the Howard Gray song?"

12:00   *"What does this say to you that 20 years later he still felt shame, guilt, and regret about what he did to Howard? This just doesn't go away."*

"Who was the bully in the poem 'The Code of Silence?'"

"How do you think the author (Frankie) feels some 30+ years after he treated Tommy the way he did?"

"What does this say to you that he still feels this way after so many years?"

15:00   *"Some of you may not feel good about how you treated or were treated by someone in this room. You don't have to go one more day let alone 5, 10, 15, 20 or 30+ years down the road regretting this like Lee or Frankie. Today is a (special, magical) day that you can change this. I am going to show you how very soon!"*

Activity Two

Positive Leader Words

PURPOSE
Students practice hearing and speaking leader words, incorporating them into common language for greater integration.

LEARNING OBJECTIVES
- Students will assimilate the collective leader words through recitation.
- Students will synthesize leader words to create new conduct norms.
- Students will integrate leader words through practical application.

CORRESPONDING STUDENT WORKBOOK PAGE 38
- Student Worksheets   1

Worksheet 1

Positive Leader Words

Add new positive leader words here:

_____
_____
_____
_____
_____
_____
_____
_____
_____
_____
_____

Take one of the positive leader words on your list and write three ways you will put this word into action:

1.
2.
3.

List three people who will support you with this action:

1.
2.
3.

Postive Leader Words

Compile and type the list of student generated leader words from Phase I and make one hard copy available for each student prior to Phase II. Be sure to place the corresponding leader words with the respective grade level. Any grades combined during Phase I should have a combined list of leader words. For example, if Grades 4 and 5 were together during Phase I, make a combined leader words list for Grades 4 and 5. For Activity Two, only use one hard copy of the list to pass around the circle, to cut down on possible distractions. After completion of Phase II hand out a copy of the leader words list to all students with instructions about starting their Leader Folder.

Ask the student on your left or right to read the positive leader quality at the top of the list and then pass the list on to the next person. Continue around the circle having each student read each word in order. Ask students to practice speaking like an enthusiastic leader by reading the word loudly and clearly. Continue around the circle until each student takes a turn reading a different leader word on the list.

Some lists may not contain enough leader words for every student to speak a word. An option could be to continue around the circle adding (with help from the entire class, if needed) a new positive leader word to the current list, so that every student can say a word. If the leader list has more words than students, keep going around the circle as many times as necessary until all leader words are spoken from the list. When the entire list is read, this is an opportunity for the facilitators to compliment students on speaking up like true leaders!

Mention to the students that saying the leader words is a first step toward putting them into practice: "Today is an important day to begin putting the leader words into action." If you plan to feature positive leader words during the school year, have students pick their "Top 10 Positive Leader Words" from the list. Each month during the school year, highlight one of the positive leader words chosen by students.

There are endless uses for the positive leader words, and it is good to refer to the list often. One reason advertisements and commercials have such a powerful and successful impact on all of us is the frequency with which we see and hear them. Repetitiously seeing, hearing, and using the positive leader words from many different sources (e.g., announcements, poster boards, bulletin boards, Smart Boards, school websites, etc.) can have a very powerful impact similar to commercial advertisements.

Suggestions for Positive Leader Words

- Post Leader Words throughout the school.
- Students pick the "Top 10 Leader Words" and use one word thematically each month.
- Students write or speak about the qualities and characteristics of the positive leader words and reference how they see these qualities in themselves, other students, teachers, or someone else they admire.
- Students choose someone considered to be a great leader and write or speak about which of the qualities they believe make this person a great leader.
- Use a leader word in a thoughtful reflection during daily announcements.
- Students continue the "Leader Folder" introduced in Phase I. This can be a simple two pocket folder to contain reflections, articles, and quotations about leadership. The Leader Word list can be the first contribution.

Suggestions for Leader Folder

- Journal entries about their own leadership
- Essays on a person(s) either dead or alive that model positive leadership for the student in his or her life
- Journal entries about positive leadership in the students' community and in the world
- Book reports about positive leadership
- Magazine or newspaper articles that reflect positive leadership

Positive Leader Words

TIME	PREPARATION & PROCESS	LOGISTICS
0:00	**Session Preparation**	Typing up the positive leader can be made into a student project. The students are then responsible for getting the typed list to the teacher or facilitator.

Session Preparation
- Have leader words typed ahead of time and a copy made for each student.
- Only use one hard copy of the positive leader list to pass around for students to recite from.
- Hand out copies of the prepared list to all students at the completion of Phase I.
- Student Workbook, p. 38

Process

Say: *"Here is a list of all the leader words you came up with in our first session. Great job!"*

"Is this all the possible leader words that exist? No. I encourage you to add to this list as you think of new leader words."

"Let's call in the spirit of these leader words by each of you reading one word on the list starting at the top."

"We'll start with (Student Name) on my left and go around the circle until all the words are read."

"Practice speaking loudly and clearly as a leader would!"

2:00 *"Good job! Let's be aware of these positive leader words today and in the future."*

LOGISTICS

Typing up the positive leader can be made into a student project. The students are then responsible for getting the typed list to the teacher or facilitator.

Make sure absent students get a copy of the leader word list.

Activity Three

Safety Check

PURPOSE

To create a baseline measurement based on student perception of the current reality for how safe or unsafe the social climate is in the classroom

LEARNING OBJECTIVES

- Students will learn a clear definition of what it means to be safe.
- Students will share their level of personal safety based on the Safety Check continuum.
- Students will practice assertiveness by speaking their truth about their personal safety.
- Students will hold each other accountable and take responsibility for helping themselves and others progress toward a 10 for total safety.
- Students and adults will have a language to communicate when they or others are or are not being treated like a 10.

CORRESPONDING STUDENT WORKBOOK PAGES 39-42

- Student Worksheets   4

Worksheet 2

Safety Check

The goal in the last session was
"To help myself and others get closer to a 10."

What was your first Safety Check number?   _____   (0-10)

What was your second Safety Check number?   _____   (0-10)

Did you help yourself and others get closer to a 10?   **Y**   **N**   (Circle One)

If you answered yes, what helpful things did you contribute toward accomplishing this goal?

_____

_____

_____

_____

If you answered no, what didn't you do to help accomplish this goal? Why?

_____

_____

_____

_____

List three things you will do throughout the year to accomplish this goal:

1.

2.

3.

Worksheet 3

360° Safety Diagram

During the program we used the term "Safety Check."
The Safety Check used is a continuum
from 0 being the least safe to 10 being the safest.

_____

0   1   2   3   4   5   6   7   8   9   10

LEAST SAFE   **SAFEST**

In the community circle, you picked a number that best represented you and how safe you feel with your class. This next activity is similar to the Safety Check line above, but involves a circle called the 360° Safety Diagram.

Follow the directions below.

Directions:

1. Color each of the four quadrants in the 360° Safety Diagram (on the next page) to a number that best represents you.

2. Use a different color for each quadrant (Physical, Mental/Emotional, Social, and Spiritual).

3. On separate paper, write down the number you chose for each of the four quadrants. Add and divide by 4 to get your Safety Check number.

   Example: If your Physical quadrant = 6, Mental/Emotional = 8, Social = 3 and Spiritual = 7, you would add 6 + 8 + 3 + 7 = 24, then you would divide 24 ÷ 4 = 6.

4. The Safety Check number in this example is 6.

What Does It Mean to Be Safe?

In order to create a common language in the school community, safety is defined as being totally free from physical, mental/emotional, social, and spiritual harm. The four generalized areas of 360° Safety—Physical, Mental/Emotional, Social, and Spiritual—describe behaviors that are not safe and do not lead to confidence and trust. They are contrasted with a question and possible responses to help students come to understand preferred treatment.

Physical Safety

Physical safety at a 10 means a student feels confident and trusts he or she will never be a target of the following behaviors: punching, pinching, kicking, slapping, scratching, poking, choking, tripping, biting, pulling hair, flicking, nipple twisting, or any other physical maltreatment. Facilitators can help students understand preferred treatment by asking: How would students treat you if your physical safety was a 10? Students may say they would receive hugs, high fives, hand shakes, or other appropriate physical behavior that will only increase their sense of safety and trust.

Mental/Emotional Safety

Mental/Emotional safety at a 10 means a student feels confident and trusts he or she will never be a target of any of the following behaviors:

- verbal or nonverbal put-downs
- disrespected for personal thoughts and feelings
- ostracized for clothes
- laughed at for physical appearance or the size or shape of one's body
- belittled for how one talks or walks
- made fun of for wearing braces or glasses
- called names
- sneered or jeered at for asking or attempting to answer questions in the classroom

Facilitators can help students understand a preferred treatment by asking: How would students treat you if your mental/emotional safety was a 10? Students might say others:

- Listen and accept how they are feeling without judgment
- Treat them with kindness and respect
- Will be considerate of them
- Will include them
- Give them compliments or put-ups daily
- Will support them in a way that increases their sense of safety and trust

Social Safety

Social safety at a 10 means a student feels confident and trusts he or she will never be a target of the following behaviors:

- Being the subject of rumors
- Cyberbullying (i.e., mean or cruel emails, IM's, Social Networking sites, text messages, etc.)
- Backbiting
- Sexting
- Being laughed at or ridiculed
- Being ignored or excluded
- Being embarrassed in any way

Facilitators can help students understand the preferred treatment by asking: How would students treat you if your social safety was a 10? Students might say others would be friendly to them even if they were not their friend. They would always be treated with kindness and respect. If there is a rumor other students would check it out directly with them to know the truth. Students would be considerate of their feelings and include them in activities both in and out of school. Students would ask other students not to talk about them in a demeaning way but rather would stick up for them. They would be treated socially in ways that would only increase their sense of safety and trust.

Spiritual Safety

Spiritual safety means students feel confident and trust they will never be a target of prejudice or racial, cultural, or religious slurs. This is a very sensitive and delicate topic even for adults. Even so, it is helpful to discuss this by having students describe what kind of treatment they do want. Facilitators can help students understand a preferred treatment by asking: How would other students treat you spiritually if you were a 10? Students might say they would always be treated with kindness and respect. They would not be judged by the color of their skin. They would not be criticized or judged for wearing clothing that reflects their cultural heritage. They would not be judged or harassed for their cultural or religious practices. They would not risk ridicule for saying grace before they eat or for participating in a Communion Service or Mass. They would only be treated spiritually in ways that increase their sense of safety and trust.

Read out loud each of the four generalized areas of 360° Safety, during Activity Three: Safety Check. Pause to allow students to silently come up with one number that best represents what their level of overall safety is on the continuum: 0 being the least safe and frequently subjected to unwanted behaviors, while 10 is the safest and absolutely free from any harm. When ready, ask students to state their number one at a time going around the circle. Adults are encouraged to honestly share their number as well; however, it is best to have a student begin the process.

Although a separate continuum could be established for each of the four generalized areas, one can make this activity into a math problem by adding a number for physical, mental/emotional, social, and spiritual and dividing by four to equal the Safety Check number. The best approach is to keep it simple. Students seem to naturally average the four areas of safety to establish one number that best represents their personal level of safety with classmates. An activity titled 360° Safety Diagram can be found on the next page and on page 41 in the Student Workbook. This activity consists of shading in a number for each area of safety, creating a more detailed 360° visual of personal safety.

SAFETY CHECK

| 0 | 1 | 2 | 3 | 4 | 5 | 6 | 7 | 8 | 9 | 10 |

LEAST SAFE   **SAFEST**

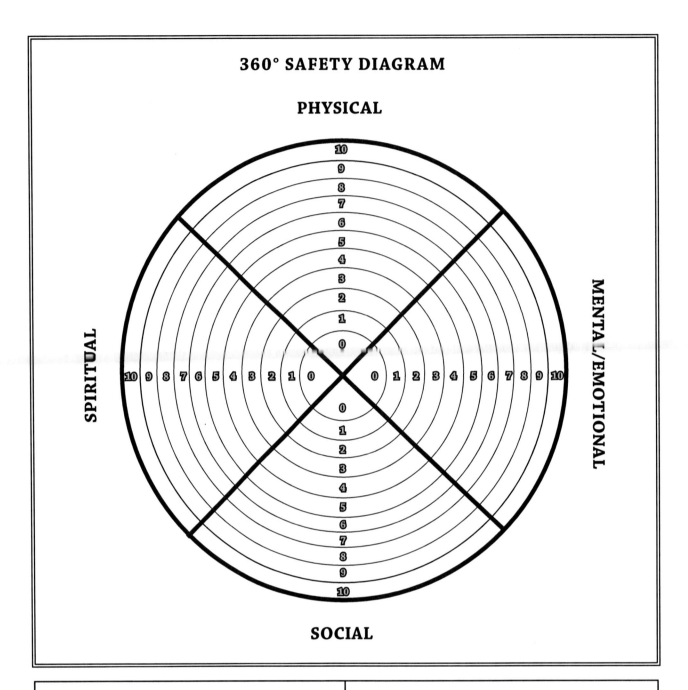

360° SAFETY DIAGRAM

PHYSICAL

MENTAL/EMOTIONAL

SPIRITUAL

SOCIAL

PHYSICAL SAFETY	SOCIAL SAFETY
NO hitting, pushing, kicking, tripping, biting, choking, slapping, poking, hair pulling, pinching, nipple twisting = 10	NO relational aggression such as spreading rumors, ignoring, excluding, backbiting, cyber assaults = 10
MENTAL/EMOTIONAL SAFETY	**SPIRITUAL SAFETY**
NO put-downs about looks, hair, size or shape of body, wearing glasses or braces, how I walk or talk, grades (good or bad), name calling, clothes or shoes, color of my skin, whether I play sports or not = 10	NO put-downs around race, culture, religious preference, or religious practices. All race, religions, and practices are supported and accepted = 10

Figure 6

The Safety Check
is important to the overall process
for the following reasons:

1. This may be new information about safety for students.
2. Students will have a reference point for what it means to be and feel totally safe.
3. When students declare their Safety Check Number, it may be the first time that they have publicly (in the classroom only) admitted how safe or unsafe they feel.
4. When students share their Safety Check Number, it becomes glaringly apparent (current reality) that not everyone is a 10.
5. Knowing everyone is not a 10 creates tension and a natural propensity among students to seek resolution. (This is good!)
6. The Safety Check Number becomes a baseline marker from which to communicate and measure student progress.
7. Any movement toward a 0 is cause for concern and intervention.
8. Any movement toward a 10 is cause for celebration.
9. The Safety Check continuum gives students a reference point from which they can determine what behaviors are safe and unsafe for themselves and others.
10. The Safety Check continuum can be a guide with which students can hold each other accountable.

Safety Check Group Process

Have students close their eyes briefly. Ask them to silently and honestly identify the number that best represents how safe they feel on a continuum from 0 to 10, with 0 representing the least safe and 10 representing the most safe. The Safety Check number they choose is one number—not four numbers—that best represents how safe they feel on average in all four areas. Have students open their eyes and raise their hands when they have the number. Let students know it is important to stick with

the Safety Check number they believe best represents them in this moment. Ask them not to change the number based on the number other students have chosen. Mention that they may judge for themselves whether their own number is too high, too low, or not the same as their classmates when everyone shares their Safety Check number. This challenge is good practice for being a leader by "holding your ground... taking a stand...standing in the fire and not changing your number in spite of the pressure you might feel to do so." Ask students to be willing to stand by what is true for them.

Start with the student on your left. Have the student say his or her number and continue around the circle until each student has shared a Safety Check number. The facilitators in the circle can opt out if they choose to, but it is good modeling for facilitators to share a number as well. Students will be able to measure progress with facilitators at the end of Phase II. Facilitator participation is servant leadership in action modeled by Jesus.

After everyone in the circle has stated a Safety Check number, ask students to pretend to be scientists and hypothesize what it means to have the range of numbers presented. This can be done by repeating the lowest number and the highest number that was shared. For example: "The lowest number I heard was a 3 and the highest number I heard was a 9. What can we hypothesize knowing our class is a range from 3 to 9 on the Safety Check continuum?"

Listen to the responses students share. The most important hypothesis—and one that many classes do not catch—is not everyone in the class is a 10. If everyone were a 10, the class would already be the most amazing class on the planet, but this is not the current reality. The reality is the class perception is a range from x to y. If students do not bring up as a hypothesis that not everyone in the circle is a 10, bring this up for them because the Safety Check measurement is a critical marker distinguishing current reality and the desired result during the Phase II process.

Important Groundwork for Activity Five

This activity is a way to establish the overall goal—to help myself and others progress (move) closer to a 10 on the Safety Check—for Activity Five: Clear Talk and beyond.

Ask students to raise their hands if they are willing to commit to this goal. If any student does not raise a hand ask why. Respond accordingly. Usually it just requires additional explanation or clarification before all students are willing to commit to the goal. Now have the students repeat the following:

> *I will help myself* (point to self) *and others* (point to each student around the circle) *get closer to a 10* (put up 10 fingers).

Student Accountability

Encourage students to use the Safety Check language to help them gauge and communicate incidences of peer maltreatment to adults or to challenge offending students. For instance, if a student sees another student being mistreated, he or she could say: "I notice you're not treating (*Student Name*) like a 10 and we don't treat each other less than a 10 here at our school." Students can also ask the question: "Do you think you are treating (*Student Name*) like a 10?"

Questions can be cause for pause for offending students, encouraging them to rethink and redecide how they are choosing to treat the targeted student. Although subjective, this simple measurement is a way for students to practice observation and communication skills. When reporting, a student could communicate with an adult an interpretation of the incident by describing the level of severity on the 0-10 continuum.

Worksheet 4

Getting to 10

What or who is getting in the way of my being a 10? (10 = totally safe and thriving at my school)

_____

_____

_____

Whom do I need to do Clear Talk with to help me get closer to a 10?

_____

_____

How might my behavior get in the way of others being a 10?

_____

_____

_____

Whom do I need to do Clear Talk with so I can help them get closer to a 10?

_____

_____

_____

List three action steps you will take to make progress toward helping yourself and others get closer to a 10:

1.

2.

3.

Share this worksheet with your teacher or a parent.

Safety Check

TIME	PREPARATION & PROCESS	LOGISTICS
0:00	**Session Preparation** • Draw a straight horizontal line on the board or flipchart. • Write the numeral 0 at the far left and 10 at the far right of the continuum. • Under 0 write the words "Least Safe" and under 10 write the word "Safest." • Student Workbook, pp. 40-41	Another option is to have students do the 360° Safety Check Diagram at the end of the detailed lesson prior to this activity for reference.
1:00	**Process** **Say:** *"Let's do a Safety Check."* *"On a continuum* (point to the board or flipchart) *with 0 being the least safe and 10 being the most safe, pick the number that best represents you."* *"As you think about this, let me define safety for you."* *"When we talk about safety, we mean 360° Physical, Mental/Emotional, Social, and Spiritual Safety."*	Facilitators are encouraged to make note cards referencing the definitions of the four generalized areas of 360° Safety found in this section.
2:00	*"Physical safety means..."* Read definition of Physical Safety on p. 98. *"How would students treat you or you them if you are safe physically—a 10?"* *"If you don't trust you can be a total 10 with your classmates or they with you, pick the number from 0-10 that best fits you."*	All Safety Check definitions can be found on pp. 98-99.
3:00	*"Mental/Emotional safety means..."* Read definition of Mental/Emotional Safety on p. 98. *"How would students treat you or you them if you are safe mentally/emotionally—a 10?"* *"If you don't trust you can be a total 10 with your classmates or they with you, pick the number from 0-10 that best fits you."* *"Social safety means..."* Read definition of Social Safety on p. 98. *"How would students treat you or you them if you are safe socially—a 10?"* *"If you don't trust you can be a total 10 with your classmates or they with you, pick the number from 0-10 that best fits you."*	

Safety Check

TIME	PREPARATION & PROCESS	LOGISTICS
4:00	*"Spiritual safety means..."* Read definition of Spiritual Safety on p. 99. *"How would students treat you or you them if you are safe spiritually—a 10?"* *"If you don't trust that you can be a total 10 with your classmates or they with you, pick the number from 0-10 that best fits you."* *"Close your eyes for a brief moment."* *Note.* This is an important reflective moment even though you will only allow for about 10 seconds.	
4:15	*"When you have the number, open your eyes and raise your hand."* *"We are going to start to my left with (Student Name) and go around the circle."*	
6:00	*"Please don't change the number you have right now."* *"You might feel some pressure to change your number based on what others say. This is a chance to practice being a leader by stating what we believe to be true about ourselves."*	
7:00	*"(Student Name), please start us off by saying your Safety Check number."* *"Thank you all for sharing your Safety Check numbers!"*	
8:00	*"Now, let's pretend we are all scientists."* *"What I heard as you went around the circle is that we are a range from (lowest number stated) to (highest number stated)."* *"Did I hear you correctly?"* *"Thank you!"*	
9:00	*"What can we hypothesize about what it means to be a range from (lowest number stated) to (highest number stated)?"* *Note.* Listen to all the possible hypotheses students present and acknowledge each. Listen carefully for the most important one: Not all students in the circle are a 10. If no one shares this hypothesis, state it for the group.	

Safety Check

TIME	PREPARATION & PROCESS	LOGISTICS

"There is one hypothesis that is key to what we are about to do today and that is not everyone in the circle is a 10."

"Wouldn't it be ideal if everyone was a 10 on their Safety Check?"

"That's our goal today, that everyone moves closer to being a 10."

"If you are willing to commit to this goal, please raise your hand."

10:00   *"Repeat after me:* **I will help myself** (gesture to yourself) **and others** (gesture to others) **get closer to a 10** (hold up 10 fingers)."

Note. If students are not in sync with this first "repeat after me" do it again so they will feel more united around the goal.

Energizers/Ice Breakers

PURPOSE

To playfully engage students in energizers/ice breakers to increase classroom cohesiveness and safety

LEARNING OBJECTIVES

- Students will create classroom cohesiveness through fun and active processes.
- Students will build trust through community building.
- Students will increase energy and enthusiasm through physical activity.

MATERIALS NEEDED

- One hula hoop
- Stopwatch or clock with second hand

Energizers/Ice Breakers

Physical movement is fun and healthy. Getting the body moving is energizing and increases blood flow, respiration, and heart rate. This increases oxygen to the brain, which helps improve concentration, focus, and brain activity. Physical activity will also engage students interpersonally and "grease the skids" for Activity Five. These Energizers and Ice Breakers are designed to promote fun and laughter, while simultaneously building connectivity and cohesiveness among students.

Rules
1. Play Hard (Participate energetically)
2. Play Fair (Respect others at all times)
3. Nobody Hurt (Be considerate of others' space)

"The Wave"
Ask for one student to volunteer to start the wave. Ask the student which direction the wave will go and how many times it will travel around the circle. Make sure it is reasonable (e.g., five times counterclockwise and five times clockwise). If the students do not jump out of their chairs with enthusiasm and/or make noise, encourage them to do so. We want to increase the energy level in the class. This activity is great for getting the energy going and is usually a fun and familiar "ritual."

"I like People Who _____!"
Take one chair out of the circle for this activity. The facilitator steps in the center and reminds the class of the rules: Play Hard, Play Fair, and Nobody Hurt. When students hear the kind of person described and it "fits" them, they are to leave their seats and move to chairs across the room (not the seats right next to them). The facilitator starts the activity by saying the phrase: "I like people who ___!" Finish the sentence with something that is inclusive, such as "eat pizza, like ice cream, are wearing school colors, like to laugh, watch movies, play video games," etc. The person standing without a chair moves to the center of the circle and repeats the statement, "I like people who ____!" This activity increases the energy level in the class and helps scramble students away from the comfortable configuration in which they started. This activity also gets students used to stepping into the center of the circle, which is helpful for the upcoming interpersonal activity.

Hula Hoop Exercise
Hula hoop needed. Have students hold hands or wrists, if they choose. Place the hoop between two students with their hands joined inside the hoop. Have the two students decide which direction the hoop will travel. The students are to negotiate the hoop over their arms, heads, and bodies all the way around the circle and back to the starting point without breaking hands. This activity is a great coordination, balance, and cooperation activity. Get a "baseline time" for the hoop making a complete circle starting and ending in the same position. Ask students what they can do to better their time the second time around. Note the first time around, students are often laughing at others for not being as quick or efficient in getting the hoop over their head and body. Also note that students may not be focused, exhibited by talking to others, and may not be fully engaged in the process.

Energizers/Ice Breakers

TIME	PREPARATION & PROCESS

Session Preparation

0:00
- Be familiar with and know ahead of time what ice breakers you want to do.
- There are no props necessary for the first two energizers. If you opt to do the hula hoop exercise, make sure you arrange to have a hoop available.
- Facilitators are encouraged to participate, but if you or any students have a physical limitation, please make sure all who need to opt out for safety reasons.

Make sure the chairs are not too crowded for the ice breakers

Process

Say: *"For this next activity there are three rules:*
> *1. Play Hard*
> *2. Play Fair*
> *3. Nobody Hurt."*

"Raise your hand if you agree to these rules."

1:00

"Thank you for agreeing to these important rules."

0:00 **Energizer/Icebreaker #1 The Wave Activity**

"Let's do The Wave!"

"Raise your hand and I will choose someone to lead us in The Wave."

"Thank you, (Student Name). Pick the direction The Wave will go."

"Class, is that direction clockwise or counterclockwise?"

"Very good."

"(Student Name), how many times will The Wave go around the circle?"

2:00 Note. Make sure the number of times is reasonable. Five to ten max.

"Okay, (Student Name), start us off with some enthusiasm!"

Note. Encourage students to jump up and make noise with this activity. Remember, we want to get them moving to increase the energy and enthusiasm.

4:00 *"What did we need to do in order for the wave to go around the circle?"*

Possible responses: We had to watch or observe each other. Teamwork. Cooperation. Good timing.

"Good job! You looked like you were having fun doing The Wave."

5:00 *"Let's try another game!"*

Energizers/Ice Breakers

TIME	PREPARATION & PROCESS	
0:00	**Energizer/Icebreaker #2 I Like People Who _____?**	Remove one chair from the circle.
	"This game is called "I like people who _____?"	
	"The person standing in the center says, 'I like people who _____?' and finishes the sentence with what he or she likes."	Teacher should stand in the center of the circle when introducing this activity.
	"If what the person in the center says fits—you like the same thing—leave your chair and quickly and safely find another chair across from you."	
1:00	*"Do not sit in the chair right next to you."*	
	"What is going to happen if we are all rushing to get a chair?"	
	"That's right! There will be a lot of mayhem in the center of the circle and I'm not going to play traffic cop."	
2:00	*"Turn to someone next to you and say: PLAY HARD, PLAY FAIR and NOBODY HURT!"*	
	"I'll start us off. I like people who eat pizza!"	
3:00	*"Okay, (Student Name), it's your turn to say, 'I like people who_____!' and finish the sentence."*	Continue this activity with about five to ten students getting "caught" in the circle.
	"It is great to see everyone laughing and having fun!"	
5:00	*"Let's have more fun!"*	
0:00	**Energizer/Icebreaker #3 Hula Hoop Activity**	
	"Stand up and hold hands or wrists."	
	"(Name of student) and (Name of student) I am going to put this hula hoop in between the two of you."	
	"Hold your hands or wrists again with the hula hoop on top."	
1:00	*"Start the hula hoop to the left of the circle. Begin."*	
	Note. Time the first round. Usually during the first round students are not focused and get the hula hoop back to the original point in 3:00 minutes or more. Use the following analogy to challenge the students to do the exercise again. Most classes can improve their time significantly the second time around. This is a great boost for the class!	
4:00	*"Your time was_____."*	
	"Do you think you can improve on this time?"	
	"Imagine we are all in the gym and I time each of you individually running as fast as you can from one end of the gym to the other."	

Energizers/Ice Breakers

TIME	PREPARATION & PROCESS

"While you are running all the students in your class are on the sideline, booing you, hissing you, saying that you can't do it, you're a loser, etc. After everyone runs across the gym I add up all the individual times. This is Round One, Group A."

"Now we do Round Two, Group B, but this time all the students in your class are clapping and cheering you on, saying very positive and encouraging statements about how great a runner you are and how you can do it. Everyone is focused on you and your success."

5:00   *"I add up all the individual times for Round Two, Group B."*

"Which group will have the best collective time, Round One, Group A or Round Two, Group B?"

Expected Response: Round Two, Group B!

"Why?"

Probable Responses: Because we were encouraging, supportive, focused on each individual's success and wanting each person to do well.

"That's right! Now imagine us being this way with each other all the time— in everything we do."

6:00   *"If we always work as a team and have a 'my success is your success' attitude, we will all be winners all the time!"*

"Now let's do a Round Two, Group B with the hula hoop and see if supporting and encouraging each other really does help us improve our time!"

Note. When students accomplish the task, praise them!

"Did it work?"

8:00   Expected Response: Yes!

"Remember this activity and what it took to improve on your time. The same ingredients are necessary in everything we do."

"I am going to say it again: If we always work together as a team or Christ-centered community and have a 'my success is your success' attitude, we will all be winners all the time!"

10:00   *"When I see you working together as a team I will let you know and if I don't see this happening I will be sure to remind you!"*

110   **PHASE II**
Dignity for All   *Peace Be With You*
MANUAL

Activity Five

Clear Talk

"The whole idea of compassion is based on a keen awareness of the interdependence of all living beings, which are all part of one another and all involved in one another."

FR. THOMAS MERTON

PURPOSE

To heal brokenness between students through experiential practice of reconciliation and forgiveness in an effort to strengthen a Christ-centered school

LEARNING OBJECTIVES

- Students will develop skill sets around a five-step communication process called Clear Talk.
- Students will have the opportunity to practice reconciliation and forgiveness.
- Students will learn compassion by practicing CLEAR Listening.
- Students will increase emotional intelligence (EI) by learning how to identify and communicate feelings.
- Students will increase social intelligence (SI) by enhancing social awareness and social facility.
- Students will increase understanding of personal responsibility and accountability.

CORRESPONDING STUDENT WORKBOOK PAGES 43-52

- Journal Entries   2
- Student Worksheets   4

Clear Talk

Step **1** Thank you!

Step **2** Data (What happened?)

Step **3** Feelings: Mad, sad, glad, afraid, ashamed

Step **4** My/Your behavior said....?

Step **5** Wants

Use Clear Talk often to help build your communication skills and strengthen your relationships.

Journal Entry

Peace Circle

Journal what you learned about yourself in the Peace Circle.

Clear Talk

At an ending point in Activity Four (Energizers/Icebreakers) the facilitator announces, "It is time to move on to the next activity!" Activity Five is called Clear Talk. The facilitator brings out a "talking stick" and walks into the center of the circle. Find a fairly straight, sturdy stick ahead of time for this particular process. It should be approximately one to three inches in diameter and at least shoulder height. Any rough spots on the stick should be smoothed over with a knife, file, or sandpaper at home. Do not bring a knife to school!

Some classes over the years have made it a project to decorate a class talking stick utilizing school colors and gluing special adornments on the stick. Have the talking stick in the room when you begin Phase II in anticipation of this activity. Students usually comment or ask about the stick and are very curious about it. This is good! There is no need to explain what the stick is until you get to Activity Five. Kindly hold students off by letting them know you are glad they want to know about the stick and you will let them know what it is for very soon.

When conflict or unfinished business exists between two or more people, there is often a negative emotional charge. The talking stick is a way to metaphorically "ground" this negative charge in a similar way to a lightning rod. Students like the "magical" aspect of this metaphor. Ask them to describe what a lightning rod is and how it is used. There is usually at least one student who is happy to share his or her knowledge. If for any reason students do not know, you can inform them that a lightning rod is a metal rod or pole that is placed on top of a structure such as a house, barn, or tall building. The lightning rod is intended to attract the lightning and channel its potentially damaging charge into the ground via a metal cable that extends into the ground from the rod itself. This will prevent the structure

---

Worksheet 1

Clear Talk Practice

Imagine Howard Gray did Clear Talk with author Lee Domann
while they were still in school. Using the five steps in Clear Talk,
write what you think Howard might say to Lee.

Step 1   Thank you!

Step 2   Data (What Happened?)

_____

Step 3   Feelings (Mad, Sad, Glad, Afraid, Ashamed)

_____

Step 4   Your behavior said.....?

_____

Step 5   Wants

_____

Do you identify more with Howard or with Lee? Why?

_____
_____
_____
_____
_____
_____

Worksheet 2

Clear Talk Practice

Imagine Frankie (bully) did Clear Talk with Tommy (target)
while they were still in school. Using the five steps in Clear Talk,
write what you think Frankie might say to Tommy.

Step 1   Thank you!

Step 2   Data (What Happened?)

_____

Step 3   Feelings (Mad, Sad, Glad, Afraid, Ashamed)

_____

Step 4   Your behavior said.....?

_____

Step 5   Wants

_____

Do you identify more with Frankie, Tommy, or Eric (active bystander)? Why?

_____
_____
_____
_____
_____
_____

from sustaining any costly damage from a fire or electrical short.

This metaphor is an opportunity to help students understand that when there is a negative charge between people, it is like lightning and can do some serious damage to the relationship. The talking stick isn't metal but acts as the lightning rod for the Phase II process during each of the Clearings. Let students know that when they participate in Clear Talk, both the speaker and the listener are holding the talking stick and magically sending any negative charge down through the stick and into the ground away from both of them. Feel free to be as theatrical as you like when explaining this part of the process.

As the facilitator enters the circle holding the stick upright, it is important to make a connection to the reason for doing this activity. Mention that Frankie would have loved to have been able to do this with Tommy and Eric in order to Clear with them and not carry his guilt with him for more than 30 years after seventh grade. Mention that Lee would have wanted this opportunity to Clear with Howard and not carry his guilt with him for more than 20 years after seventh grade. As the facilitator, you could also share how this process would have been beneficial for you as well—if it is an honest statement—when you were in school. Assure the students that hundreds of students just like them have stepped into a circle and magically cleared with another student, just as they will. Note that this process was conducted with Grades 4-12 for close to 10 years in more than 60 schools, prior to the publication of this book.

Emphasize that this process is an opportunity for them to magically undo any wrong they have done or that has been done to them by another student. Let students know you do not want them to have regrets about how they were treated or how they have treated someone else a day longer, let alone 5, 10, 15, 20 or 30

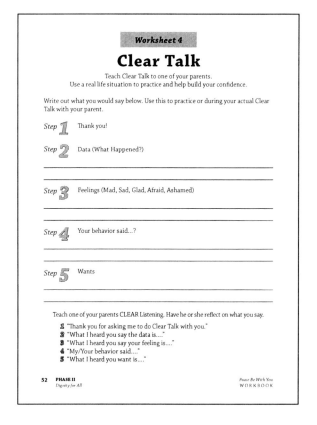

Worksheet 3

Clear Talk Practice

Write out a Clear Talk you want to do with a classmate.
Only follow through with this Clear Talk in a class meeting with
your teacher or school counselor present to support you.

Step 1 Thank you!

Step 2 Data (What Happened?)
_____

Step 3 Feelings (Mad, Sad, Glad, Afraid, Ashamed)
_____

Step 4 Your behavior said.....?
_____

Step 5 Wants
_____

What is at risk if you follow through with this Clear Talk?
_____

What is at risk if you don't follow through with this Clear Talk?
_____

Peace Be With You
WORKBOOK   **PHASE II** 47
                                       Dignity for All

Worksheet 4

Clear Talk

Teach Clear Talk to one of your parents.
Use a real life situation to practice and help build your confidence.

Write out what you would say below. Use this to practice or during your actual Clear
Talk with your parent.

Step 1 Thank you!

Step 2 Data (What Happened?)
_____

Step 3 Feelings (Mad, Sad, Glad, Afraid, Ashamed)
_____

Step 4 Your behavior said...?
_____

Step 5 Wants
_____

Teach one of your parents CLEAR Listening. Have he or she reflect on what you say.

1 "Thank you for asking me to do Clear Talk with you."
2 "What I heard you say the data is...."
3 "What I heard you say your feeling is...."
4 "My/Your behavior said...."
5 "What I heard you want is...."

52 **PHASE II**   *Peace Be With You*
    Dignity for All   WORKBOOK

years down the road! Remember, unfinished business between students is essentially a covert contract which has serious implications for the school climate. This process is a critical step to a safe school by creating an opportunity for students to reconcile, possibly sparing them from a lifetime of regret and the negative rippling effect these regrets can have with others.

In order to accomplish this very important mission, students will need to tap into many of the positive leader qualities they brainstormed in the last session. They are not just talking about leader words now, but living them in this experience. The Phase II circle is a wonderful life laboratory, where students can practice honesty, integrity, courage, compassion, etc.

Now, place the stick on the floor in the center of the circle and sit in the circle with the students. Let students know you are thinking about a situation that happened and you want to do Clear Talk with another student. Take time here to demonstrate the process through a role play between yourself and another student. It is recommended that you role play being a student, and not "the teacher" or adult in this process. Do not make this a real-time demonstration. Tell students that you are going to role play a situation that you want to Clear. Walk into the center of the circle, pick up the stick, and invite a student into the center with you. Both of you hold the stick facing each other. Begin with the first step by thanking the student for helping you role play Clear Talk.

Ask students to notice the entire process is in a "spirit of gratitude." Blaming another student is not tolerated in or out of the circle. The student asked to role play with you does not talk, only listens attentively. Walk students through each step with a predetermined role play scenario.

Five Steps to the Clear Talk

Step **1** Thank you!

Step **2** Data (What happened?)

Step **3** Feelings: Mad, sad, glad, afraid, ashamed

Step **4** My/Your behavior said....?

Step **5** Wants

Post the above for student reference during Clear Talk.

Emphasize with students that they can magically undo any wrongs with each other by doing Clear Talk. This is an important time to share with them the sacredness of the circle and the power of reconciliation and forgiveness with the community. Let them know that they can enter the circle in one of two ways:

1. Student "wronged" (mistreated) another.
2. Student was "wronged" (mistreated) by another.

More Detail on Clear Talk Steps

Step **1** **Thank you!**

As a first step, "Thank you" sets the intention around a process that goes much deeper than just good manners. Students entering into this process display tremendous courage as they navigate through a challenging circumstance— a willingness to move beyond something that has been of negative consequence most likely affecting the school climate. Saying, "Thank you for entering the circle with me," honors and respects both parties, welcoming them into a spirit of gratitude. God created the world and then took time to see that His work was good. God was appreciative, which in many ways is the highest spiritual state. When we are appreciative, we don't put ourselves first. There is less ego involved, and we are less likely to complain or blame with a thankful heart. Let students know this is sacred practice in "seeing Christ in each other."

Setting an inviolable intention around this process encourages students to be compassionate with each other. Our culture is expedient and literally encourages youth and adults to treat each other as objects, things, or "its." The latter creates anxiety and mistrust among people. The act of holding a stick together and standing across from another person, while looking him or her in the eye is a very honoring, humbling, and human experience. The Phase II process creates a safe container that encourages a multitude of opportunities to practice what it is like to be in a reverent community.

Ask students if they have ever seen in a movie—or in real life—two people face each other and bow. Students always report they have witnessed such an action between two people. When asked what the two people are communicating, students clearly understand the act is about honor, respect, dignity, or caring; words don't even have to be used to convey this message. We are essentially saying, "I see the Christ in you and I invite you to see the Christ in me."

Step 2 Data (What happened?)

Describe just the facts of the incident that caused harm, noting the physical, mental, emotional, social, or spiritual offense.

This step instructs the student who initiated Clear Talk to state only the facts about what happened. Stating what happened is, of course, the student's perception. Remember, perception is in the eye of the beholder and part of honoring is not questioning what a student believes he or she has done or what has been done to him or her by another student. Articulating one's perception using just the facts is often very challenging for students. If a student is too quick to "jump" to other steps, the facilitator can gently guide the student to describe only the facts surrounding the incident. Students

may also choose to leave out certain details because the material may be emotionally charged or embarrassing to repeat. Forcing students to discuss the details surrounding a difficult incident is discouraged. Facilitators must keep in mind, however, that "secrets" are what perpetuate bullying behavior and rob students of the opportunity to truly reconcile.

For instance, students at times want to generalize by saying "he called me names" or "she disrespected me." Although this glimpse of fact is true, it omits the names the target was called. Simply stating "she called me names" is much easier to dismiss by all the students. This omission perpetuates the covert contract. Stating the specific names called exposes the covert contract making the nature of the disrespect and the incident very real. For example, "The data is that you called me a slut and a whore in gym class." Another example is for a student to specifically state, "I was slapped in the face... punched in the arm...or kicked in the privates," which takes the clearing to a much deeper level than if we allow the student to just say "he disrespected me." It is very easy to refute the latter generalization, which is a judgment, but much more difficult to refute the specifics surrounding the former. Gently encourage students to use critical details in this step to bring out covert contracts.

Step 3 Feelings

How do I feel about being treated or having treated you this way? This step is an important opportunity for a student to state how he or she feels about the incident. The act of identifying feelings and expressing them out loud is very powerful and healing. Students and adults can do a much better job at identifying and communicating feelings. This step is great practice for students and will help them feel supported and accepted for their feelings. Additionally, tell the students that to use another student's feelings against them in any way, in or out of the circle, will not be tolerated. Reinforce confidentiality.

This step is a wonderful teaching piece around the five basic feelings (mad, sad, glad, afraid, and ashamed) in an effort to increase emotional intelligence (EI). There are many variations of these five basic feelings that students are welcome to use. Discourage them from saying they feel "bad," "terrible," or "fine." Even the word "depressed" is a condition or state of being and not a feeling. Encourage students to use the five basic feelings or some variation thereof. It is very common and acceptable for students to identify and report more than one feeling in response to the incident described.

It is highly recommended that you have each of the feelings written down next to Step 3 on the board or flipchart. Visual learners will also benefit from having faces—caricatures or photographs—displayed on a separate medium identifying the five feelings. Free images of feeling faces can be downloaded online.

Step 4   My/your behavior said.....?

This step assists students in understanding and recognizing how behaviors have consequences.

Students don't always consider the impact their behavior has on others. For students to use another as the brunt of a joke and then abdicate responsibility by hiding behind the statements, "I was just kidding....I didn't mean it" is not acceptable. Every word and every action—positive or negative, direct or indirect—toward another human being has either positive or negative consequences. Remember the pebble in Phase I? Our behavior is the pebble and the rippling effect is the consequence of our actions. This step asks students to identify and vocalize how their behavior and/or another student's behavior has impacted them. This is a critical step in creating a community of reverence.

Use the two "complete the sentence" options below to help students interpret cause and effect:

1. My behavior said.....?
2. Your behavior said.....?

These can be written on the board as follows: Step 4: My/Your behavior said.....?

If a student stepping into the center has "wronged" another student, the following incomplete sentence would be used: "My behavior said....?" If a student stepping into the center has been "wronged" by another student, the following incomplete sentence would be used: "Your behavior said....?" Step 4 is student perception and an important part of helping students understand how behaviors are interpreted and misinterpreted. If a student appears stuck on this step, use these optional questions:

- **Option 1**: Student "wronged" another student. Student asks self: Did my behavior consider the other person? If not, then complete the sentence: My behavior said...?
- **Option 2**: Student was "wronged" by another student. Student asks self: Did the behavior of the student who wronged me consider my feelings, space, belongings, etc.? If not, then complete the sentence: Your behavior said...?

Step 5   Wants

- What damaging behaviors don't I want to continue in our relationship?
- What supportive behaviors do I want in our relationship?
- What are some hopeful things we could look forward to in our relationship?

In order to make this clearer for students it is important to help them identify an action that is more "behavioral specific." By doing so, both students—speaker and listener—can connect with a more concrete plan for future change. In order for him or her to achieve this, it is necessary to ask a follow-up question. This will take the student one step further in describing a specific Positive Replacement Behavior (PRB) that will help the student get to the core "want."

Here are a few examples of follow-up questions to identify the PRB helping students get more of what they do want:

Possible Response	Follow-Up Question
"I want to be respected."	"What would Greg be doing specifically that says to you he respects you?"
"I want to be appreciated."	"What would Jessica be doing specifically that says to you she appreciates you?"
"I want to be supported."	"What would Sandra be doing specifically that says to you she supports you?"

Students will range in ability and maturity about speaking up or not speaking up about unwelcomed treatment from their peers. There are students who are skilled at speaking up (assertive) when targeted and other students who will not speak up (non-assertive) and everything in between. Students often struggle with coming up with what behavior(s) they do want in the relationship. For a student to assert that he or she does not want a specific behavior to continue is very important and takes tremendous courage. Even if, ideally, we could get all students to voice objections about peer maltreatment, most students (even the assertive ones) have difficulty stating what kind of treatment they would prefer.

Having a student state what kind of treatment he or she does not want or for a student to make a promise not to continue to treat another a certain way is a great start, but it is incomplete. Helping students to be clear about specific ways they want to be treated and to verbalize them is an important part of the process because unless students know how to encourage wanted behavior, the unwanted behavior will most likely continue.

Therefore, we would be remiss, if the five-step process ended with what students don't want or promises not to continue certain treatment. Facilitators can take each "don't want" and help a student turn it into a "want." Unless a student identifies and expresses a Positive Replacement Behavior (PRB)—what he or she wants instead—the student is more likely to have the unwanted behavior continue.

If a student reports he or she doesn't want to be hit, called names, or have rumors spread about him or her, they are 50% complete with the fifth step. After the student has expressed all the damaging behaviors, the facilitator or class can then ask what behavior(s) the student wants instead—PRB. When the question, "What do you want instead?" is asked the student may have a very confused look on his or her face. This is good because the student is in a wonderful spot to come to understand the difference between "don't wants" and replace them with "wants."

The following chart contains a few examples of questions to ask that will help flip a "don't want" into identifying the behavior a student does want.

Don't Want	Question to Help Clarify Wants
"I don't want to be hit."	"How do you want Greg to treat you instead of hitting you?"
"I don't want to be called names."	"How do you want Jessica to treat you instead of calling you names?"
"I don't want to be a topic of rumors."	"How do you want Sandra to treat you instead of spreading rumors about you?"

Often when responding to one of these questions, students generalize by saying they want to be treated with respect instead. We can assume that all unwanted behaviors are disrespectful in some way. In essence, the opposite of what I don't want is what I do want: "I don't want to be disrespected, but I do want to be respected....I don't want to be hit, but I do want to be appreciated.... I don't want to be put down, but I do want to be supported," etc. It is powerful when a student can identify that he or she wants to be respected, appreciated, and supported. Recognizing the opposite to "what I don't want" is important, but it is too vague for behavioral change to occur.

Spiritual Perspective

Clear Talk mirrors the steps for the Sacrament of Reconciliation in the Catholic faith and the communal experience deepens an appreciation of the Sacrament. "The Lord Jesus Christ, physician of our souls and our bodies...has willed that His Church continue, in the power of the Holy Spirit, his work of healing and salvation" (Catholic Church, 2010). As we understand this Sacrament more fully, we are able to enter into the healing and salvation work of the Spirit with us.

When we come to the Sacrament:

- Thank You: We come with gratitude for Jesus' healing mercy.
- Data: We share how long it has been since our last Sacrament visit and confess our sins.
- Feelings: We come with true sorrow and contrition.
- My/Your Behavior said: We have sinned against God and against our brothers and sisters.
- Want: We desire to amend our lives, change our behaviors, to do penance, atone, and receive absolution.

To properly celebrate the Sacrament, "we are asked to look into our souls and, with an honest and unblinking gaze, identify our sins. This opens our minds and hearts to God, moves us toward communion with the Church, and offers us a new future" (Catholic Church, 2010, §37).

Similar customs are found in other faith traditions, and it is the internal ownership of sin and wanting to change that is essential. This is the same approach of Clear Talk. Rather than telling the bully he or she is wrong and needs to stop and apologize, a sacred space is created to look at the bullying act. All present look at the bullying act and personally identify participation in the action. Deep internal ownership happens, and a shift in behavior begins.

Clear Talk and compassionate listening are expressed powerfully in the Scripture story of the prodigal son in Luke 15:11-32. Jesus tells the story of a man who has two sons. The younger demands his share of his inheritance while his father is still living and goes off to a distant country "where he squandered his inheritance on a life of dissipation" and eventually has to take work feeding the pigs—clearly a low point, as swine are unclean in Judaism. There he comes to his senses and decides to return home and throw himself on his father's mercy, thinking that even if his father does disown him, that being one of his servants is still far better than feeding pigs.

Using Clear Talk phraseology, the youngest son comes to terms with his actions and takes ownership. On his way to his father's home, the father "ran to his son" in a celebration gesture of gratitude (*Thank You*) meeting on the path to the house. The son gives the *Data*: "Father, I have sinned against heaven and against you; I no longer deserve to be called your son; treat me as you would treat one of your hired workers." The son's *Feelings*: repentance and sorrow. *His Behavior Said*: "I have disrespected you....I no longer deserve to be called your son. I deserve to be treated as one of your paid servants." The son's *Wants*: "here am I, dying from hunger."

The father gets it! He runs to greet his son with open arms and comes face-to-face to create healing (*Thank You*). The father's *Data*: "this son of mine was dead, and has come to life again; he was lost, and has been found." The father's *Feelings*: "filled with compassion" when he saw his son approaching. He was also filled with joy, calling for a celebration. The father's *Behavior Said*: "Quickly bring the finest robe and put it on him; put a ring on his finger and sandals on his feet." The father's *Wants*: To kill a fattened calf for a feast—to celebrate my son who "has come to life again; he was lost, and has been found."

The rippling effect of this celebration and healing reaches the eldest son. When the eldest son realizes his brother has returned and his father is throwing a party, he acts out his anger and refuses to join. The father comes out to plead with his son to join the party. The son's anger, jealousy, and resentment keep him from entering into celebration. The father's expression of love for his eldest son falls on deaf ears because there was not a compassionate heart listening: "My son, you are here with me always; everything I have is yours. But now we must celebrate and rejoice, because your brother was dead and has come to life again; he was lost and has been found."

Below are two versions of a scenario between David and Andrew to help with the flow of the five-step process. In both examples, David is the student initiating the five-step process by stepping into the circle first.

Scenario Version 1

David was wronged by Andrew. David was walking into the classroom one day and Andrew was standing in the doorway. As David crossed the threshold of the door, Andrew impulsively stuck out his foot, tripping David and sending him stumbling into the room. As David staggered he caught himself on the desk in front of him, nearly striking his head. Everyone in the class laughed, including Andrew, as they witnessed the event.

Step **1** Thank You!

David simply says: "Thank you, Andrew, for stepping into the circle with me."

Step **2** Data (What Happened?)

David says to Andrew: "I was walking into the classroom the other day and you stuck out your foot. I tripped and fell, catching myself on a desk, almost hitting my head and everybody laughed."

Step **3** Feelings: Mad, Sad, Glad, Afraid and Ashamed

David says to Andrew: "I feel angry that you tripped me. I feel afraid that you did that to me. I feel embarrassed because everyone laughed."

As a facilitator, it is not our job to ask why or have a student justify his/her feelings. All we need to do is support the student by allowing him or her to speak the specific feeling(s).

Step **4** My/Your Behavior said....?

David says to Andrew: "Your behavior said that you weren't feeling very good about yourself when you did this to me and you tried to make yourself feel better by putting me down and getting everyone to laugh."

Step **5** Wants

David says to Andrew: "I don't want you to trip me or anything else like that again...." Facilitator asks what David wants instead. David may respond with: "I want you to respect me." Facilitator then asks: "What would Andrew be doing specifically that says to you he respects you?"

David may respond with: "I want you to use put-ups with me....I want you to say you're sorry and I want you to be open to sitting with me at lunch." The facilitator can make the "want" even more likely to happen by having David get even more specific by asking the question: "When would you like to sit with Andrew at lunch?" Of course, Andrew has a choice to agree or not agree to follow through with the requested behavior.

Scenario Version 2

Andrew was wronged by David. Andrew was walking into the classroom one day and David was standing in the doorway. As Andrew crossed the threshold of the door David impulsively stuck out his foot tripping Andrew and sending him stumbling into the room. As Andrew staggered, he caught himself on the desk in front of him, nearly striking his head. Everyone in the class laughed, including David, as they witnessed the event.

Step 1   Thank You!

David simply says: "Thank you, Andrew, for stepping into the circle with me."

Step 2   Data (What Happened?)

David says to Andrew, "You were walking into the classroom the other day and I stuck out my foot. You tripped and fell, catching yourself on a desk, almost hitting your head and everybody laughed."

Step 3   Feelings: Mad, Sad, Glad, Afraid and Ashamed

David says to Andrew, "I feel angry at myself for tripping you. I feel ashamed that I did that to you."

Step 4   My/Your Behavior said....?

David says to Andrew: "My behavior said that I wasn't feeling very good about myself and I tried to make myself feel better by putting you down and getting everyone to laugh, but it was at your expense."

Step 5   Wants

David says to Andrew: "I want you to know that I will not trip you or disrespect you in anyway ever again. I want you to know I am sorry."

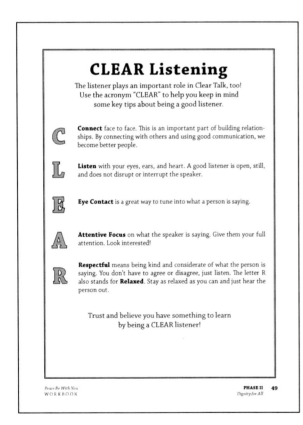

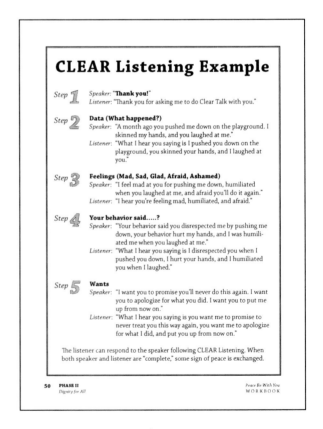

Facilitator asks this possible sequence of questions:

"What do you want instead?"

"I want you to know I will put you up from now on and not trip you down."

"What specifically will you do to put up Andrew's leadership?"

"I will use put-ups with you when I see you doing something well. I want you to sit with me at lunch tomorrow."

CLEAR Listening

The entire CLEAR Listening section in the Student Workbook can be found on pages 49-52.

Following the mock five-step process, ask the class if they believe the volunteer student was listening to you. Then ask them what he or she was doing that let them know he or she was being a good listener.

Students will often point out the student used good, non-verbal behavior such as eye contact, nodding, didn't interrupt, etc. These are all important parts of listening and we want to reinforce them as much as possible. Have the

class reinforce good listening by giving the listening student one clap, two claps, and three claps.

This is a good time to take listening to the next level by introducing active listening or what we call "CLEAR Listening," which can be found in the Student Workbook on page 49. CLEAR is an acronym for:

 Connect face-to-face. This is an important part of building relationships. By connecting with others and using good communication we become better people.

 Listen with your eyes, ears, and heart. A good listener is open, still, and does not disrupt or interrupt the speaker.

 Eye contact is a great way to tune into what a person is saying.

 Attentive focus on what the speaker is saying. Give them your full attention. Look interested!

 Respectful means being kind and considerate of what the person is saying. You don't have to agree or disagree, just listen! The letter R also stands for **Relaxed**. Stay as relaxed as you can and just hear the person out.

Ask the students if they have ever heard someone say something to them and it went in one ear and out the other. They will all agree that they have done this. Explain that CLEAR Listening is much different than this. Have the students hold up one of their hands. Now ask them to place this hand over their heart. Ask them to follow your lead as you make the sound in the rhythm of a heartbeat. Do this for about 10 to 15 seconds or so, making sure students do this in silence and get connected to the rhythm. Ask them what this is. Of course they will all say it is a heartbeat. Emphasize that CLEAR Listening is much more compassionate; it's about

---

CLEAR Listening

Journal Entry

Journal about a time when you were a CLEAR Listener.

_____

_____

_____

_____

What was the speaker's reaction to your CLEAR Listening?

_____

_____

Whom in your life do you go to for CLEAR Listening?

_____

_____

What are the gifts of being a CLEAR Listener?

_____

_____

_____

What are the gifts for us when we receive CLEAR Listening?

_____

_____

_____

being attentive and that hearing the person comes from the heart.

This is your segue into teaching the active part of CLEAR Listening. Here's how it works:

Ask the student volunteer to start with Step 2: Data and "mirror" to you what he or she heard you say is the data about the situation. Explain that "mirroring" is just reflecting back to the person what you heard him or her say. You can start the reflection by saying, "What I heard you say is...." When they reflect Step 2, ask the class if (Student Name) did a good job of reflecting Step 2. If not, have the student try again with help from the class. When the group says the student "got it" say, "Good job, (Student Name)!" Reinforce good listening whenever possible by having the circle of students clap once, twice, and three times. Remember that when students go "live" with this, that it is important to ask the speaker whether or not the listener "got it."

Now go to Step 3: Feelings and ask (Student Name) what feeling(s) he or she heard in Step 3. After the student reflects the feeling(s) ask the class if he or she "got it." If the student does not reflect the feelings exactly like the ones shared, let the class know that it is important to reflect what you have heard, especially the feeling words used. Have the student try again if he or she missed the feeling word(s). If the student needs help, it is okay to get it from the student circle. Then ask the circle if the student "got it?" If they say, "Yes!" then again reinforce good listening with three claps.

Now move to Step 4: My/Your behavior said....? and have the student reflect the cause and effect of the behavior(s). It is best to have the student begin this by saying: "What I heard you say is that your behavior said to you that...." The wording of this will be dependent on what is presented in Step 2. When finished, ask the circle if (Student Name) "got" Step 4. Again, have the student get help if needed and when this step is complete, reinforce the effort.

Now move to Step 5: Wants, the final step. Have the student say: "What I heard you say

you don't want is.... What I heard you say you do want is....." When you do this step in real time you will need to check out whether some of the wants are mutual for the listener. It is one thing to state what it is I want and another to have someone agree to the want. Most students are very amenable to the wants requested.

Use the same scenario you role played and run through the other option. It is more understandable for students when you walk them through the same scenario as the first role play by simply flipping the script. If you used option #1, I wronged you, then use option #2. you wronged me to demonstrate. Briefly run through the second version. Tell them that you know (Student Name) is a good listener so you are not going to take time to have him or her practice active listening with this second role play, so they can have more time to practice in real time.

Reminder! Be sure to let students know they can enter the circle in one of two ways:

1. Student "wronged" (mistreated) another student.
2. Student was "wronged" (mistreated) by another student.

Spiritual Perspective on CLEAR Listening

The act of listening is in and of itself a very spiritual experience. When I listen to my brothers and sisters in order to hear them, there must be at least some aspects of compassion, love, generosity, healing, and authenticity present.

Father Edward Hays (1998) in his book, *Psalms for Zero Gravity*, describes a deeply empathic response to another human being as

> a true communion of sorrow involves feeling sick myself, suffering another's anguish, pain, sickness and loss. Grant me, O God, a measure of such compassion. My beloved, give me the gift not so much to be patient with those who are suffering but to be a patient who suffers with the suffering. (p. 204)

Clear Talk
Facilitation Considerations

#1

Prior to facilitating the Phase II process, write down each of the five steps on the board or a separate flip chart. Make it easy for the students, especially those in the center of the circle, to reference. Assure students they will not need to memorize the steps and encourage them to refer to the five steps on the board when clearing with another student. The sequence of the five steps is critical and any deviation from the process is strongly discouraged.

#2

Phase II facilitation should be conducted with co-facilitators. It is best to have a neutral and respected adult—such as the school counselor or school nurse—co-facilitating with the classroom teacher.

Co-facilitators are expected to clear their schedules and be present for the entire Phase II process. The principal or school disciplinarian is discouraged from facilitating the process. They are certainly welcome to be in the room, but only on the periphery as passive observers.

#3

Facilitators must be vigilant about keeping the process safe at all times. Students are never to be coerced or cajoled into participating during any part of the process. If a facilitator has information about student conflict he or she is never to impose an agenda by even as much as mentioning that two students should do Clear Talk. This process is only to be initiated by and generated by students. The approach is always "challenge by choice." A facilitator can support, encourage, and/or challenge when a student initiates the process. Everything in Phase II is offered as an invitation for students to participate in a discovery process. Resistance to change is very normal and facilitators must maintain a posi-

tive presence, always conducting themselves in a spirit of gratitude.

#4

Facilitators must believe they have the power to effect change in the school climate. Following the proposed approaches in this curriculum will give you some powerful tools for creating a new reality together. Be honest with yourself about whether you are the person to facilitate this process. Only facilitate Phase II if you are willing to journey with the students in this process. It is okay to defer facilitation to someone else, but do not sell yourself short.

#5

During Clear Talk, facilitators are encouraged to be aware of the nonverbal behavior of students both in the center of the circle, as well as the circle itself. If a student is Clearing about being called a name or being hit, but has a smile on his or her face, let the student know that this is incongruent. If a student doesn't want a certain behavior to continue, conveying verbal and nonverbal congruity is imperative. A smile encourages behavior and does not discourage it.

One way to demonstrate incongruity is by telling students you feel angry—really angry—but have a smile plastered on your face when you say this. You can even have the entire group try this together. They will laugh about how strange and truly absurd this feels. All the students will understand from this demonstration that saying we feel a certain way, but not having a facial gesture to match or support the feeling being reported, sends a very mixed message. The mixed message makes the feeling and even the data being shared unbelievable or insincere even though good intentions may be present.

Include the circle by asking what mixed messages students picked up between the nonverbal behavior shown and the way the data is being presented. A student's report should never be challenged for the content of what is being said, only how it is being said. You can do this by simply asking the group and/or the listener questions like: "Do you trust what (Student Name) is saying by the way he is saying it? Is (Student Name) looking and sounding sincere with how she is reporting the data?"

Co-facilitators must also be aware of the nonverbal in the circle itself. Students laughing or gesturing inappropriately during a Clearing is not to be tolerated. It is, however, important and reflective of how students treat each other. Students who feel uncomfortable with silence or emotion will try to break the tension with laughter. Laughter that is out of turn can be harmful and does not lend itself well to creating a safe school climate. We want to encourage laughter when it is appropriate. Facilitators are encouraged to deal with inappropriate laughter as soon as it happens, but are discouraged from dealing with it directly. Place the responsibility for dealing with inappropriate laughter or gestures on the students.

For instance, if a student in the circle laughs at a student doing a Clearing who is sharing sad feelings, immediately ask, "How did that make you feel when (Student Name) laughed at the feeling you just shared? Did that behavior help you move closer to a 10 or did it move you the other way closer to a 0? I understand, then, that you are telling me that when (Student Name) laughed, that made you feel less safe. Am I correct in saying this?"

Facilitators can also ask the circle: "How do you think that made (Student Name) feel when (Student Name) laughed? How would you feel if someone laughed at you for sharing your feelings? Did that behavior help you move closer to a 10 or did it move you the other way closer to a 0? I understand, then, that you are telling me that when (Student Name) laughed, that made you feel less safe. Am I correct in saying this?"

Students are very perceptive and when they challenge a student on incongruities it is very powerful. In order for social climate change to occur and move in the direction of a safe school culture, student feedback is critical. This feedback increases their EI and SI. Leadership is about being congruent in thought, feeling, and

action. Guiding students toward nonverbal and verbal congruity is a valuable awareness. We teach people how to treat us; congruity in our thought, feeling, and action will encourage and even persuade others to behave in ways that support us.

#6

Involve and engage the circle as much as possible. This activity is a community building process and is not just about the two students in the center of the circle. Ways to involve the circle were mentioned in the previous consideration (#5) regarding incongruities in verbal and nonverbal behavior. Give the circle permission to be involved in the process by speaking up (assertion skills) about incongruities they see. This practice helps them develop skills of observation, interpretation, and feedback. Welcoming student input creates opportunities for students to give voice where they may not have had permission and courage to hold others accountable when they didn't have the strength or skills before.

#7

When you demonstrate with the initial mock Clearing for students, make sure you know exactly what scenarios you will use. Have both a scenario one: "I wronged you" and a scenario two: "You wronged me" in mind before you facilitate Phase II. Write them down (or brief prompts) and refer to them if need be. Students need to see both of these scenarios demonstrated in a way that seems effortless and seamless. Seeing the facilitator grope through the process will not instill confidence. Use your own role play scenario or use the ones provided. If using the latter, just substitute yourself and the volunteer student for the David and Andrew characters. Facilitators are discouraged from having two students do the role played Clearing. Facilitators are also discouraged from doing a real-time Clearing to demonstrate the process.

The demonstration is an important part of teaching each step in the process. If the facilitator uses a live demonstration to teach the process, it could take away from a real-time Clear Talk experience. Use a role play only so that you can take the necessary time to explain each step thoroughly. Your clarity in teaching the steps ensures that students will succeed during their Clear Talk experience. Make sure students know what you are doing is a mock Clearing or role play and not real. When they step into the center of the circle it will be live—Real Time.

#8

When you are ready to begin the process, it is natural for students to have questions. Gently discourage lengthy question and answer time and let them know as they practice and trust the process that it will get clearer for them. One of the most frequently asked questions and an important one to address is if they can ask more than one student at a time into the center of the circle. Facilitators are discouraged from allowing more than one student at a time to enter the process, because it can get complicated and sometimes confusing. Encourage students to ask only one student into the center of the circle. If more than one student is involved with the incident, have the student pick one person to represent all involved. Once you get a handle on what is going on, you may at some point find it helpful to bring in the other students. Two special circumstances scenarios are included on the following pages to help facilitators understand a way more students can successfully enter the circle.

#9

After the role play demonstrating the five-step process, assure students they will not be on their own in the center of the circle; you will help guide them through the process. Place the stick down on the floor in the center and sit with students in the circle. When you ask, "Who would like to start," pause, allowing the tension to build. Most groups have at least one student that will jump in the center right away. Other groups may take a little while. As the

tension mounts, look each student in the eye, going clockwise around the circle. Keep doing this in silence until a student enters the circle. This tension is very useful because it will motivate a student to break the tension by stepping into the center. If the facilitator feels uncomfortable with the tension and breaks the silence, he or she will reduce student tension and possibly decrease motivation. The result will be a longer waiting period. Go back to silence and look at each student going around the circle.

If this doesn't work, a facilitator could say: "The goal is to help ourselves and others get closer to a 10. This class had a Safety Check range from (4) to (10). Does this mean this class is satisfied being a range from (4) to (10) and has no motivation to help each other get closer to a 10?" Pause, allowing the tension to build. Someone will eventually step in to the circle. You can also let students know they must not have the maturity to handle the process yet, because it takes a lot of maturity to be a leader. Saying this will likely cause a student to dive for the stick!

#10

What do you do if a student refuses to do Clear Talk with the student who initiated the process?

Nothing! This is a voluntary process and students should not be forced or coerced into it. Usually the positive peer pressure will propel the student to enter the circle when invited. The authors have experienced only one time that a student refused to enter the circle when asked. The principal reported later that the student who refused to enter the circle went to the other student's home that same night and did Clear Talk with him there. What a success story!

#11

What do you do if two or more students enter the circle and all try to grab the stick? Have all students in the circle stand by the stick, but not touch it. Let the students know that you are very encouraged by their enthusiasm to do Clear Talk! Ask them to respectfully discuss with each other and choose within 30 seconds who will be next and in what order—first, second, third, etc. This is a wonderful real-time community problem-solving exercise. Know that you will not facilitate every student interested in doing Clear Talk during this session. (See Consideration #18).

#12

Clearings vary in duration, but usually are not much more than 5 to 10 minutes in length from start to finish. There is no objective to rush through the process. It is important to guide, but also to allow the five-steps to unfold. Students at times have a tendency to want to quickly get to Step Five (Wants) because it feels better than the other steps. It is okay to slow them down and have them get clear through each step. This is important because the clearer each step is, the easier it is for the listener to be a compassionate listener. Most miscommunication occurs because the sender isn't clear with the message he or she is sending, even though he or she wants to be understood. It is much easier to be attentive when we reflect understandable (Clear) communication.

#13

When complete with the Clearing, ask both students to state their Safety Check Number— the original number from 0 to 10 shared with the circle. Begin with the student who initiated the process. Then ask if the number changed at all with what he or she just did. Have the class notice the progress closer to a 10. Any movement—even if a student says they moved a half of a point—is progress. Now turn to the student-listener and repeat the same process. If there was no movement ask either student what he or she needs to do next to help get closer to a 10. Have the class reinforce what the students have accomplished (no matter how small an increment) with one clap, two claps, three claps! Any movement closer to a 10 is a victory and worth celebrating!

#14

Ask the circle who was aware of the data surrounding the situation with the students who just did Clear Talk. Usually at least several hands will go up. This demonstrates and confirms for students the impact of the negative rippling effect—consequences—surrounding an action. This is a wonderful opportunity to ask students what they did when they saw or became aware of the incident. Generate discussion around active and passive bystanders with the following questions: What did you do about it? What was the result? What didn't you do about it? What was the result? How did you feel when you saw it and what did you do with the feeling? If you see it happening again, what can you do about it? The questions will raise critical awareness around eliminating covert contracts, increasing accountability, and taking responsibility for creating a community of reverence.

#15

Before you begin another process, ask students what they learned from what (Student Name) and (Student Name) just did. If you hear compliments of the two students make sure that this feedback is directed to the student they are complimenting. This is powerful real-time feedback for students. If students say their number moved closer to a 10 because of what the two students just did, ask for more specifics. Ask:

- What did (Student Name) and (Student Name) do specifically to help you move closer to a 10?
- What did (Student Name) and (Student Name) do to drop a positive pebble in the room?
- What positive rippling effect did your classmates have on you with what they just did?
- What did you learn from what they just did?
- What did (Student Name) and (Student Name) do to create a different reality with each other?
- What happens when we don't say anything and just let things go? Does the conflict get bigger or smaller? Does stuff accumulate and get worse or does it get better?
- When an incident is left unfinished and not Cleared do we trust each other more or less?
- When an incident is left unfinished and not

Cleared am I open to you or do I begin to doubt you and hold back?
- Does not doing a Clearing raise or lower Safety Check Numbers?
- What happened to the Safety Check Numbers of (*Student Name*) and (*Student Name*) after doing Clear Talk with each other?

#16

After debriefing each Clearing, have students stand. They have been sitting for a while and getting them moving will help keep the energy up. Ask the students what they would like to magically toss out of the room to help us all get closer to a 10. They will say things like: rumors, hatred, put-downs, etc. Have them kneel down, drum on the floor and make noise. Next have them pretend they are "wadding up" the negative stuff in their hands and launching it up and out through the roof of the room. Now ask them what they would like to bring into the room to help get them all closer to a 10. They will say things like peace, caring, respect, understanding, etc. Have them make a vacuum noise as if they are drawing this in from the sky into the room. Students enjoy doing these energizers after each Clearing and will often volunteer to lead them.

#17

Before the next Clearing have students sit back down in their seats and pause in silence for a short while (10 seconds). Ask them all to take another big "belly breath" and ask, "Who would like to go next?" Usually there is no hesitation for this next round. When the next student steps into the center of the circle and takes the stick, again ask students what he or she modeled by going next. This is important reinforcement for calling attention to leadership qualities and good practice for students to verbally acknowledge the student through put-ups.

#18

Continue doing Clearings with as many students as time and energy will allow. Depending on the nature and duration, you can expect to do about five Clearings. About 15 minutes before the scheduled ending time, ask if there are any students that would have stepped into the center of the circle to Clear with someone if more time was available. Ask students with their hands up to stand and go to the person they would have asked into the center and plan a future date, time, and place—before school, at lunch, at recess, another free period, or after school—to do Clear Talk with each other. Have them come up with a plan for when, where, and with whom they will do their Clearing. Have them decide who will help facilitate—a teacher, counselor, or another student. Encourage them to do their Clearing sooner rather than later and within a few days.

#19

Facilitators and schools can help students integrate Clear Talk in the following ways:
- Ask students before class starts if there are any Clearings that need to take place. If yes, take no more than 5 minutes to do the Clearing. If there is more than one, have the students take 30 seconds to decide which one of the Clearing is the "hottest."
- Clear Talk can be done during classroom meetings or community building time.
- Use the language from the program.
- Have students journal or write a reflection paper about what they are learning from the program.
- Have students write about their Clearings.

#20

Save the last 5 to 10 minutes for closure. A "Check Out" looks like:

- Go around the circle and say, "State the Safety Check number you had when we started today. If you helped yourself and others move closer to a 10, what is your new number?"
- Say one word that describes your experience today.
- Facilitators model this for students: "I was a number 6, now I am a number 9. Awesome!"

- Facilitators are encouraged to share a Safety Check and word that honestly describes their own personal experience.
- Say something honest and sincere in your own words to congratulate the class for all their hard work today and let them know how proud you are of what they accomplished together.
- Give one clap, two claps, three claps!

Special Circumstances: Case Study A

During the process, the facilitator may identify a special circumstance which involves more than just the two students Clearing in the center of the circle.

A student entered the circle to Clear with another boy about how he (the initiator) had wronged him (the student brought into the circle). As the initiating student was going through the steps, he said "we" treated you this way. That was a clue that more students were responsible for reducing safety in the class. After the speaker went through each step and both boys were "complete," the facilitator asked them for permission to take the Clearing a step further. Both boys agreed. It is imperative to not assume the process can be taken to another level without asking for permission first.

The facilitator said to the speaker (Brent), that he used "we" at one point when describing the maltreatment of the other student (Jake). Brent admitted he said this. The facilitator then turned to the group and asked that any student who believed they had ever mistreated Jake to please stand behind Brent.

All but four of the entire class stood behind Brent. The facilitator then placed the stick on the ground representing the invisible line drawn between Jake and the rest of the students and asked the students if they were aware of the division they had created between themselves and Jake.

Students were aware of the isolated incidents (covert contracts), but for them to experience this visually was very profound. The facilitator asked Jake how he felt to be "over there"

intentionally disconnected from his peers. He reported feeling empty, sad, lonely, depressed, angry, and even suicidal at times. As he shared, many of the students on "the other side" began to cry. This is the very first time the students could actually feel the enormity and gravity of this situation and how they were all directly responsible for another person's pain.

The facilitator asked the students what needed to happen in order for them to get back in integrity with Jake and to help him and themselves get closer to a 10. The students collectively decided they would each do their own Clearing with Jake. Of course this took a while, but they may have saved a life—or at least a lifetime of pain. When each student finished Clearing with Jake they spontaneously circled around him as a gesture of support and "we've got your back!"

Witnessing the students make this shift from the negative social norm they had created—division and exclusion—to a new social norm of inclusion and acceptance was nothing short of a miracle. They had, in fact, created a new reality together. One of the female students commented her joyous surprise of the new reality, saying she thought Jake would be treated poorly all year and that nothing would change it.

Special Circumstances: Case Study B

Two fifth-grade girls entered the circle: Amanda and Danielle. Amanda asked Danielle to Clear with her. After thanking Danielle (Step 1), Amanda admitted she slapped Danielle (Step 2) and felt ashamed (Step 3) about doing so. Amanda stated, "My behavior said (Step 4) that I seriously disrespected you." Amanda wanted Danielle to know that she (Amanda) was very sorry and apologized for what she had done and was hoping that Danielle could forgive her. Amanda continued saying she wanted to hang out at recess and swing on the swings together.

The facilitator asked if Amanda was "complete" and she responded that she was. Danielle did a great job being a compassionate listener, reflecting what she heard Amanda say. Danielle said she too was "complete." The two girls hugged as a sign of peace. The facilitator asked Amanda what her original Safety Check Number was and if there was a new number that better represented where she was now after this Clearing with Danielle. Amanda said her first number was a 6 and now she was a 9. The facilitator then asked Danielle the same question and she said her first number was a 3 and now she was a 9.

Clear Talk was very successful and could have ended there, but the facilitator asked the girls to take the process one step further. Both agreed. The students were asked to use the Clearing to identify who played what role in the Bullying Triangle. Right away Amanda was identified as the bully and Danielle as the target. When asked who the active or passive bystanders were the room got very quiet. The facilitator asked if anyone in the class was aware that Amanda had slapped Danielle. Eleven students stood up, both girls and boys. The facilitator thanked them for their honesty. Without even asking the question, all the students admitted collectively that they were all passive bystanders. It was critical at this point to use the situation in retrospect to increase awareness of how bystander behavior perpetuates covert contracts.

The following questions were asked to increase student awareness and prevent repeating history:

- What did you do when you saw Amanda slap Danielle?
- *General response:* Nothing.
- What did you think about doing as you witnessed Amanda slap Danielle?
- *General Response:* Lots of stuff was thought about, such as saying something to Amanda about her behavior, saying something to the teacher or the counselor.
- What kept you from following through with the thought you had? Why didn't you put the thought into action?
- *General Response:* Most said they were afraid that Amanda might retaliate. One said that he thought he heard Amanda apologize to Danielle after she did it, so he let it go. One said he really didn't think much of it, just dismissed it.
- Do you all think you owe Danielle an apology?
- *General Response:* Yes! (Which they all did)
- Danielle, what did you do when Amanda slapped you?
- *Danielle's response:* Nothing.
- What did you think about doing after Amanda slapped you?
- *Danielle's Response:* Hitting her, saying something to her, saying something to the teacher or counselor, telling the principal, telling my parents.
- What kept you from following through with the thought you had? Why didn't you put the thoughts into action? Why didn't you speak up for yourself?
- *Danielle's Response:* I don't know. Maybe I was afraid.
- What will you all do if something like this happens next time?
- *General Response:* Speak up, tell the bully or ask for help from an adult.

Clear Talk

TIME	PREPARATION & PROCESS	

0:00

Session Preparation
- Read Clear Talk Facilitation Considerations (pp. 123-129).
- Write the five steps and a description of each step on a note card.
- Write the five steps on the board or flipchart for student reference.
- Post "feeling faces" for visual reference.
- Classroom should remain in a circle with no obstructions.
- Student Workbook, pp. 43-52

(margin) Write down the five steps of Clear Talk on a flip chart or board.

Post feeling faces.

Process

Say: *"Let's do another activity!"*

Note. At this point pick up the "talking stick/lightning rod" from a point in the room or near you. Walk into the center of the circle.

"This is a talking stick and is similar to a lightning rod and will be helpful to us during this activity."

"Who can tell me what a lightning rod is?"

Possible Response: A metal pole that draws the lightning to it and channels it into the ground so that a building won't get damaged. Work with student responses.

1:00

"That's right! When there is a conflict between two people it's like a negative electrical charge, similar to lightning which can do some serious damage in our relationships."

"The lightning rod is magically going to help us channel any negative charge between students, down through the stick down, into the earth and away from them."

"(Student Name), will you come up and help me role play what we are going to do in this activity?"

"I would like everyone to look up at the board/flipchart right now at five simple steps called Clear Talk."

"Let's start with Step 1. 'Thank you, (Student Name) for volunteering to step into the circle with me.'"

"Why do you think saying 'thank you' is an important first step?"

Possible Responses: It is good manners....It's nice....It's kind....It's respectful because it took a lot of courage for (*Student Name*) to come into the center of the circle.

2:00

"You are so right! It is so important that we have an attitude of gratitude not only when we do this activity, but whenever and wherever possible."

Clear Talk

TIME	PREPARATION & PROCESS

"Raise your hand if you have ever seen in a movie or in person two people standing facing each other and bowing like this?"

Note. It is good to model what this looks like as you talk about it. It is your decision on whether or not to place your own hands together as you bow.

"Thank You!"

"What are these two people communicating with each other without even using words?"

Possible Responses: Respect...honor...caring...kindness...thank you.

"You are so right! For this activity saying 'Thank You' as a first step is about respecting, honoring, being kind and caring for the person across from you."

Note. Use the actual words the students come up with as a response to the last question. If they do not come up with words that go beyond a thank you as just good manners, help them go deeper with this.

3:00

"I asked (Student Name) into the circle because there is something not okay that happened and I want to make it right between us. I don't want the negative charge to do any damage."

"In Step 2, I tell the data of what happened between (Student Name) and me. I am only describing what happened. This is just a role play right now. But when you step into the circle, it will be for real."

"The data is, (Student Name), you were walking into the classroom the other day and I stuck out my foot. You tripped and fell, catching yourself on a desk, almost hitting your head and everybody laughed."

"That's the data, now in Step 3 I share how I am feeling about treating (Student Name) this way."

"Feelings are so important and it is important that we communicate what we feel to others in a clear way."

"There are five basic feelings. They are mad, sad, glad, afraid and ashamed."

"There are many variations of these five basic feelings."

"What is a variation of the feeling mad?"

Possible Responses: Angry, upset, irritated, annoyed.

4:00 *"Good!"*

Clear Talk

TIME	PREPARATION & PROCESS

"What are some variations of sad?"

Possible Responses: Hurt, blue, depressed, down.

"You've got it!"

"How about glad?"

Possible Responses: Joy, happy, elated, excited.

"Yes!"

"How about ashamed?"

Possible Responses: Embarrassed, guilt, shame, red-faced.

"Great! You guys really know what feelings are!"

"I feel angry at myself for tripping you (Student Name). I feel ashamed that I did that to you."

5:00   *"In Step 4, I share an observation about why I think this happened. I can use a couple of incomplete sentences to help me with this: My behavior said? Your behavior said?"*

Note. Make sure you have the incomplete sentences written next to Step Four on the board/flipchart or place them in a separate location as a visual reference.

"My behavior said that I wasn't feeling very good about myself that day and I tried to make myself feel better by putting you down and getting everyone to laugh, but it was at your expense. My behavior said that I disrespected you."

6:00   *"In Step 5 I share what I want. I know what happened between us isn't okay and I want our relationship to be different than the way it is right now."*

"(Student Name) I want you to know that I will not trip you or disrespect you in anyway ever again. I want you to know I am sorry and I want you to forgive me for what I have done to you. I want you to know I will put you up from now on and not trip you down. I want you to sit with me at lunch tomorrow."

Note. After Step 5 begins an important transition to active listening.

"This completes the five steps for the speaker. Now it's time for (Student Name) to practice being a good listener."

"Do you think (Student Name) listened to what I said to him or her?"

"What ways did you see him or her demonstrate good listening?"

Clear Talk

TIME	PREPARATION & PROCESS

Possible Response: The student made good eye contact, nodded, didn't interrupt, didn't fidget, seemed interested, etc.

"Let's give (Student Name) one clap, two claps, three claps!"

"Yes! I feel heard by (Student Name) and think he or she did a great job at non-verbal listening which is all those things you mentioned like good eye contact, nodding, not interrupting, not fidgeting, looking interested. He or she was really paying attention to me."

7:00 *"How many of you have ever heard someone say something to you and it went in one ear and out the other?"*

"We probably all have done this."

"When we are talking and the other person is not paying attention to us how does that make you feel?"

Possible Responses: Unimportant, unwanted, devalued, disrespected, annoyed, angry, etc.

"This doesn't feel good at all and I think poor listening can cause people to lash out. Poor listening doesn't help us feel safe."

"How do you feel when the other person is paying attention like (Student Name) just did with me?"

Possible Responses: Important, special, wanted, valued, respected, etc.

8:00 *"I want to show you a way we can be even better listeners."*

"Hold up one of your hands. Now place your hand over your heart. Follow my lead."

Note. Have students follow your drum beat of a heart rhythm for a few seconds.

"CLEAR Listening is listening to another person with compassion. When someone is sharing something with you, it goes in one ear and then it is channeled through the heart."

"As we listen to each other today, let's practice being compassionate with CLEAR Listening."

"CLEAR Listening starts with Step 1 by saying to the speaker what you heard him or her say in each step."

"It is important to mirror or reflect back what the speaker said as close as possible, but you don't have to remember every word."

Clear Talk

TIME	PREPARATION & PROCESS

9:00   *"Mirroring is just reflecting back to the person what you heard them say."*

"Know that it is okay to get help with this and that the speaker and the class are here if you get stuck."

"One of the best ways to start CLEAR Listening is by saying, 'What I heard you say is...' or 'I heard you say...'"

"Now (Student Name) I would like you to practice CLEAR Listening by saying what you heard in Step 1."

Note. Have the class help the student listener in any of the steps if needed. The following dialogue is an example of successful mirroring of what the speaker said.

Student Response: "What I heard you say is "Thank you." What I heard you say is (Data presented by speaker in Step 2)." What I heard you say you are feeling is (feeling word or words shared)." "What I heard you say your behavior said is (behavior described)" or "What I heard you say my behavior said is (behavior described)."

"Class did (Student Name) get it?"

"Yes! Let's give him or her one clap, two claps, three claps!"

"Continue with what you heard are the feelings in Step 3."

Student Response: "What I heard you say you are feeling is (Feelings Expressed)."

"Class did (Student Name) get it?"

"Yes! Let's give him or her one clap, two claps, three claps!"

Note. You may want to let students know that it is most helpful to reflect back the exact feeling stated by the speaker, because it best reflects what they are feeling. For instance, if the speaker says he or she feels angry and the listener reflects back that he or she is upset it tends to minimize what the speaker is really feeling.

"Continue with what you heard the behavior said in Step 4."

Student Response: I heard you say (My/Your behavior said?).

"Class did (Student Name) get it?"

"Yes! Let's give him or her one clap, two claps, three claps!"

10:00   *Note.* If there is any step that students usually need help with it is this one. Remember, the wording of this will be dependent on what is presented in Step Two. Guide the student to the best possible sentence completion. (My/Your behavior said to me....My/Your behavior might have said to you....)

"Continue with what you heard are the wants in Step 5."

Clear Talk

TIME	PREPARATION & PROCESS

Student Response: What I heard you say you want is (Wants Expressed).

"Class did (Student Name) get it?"

"Yes! Let's give him or her one clap, two claps, three claps!"

"Great job (Student Name)!"

Note. Have the student remain standing with you and transition to the second option for entering the center of the circle.

"There is one more way you can step into the circle."

11:00 *"Let's take the same role play and just flip the script."*

"In this version of the role play (Student Name) wronged me."

"(Student Name) was walking into the classroom one day and I was standing in the doorway. As I crossed the threshold of the door (Student Name) impulsively stuck out his or her foot and tripped me, sending me stumbling into the room. As I staggered I caught myself on a desk and almost hit my head. Everyone in the class saw what happened and laughed, including (Student Name)."

"Here's how the other option would go."

"Step 1: Thank you, (Student Name) for stepping into the circle with me."

"Step 2: Data. I was walking into the classroom the other day and you stuck out your foot. I tripped and fell, catching myself on a desk, almost hitting my head and everybody laughed."

12:00 *"Step 3: Feelings. I feel angry that you tripped me. I feel afraid that you did that to me. I feel embarrassed that everyone laughed."*

"Step 4: Your behavior said to me that you weren't feeling very good about yourself when you did this to me and you tried to make yourself feel better by putting me down and getting everyone to laugh. Your behavior said that you disrespected me."

"I will not have (Student Name) practice good listening for this role play because of time, and he or she already demonstrated he or she is a good listener in the first role play."

"When we are complete with the process, we will exchange some sign of peace."

Clear Talk

TIME	PREPARATION & PROCESS

"This could be a high five, a hand shake, bump fists, or a hug."

13:00

Note. As you are giving peace sign options demonstrate them with the student volunteer. Only demonstrate the hug option if the student (and you) are comfortable doing so.

"If it is a hug, it needs to be mutual, because not everyone wants to be hugged."

Note. It is natural here for students to have questions about the process. Gently discourage a lengthy question and answer session letting them know the process will get clearer for them with the practice coming next.

"Please sit up straight and tall and close your eyes."

"Go inside yourself and ask who in the circle you need to Clear with in order to help you and others get closer to a 10."

"Keep your eyes closed and when you have a person in mind, raise your hand."

"Now, keep your hand up, take a big belly breath and open your eyes."

"Notice that you are not the only one who needs to do Clear Talk with someone in the circle."

14:00

"Who would like to start?"

Note. Groups vary on the length of time it takes for the first student to enter the circle. Be patient here if it takes students a little longer than you would like for them to get started (see Clear Talk Facilitation Tips, pp. 123-129).

"Thank you, (Student Name), for starting us off!"

"What did it take for (Student Name) to step into the circle?"

Possible Response: Courage...leadership...determination, etc.

"Yes! It does take courage, leadership, and determination to be the first one into the center of the circle."

"How do we let someone know that we admire these qualities in them?"

Possible Response: The group will clap and cheer or will do one clap, two claps, three claps!

15:00

"(Student name), whom do you want to ask into the circle with you?"

Student Response: I would like (*Student Name*) to come in with me.

Note. Often students are quiet at this point as well.

TIME	PREPARATION & PROCESS

"What did it take for (Student Name, Listener) to step into the circle with (Student Name, Speaker)?"

Possible Response: Courage...leadership...fear, etc.

"Yes! It does take courage and leadership, and (Student Name, Listener) may feel fear about being the first one asked into the center of the circle."

"How do we let someone know that we admire these qualities in them?"

Possible Response: The group will clap and cheer or will do one clap, two claps, three claps!

Note. The two students in the center of the circle should be facing each other at this point and each holding a part of the talking stick. The student who initiated the process will now begin with Step 1.

60:00   Attention!
Facilitators have approximately 45 minutes from this point to facilitate Clear Talk. You will be able to conduct approximately five Clear Talk sessions including debriefing time. Do not pressure yourself to get in as many Clear Talk sessions as you can. Each one is a teaching piece and is not to be rushed. Rushing will cause confusion and miscommunication. One Clear Talk session done well is better than five done poorly.

Closure
"Let's do a 'Check Out!'"

"Go around the circle and say what your original Safety Check number was and what your new number is if you made progress toward the goal of getting closer to a 10."

"After that say one word that describes your experience today."

"I will model this for you."

"I was a (4) now I am a (9). Awesome!"

"(Student Name), will you go next?"

"Thank you, and after (Student Name) is finished please continue around the circle."

Closing Prayer: Hold hands around the circle and together say the "Our Father."

Note. Following the "Our Father" is an opportunity for facilitators and any other adults in the room to share a few brief (positive) comments in support of what students accomplished during the Phase II process. Remind students to respect "what was said here stays here." It is also a good time to say how the process will be continued throughout the year and what the parameters are (e.g., use of Clear Talk during the school day, classroom meetings and/or community time, etc.).

Phase II Follow-Up

Although Clear Talk is not counseling, emotions are common and a normal part of reconciliation and forgiveness. Any student who appears to be struggling or has a strong emotional response to the Phase II process should be referred to the school counselor for extra support as a precautionary measure.

Prior to ending the Phase II process, ask students to raise their hand or stand if they would have stepped into the center to do Clear Talk with someone if there was more time available. Ask these students to stand. Now ask them to go to the person they would have invited into the circle and make a commitment with each other to do a Clear Talk with them at a future date. Make note of who students pair up with. It is strongly recommended that during some class time—a class meeting or community-building time—that these students have an opportunity to do Clear Talk. This should be done relatively soon, ideally within one week. It is highly recommended that weekly classroom meetings be set up to encourage the Clear Talk process throughout the school year. It is always preferable to conduct Clear Talk in the presence of the entire class or classroom community rather than in isolation. It may seem expeditious to conduct Clear Talk with only two individuals in private; however, this poses the risk of promoting covert contracts. Clear Talk should only be implemented as a communal process because bullying behavior is a community problem and the responsibility of the community to reconcile.

Important Follow-Up Actions:
- Make time for students to do Clear Talk with each other.
- Have students read and complete pages 43-52 in the Student Workbook.
- Check student journal entries to support and encourage the process.
- Pair and share selected Student Worksheets.

Prayer for one about to approach another for pardon

Lord, Divine Parent,
Make me as humble and healing as our mother earth.
Make me as honest and defenseless as a child.
Make me as loving and compassionate as Your Son, Jesus.
And, Lord and Giver of True Strength,
Make me as forgiving as are You, Yourself.
Amen.

Teacher and Counselor Reflection

Congratulations! You have completed Phase II of the program. Take time to recall the reflection piece used in Phase I. Reflecting on your baptismal calling will help with these three new reflection questions. Each person is anointed priest, prophet, and king or queen. In your role as teacher or facilitator of the *Peace Be with You* process, you are invited into the communal healing ministries of Christ. Your personhood, presence, and professionalism are Christ's healing, present in the classroom.

After self-critiquing how this session transpired, take some quiet time and reflect on your Baptismal role as priest, prophet, and a person of royalty. Do you have a new appreciation of the Sacrament of Reconciliation and the power of forgiveness?

Take time after this session to still yourself. Reflect on the vulnerability of the young people. Reflect on the body language of each student as they stepped into or stood around the circle. Compare this body language with the language of their body at the conclusion of the Clear Talk. Honor your facilitating this sacred space for reconciliation, forgiveness, and healing.

Journal any shift(s) that are happening within yourself. Is there a person(s) you need to do Clear Talk with in the classroom? In the school? In your family? Or with a friend?

Peace be with you!

PHASE III

Pure of Heart

PHASE III
Pure of Heart

"For we are his handiwork, created in Christ Jesus."

EPHESIANS 2:10

PURPOSE
To deepen student understanding of the importance and power of prayer, meditation, and being Pure of Heart

LEARNING OBJECTIVES
- Students will learn how leading an impure life is sinful.
- Students will learn how busyness can lead to sinfulness and split us off from God.
- Students will learn how to be open to the gifts of the Holy Spirit.
- Students will learn about compassion for self and others.
- Students will learn the discipline of self-care and remaining pure of heart.
- Students will learn deeper levels of prayer.

TEACHER MANUAL ACTIVITIES   12

CORRESPONDING STUDENT WORKBOOK PAGES
- Prayers   2
- Journal Entries   3
- Student Worksheets   20
- Quotation Pages   6

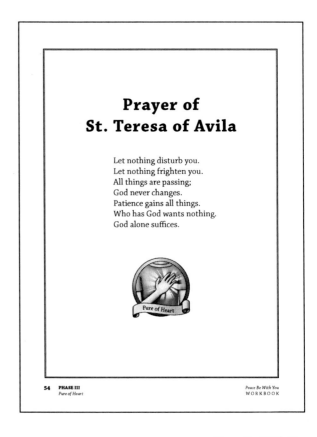

Ecumenical Impact

Before I formed you in the womb I knew you, before you were born I dedicated you. (Jeremiah 1:5)

For I have redeemed you; I have called you by name: you are mine. (Isaiah 43:1)

Phase III enters into the personal area of meditation and prayer. Scripture tells us of God's intimacy and care for us. The Trinity calls us into a relational, intimate life. Each member of the Bully Triangle—the bully, target, and bystander(s)—come to realize more fully their internal gift(s). Connecting with the Trinity, students learn of their ability to alter their own stress level and call forth the people God has always called them to be from the time they were in the womb.

Using the words from Isaiah, counselors and teachers are invited to enter quiet space and gaze into the loving face of our God. In the course of a day many names are used to address us:

- Mom/Dad
- Grandma/Grandpa
- Grandson/Granddaughter
- Aunt/Uncle
- Godchild
- Mr./Mrs.
- Teacher/Counselor/Nurse
- Principal/Headmaster/Headmistress
- Full name
- First name
- Nickname
- Baptismal name

By what name does our loving God call you? Take time to listen to His gentle voice, as He calls you by the name only He knows for you!

The Episcopal Diocese of Alabama (http://www.dioala.org/ministries/christian_formation.html) provides a list of recommended resources for its parishes. Barbara Coloroso's (2003) book, *The Bully, The Bullies and The Bystanders,* is recommended under the topic of bullying.

Our compassionate, respectful, and communal approach is the same approach the Episcopal Diocese of Alabama desires for its children. Again, we Christian schools and churches want nurturing experiences for our children, just as our God wants such experiences for us with The Trinity.

Spiritual Perspective

The Bully Triangle (see Figure 1, p. 10) represented in the inverted triangle, depicts the bully and bystanders on top, with all the negative focus downward toward the target. The Christ-centered triangle (see Figure 2, p. 16) is upright and symbolizes the Trinity which focuses on giving life. Phase III focuses on the triangle of compassion and the importance of our connection with each other and our relationship with God. One of the ways to be compassionate with ourselves, each other, and God is through prayer and solitude. The experience grounds and stills us and provides a connection with our Creator. In the Gospel of Mark, Chapter 1:32-35, the full evening of cures that Jesus performed are presented. Verse 35 tells us; "Rising very early before dawn, he left and went off to a deserted place, where he prayed." Several times, Jesus set Himself apart in stillness and silence. Jesus is also our model for meditation.

Before getting into the practices encouraged in this phase, it will serve us well to do an overview of meditation. For countless students and possibly adults, the extent of "meditation" has been a parent's punishment of "go to your room and think about what you have done." Most spiritual practices share a common thread of placing one's self in the presence of God, knowing that we are not alone. From this point, there are a multitude of spiritual disciplines concerning meditation. Four types of meditation are highlighted:

- **Visualization:** A person visualizes a scene and places oneself within the scene. This can be done by an individual or as a group.

- **Centering:** Through the use of conscious and intentional breaths and by repeating a Christ-centered mantra, one is brought to centeredness.
- **Spiritual Exercises:** An older and more structured process is the Spiritual Exercises of St. Ignatius of Loyola (composed from 1522-1524) that uses directed meditations, prayers, and mental exercises carried out over a period of time.
- **Silence:** Popular motivational writer, Matthew Kelly (2002), in his book, *Rediscovering Catholicism*, uses the phrase "the classroom of silence" (p. 40). Kelly goes on to write: "I will make two promises to you. In this silence, you will find God. In this silence you will find yourself" and "the lack of intimacy with God and self limits any possible intimacy with others" (p. 41).

Phase III introduces students to visual exercises and affirmations that can be used as mantras. These of course can become a springboard to other spiritual practices. The authors believe that people who make a profound difference in the world have an ability to visualize and take action on manifesting the desired outcome. This ability comes from "divine intervention" and is one of the great mysteries. We hypothesize that young people seldom hear they have the "God given" ability to make a major difference in the lives of others.

There are a wealth of books that talk about people making a difference and convey inspirational messages that a person is never too old or too young to begin. Examples such as Grandma Moses and Thomas Edison are often cited, but young people have the ability to make an impact and inspire others as well.

Not all of us are old enough to remember, but during the Cold War with Russia in 1982, a ten-year-old girl, Samantha Reed Smith of Maine (http://www.samanthasmith.info), wrote a letter to Soviet Communist Party General Secretary Yuri Andropov, and from her actions became known as a "goodwill ambassador" and "America's Youngest Ambassador."

Matthew Joseph Thaddeus Stepanek (www.mattieonline.com) wanted to be remembered as "a poet, peacemaker, and philosopher who played." When Mattie died at the age of 14 from dysautonomic mitochondrial myopathy, he had authored the bestseller, *HeartSongs*, followed by four more books. From his deep self-reflections, he wrote the poem "Future Reminiscing" which reads: "It is good to have a past that is pleasant to reflect upon. Take care to create such a gift for your future."

The website, www.myhero.com, focuses on heroes with a special link to children that are heroes, including Gerson Andres Florez Perez, age 16 from Columbia, nominated for the Nobel Peace Prize; Jason Crowe, awarded United Nations global peace and tolerance award; and Ryan Wayne White, 13, who was an AIDS educator. Visit the website for more inspiring stories about these modern-day heroes.

Most of us have read the diary of Anne Frank, who documented her life from ages 12 to 14 while in hiding during the Holocaust. Even at age 13, Jesus was inspiring others: "All who heard [Jesus] were astounded at his understanding and his answers" (Luke 2:47). The Scripture verse from 1 Timothy 4:12 is encouraging about youth and their calling: "Let no one have contempt for your youth, but set an example for those who believe, in speech, conduct, love, faith, and purity."

Other Scriptural insights, including the ones below, serve as an inspiration to see youth as not only capable, but endowed by the Holy Spirit from conception, with no certain way of knowing when gifts of the Holy Spirit will mature.

The word of the LORD came to me thus: Before I formed you in the womb I knew you, before you were born I dedicated you. (Jeremiah 1:4-5)

I have called you by name: you are mine. (Isaiah 43:1)

My bones were not hidden from you, When I was being made in secret, fashioned as in the depths of the earth. (Psalms 139:15)

God the Father of our Lord Jesus Christ has freed you from sin, given you a new birth by water and the Holy Spirit, and welcomed you into his holy people. (Prayer for anointing with Chrism in the Rite of Baptism)

Phase III proactively introduces prayerful meditation. Although the intent of this program is to eliminate bullying, even more important is the invitation to deepen our relationship with Christ and be on a path moving in the direction of our Holy Calling. By creating a reverent environment and giving our students the tools and resources to go deeper, we can achieve the intended outcomes:

- Reduce the busyness and stress by slowing down
- Achieve personal clarity and focus
- Find a deeper connection with God
- Pay attention to God's call for us
- Become more mindful and compassionate toward others
- Become mindful of the interconnection to all of God's creation
- Conduct ourselves in prayerful action for the greater good

Phase III is about the importance of self-care, fully embracing the body as a Holy Temple. The rippling effect described in Phase I is initially discussed as our behavior and its impact on others, moves outward. Galatians 6: 7-9 says that we reap what we sow—an awareness that what we sow in one season, we reap in another. Phase III encourages us to look at the rippling effect as an internal dynamic as well; our behavior and actions toward self and others powerfully impact us from within. Sowing a thought, reaps an action. Sowing the act frequently creates a habit. Sowing the habit produces character. Sowing character creates life-long consequences, both positive and negative.

The Fifth Commandment says, "Thou shall not kill." As we deepen our understanding of the Commandments we come to learn that the Fifth Commandment also governs care for our

own body and health and forbids other sins of bigotry and hatred, physical or emotional abuse, and violence of any kind against another person (Catholic Church, 2010).

Pure of Heart is a term used by the Catholic Church and other Christian denominations to name a condition near to Salvation. The Roman Catholic Church encourages members to seek it and codifies the required knowledge and practices with the Liturgy of the Eucharist, which serves other purposes as well. Teachings about being Pure of Heart are provided in the Liturgy of the Word which involves reading and singing.

Beatitudes

Blessed are the poor in spirit, for theirs is the kingdom of heaven.
Blessed are they who mourn, for they will be comforted.
Blessed are the meek, for they will inherit the land.
Blessed are they who hunger and thirst for righteousness, for they will be satisfied.
Blessed are the merciful, for they will be shown mercy.
Blessed are the clean [pure] of heart, for they will see God.
Blessed are the peacemakers, for they will be called children of God.
Blessed are they who are persecuted for the sake of righteousness, for theirs is the kingdom of heaven. (Matthew 5:3-10)

We are called as God's stewards in the care of our self, each other, and of the earth: "This law of human solidarity and charity, without excluding the rich variety of persons, cultures, and peoples, assures us that all men are truly brethren" (USCCB, 2006, p. 73).

Living out this solidarity with all of creation, we are called to live out the Beatitudes. The fifth Beatitude is the center of our focus in this phase. "Blessed are the clean [pure] of heart, for they will see God."

Jesus sketches out the new spirit of the kingdom of God within this discourse. The sketch includes the spirit that should animate us as children of the kingdom and about relationships with our neighbors. The Trinity mirrors the love for each other and deep respect and reverence that we are called to live out. In this phase, with the use of meditation and prayer and a focused, pure heart, we will help students gain a personal glimpse of the face of God. Interestingly being "pure of heart" comes between the fifth beatitude of "mercy" and the seventh beatitude of "peacemaker." Becoming pure of heart calls us to be solely focused on God as we live out mercy and peacemaking here on earth.

> The Beatitudes depict the countenance of Jesus Christ and portray his charity. They express the vocation of the faithful associated with the glory of his Passion and Resurrection; they shed light on the actions and attitudes characteristic of the Christian life; they are the paradoxical promises that sustain hope in the midst of tribulations; they proclaim the blessings and rewards already secured, however dimly, for Christ's disciples; they have begun in the lives of the Virgin Mary and all the saints. (Catholic Church, Part 3, Article 2, #1717)

In Baptism, every member of the Church participates "in Christ's offices as priest, prophet and king" (USCCB, 2006, p. 117). We do this in context of our lives daily within our families, schools, communities, and workplaces. The everyday gifts of ourselves in love and care for one another is our priestly offering joined to the sacrifice of Christ in the Eucharist. By words and deeds faithful to the Gospel message of Jesus, we live out our prophetic role. By seeking to build the common good of society on the basis of moral principles, we live out our kingly role. We live out the Beatitude, "Happy are the pure of heart, they shall see God" (Matthew 5:8).

Brief Background

Our accelerated pace of life has become normal and pushes us in many directions, making it easy to get out of balance. We can become irritable, agitated, less tolerant, impatient, mean, nasty, rude, angry, or frustrated and so on. When we feel this way we are more likely to take it out on someone. As mentioned in Phase I in the Choose Your Flavor activity, how a person treats oneself and others causes either a positive or negative ripple to happen. The direction we take and the kind of ripple we make is our choice. By not managing our stress, we make it easier to snap out at others. To be a good neighbor and make positive choices, we must look inward, taking responsibility for our actions and building internal competencies. Success, however, is frequently defined in terms of wealth and outward appearances. Looking inside is not a popular or common approach in a culture based on external rewards and immediate gratification.

The Peace2U Stress Less Series Audio CD (formerly The Peace Project audio CD) was released in July of 2001—two months prior to 9/11—and is a precursor to this program. Work on the CD began following the Littleton, Colorado, Columbine High School tragedy in April 1999, as a humble response to the increasing violence in schools. The original intention behind the audio CD was to help parents and children discover a fun and meaningful way to reduce daily doses of stress. Being a timeless introduction to some significant, yet highly practical stress management techniques, the CD has increased its audience to include teachers, counselors, and other youth serving organizations around the globe.

The Peace2U Stress Less Series Audio CD was not designed to be an anti-war movement or teach students how to become "peace activists." The CD is not about exploring our outer stratosphere, but is a mission headed in a much different direction—the inner stratosphere—encouraging students to become "inner-activists." As we take daily steps journeying inward, we discover our true nature and the unique treasure trove with which we are all born.

By taking these courageous steps into our inner-world, our authentic gifts become positively visible, touching and transforming to those around us. This is what it means to be a bold leader for peace!

Phase III is a spiritual, inner peace strengthening (internal asset building) set of activities to counterbalance periods of "hurried restlessness." When students do something healthy to manage their stress, they will most likely choose to treat others with respect. Practicing Phase III skills on a daily basis—or as often as possible—is an opportunity for students to take charge of slowing down their internal world, even while the external world continues to accelerate. By teaching them how to pause, we are helping students learn more about leading a balanced life and being positive leaders in creating a safe school climate. By playfully working with students on these concepts you are planting important seeds for a lifetime and creating a positive ripple in the world!

Phase III includes a digital download of the Peace2U Stress Less Audio CD as an accompaniment along with the scripted content in Appendix A. Each track contains positive, thought-provoking and educational messages: the damaging effects of put-downs, the importance of staying alcohol and drug free, the accelerated pace of our world, what stress is and how to reduce it, a simple metaphorical story about mind/body/spirit called "The Gift," specific stress reducing techniques, affirmations to boost self-confidence, as well as short and long meditations.

The Peace2U Stress Less Series Audio CD sound tracks and length in minutes:

Track 1: Introduction (2:11)
Track 2: Life in "Fast Forward" (5:19)
Track 3: Understanding Stress (2:12)
Track 4: "The Gift" (4:39)
Track 5: Relaxation Tips and Techniques (6:02)
Track 6: Short Meditation (12:27)
Track 7: Self-Esteem Affirmations (11:10)
Track 8: Long Meditation (28:54)

Through the use of relaxation techniques, meditations, and other activities, this phase assists students in learning important peace building skills, including:

- stress management
- focus and concentration
- self-control and self-discipline
- healthy body awareness
- improved self-esteem
- improved social skills
- general well being.

With regular use, the Peace2U Stress Less Series Audio CD will:

- increase respect for self and others
- reduce the incidence of alcohol, tobacco, and other drug use
- create a bully-resistant environment
- increase positive attitudes

Activity One
Life in Fast Forward
(Track 2)

PURPOSE
To establish that an accelerated cultural pace can easily lead to physical, mental, emotional, social, and spiritual imbalances, high-risk choices and a split from God, whereas being mindful and balanced in these areas calls us to be Christ-centered and generative for the world

LEARNING OBJECTIVES
- Students will explore the upsides and downsides to technology.
- Students will understand that a hurried pace splits us off from God.
- Students will learn that we must slow down to counterbalance an accelerated cultural pace.
- Students will explore how commercials and advertisements impact our daily thinking, emotions, and life decisions.

CORRESPONDING STUDENT WORKBOOK PAGES 58-59
- Student Worksheets   2

Worksheet 1
Living in "Fast Forward"

1. Write about a time when you hurried or rushed to get somewhere or do something.
_____
_____
_____

2. Who was with you? How were you treating each other?
_____
_____

3. What was physically happening inside of you while you were hurrying?
_____
_____
_____

4. What were you thinking while you were rushing around?
_____
_____

5. What were you feeling emotionally in this hurried state?
_____
_____

6. What were the consequences of this hurried pace for you and everyone else?
_____
_____
_____

Continue this exercise on the next page.

58   **PHASE III**
    Pure of Heart

Peace Be With You
WORKBOOK

Worksheet 1
Living in "Fast Forward"
(continued)

7. What does leading a balanced life mean to you?
_____
_____
_____

8. What is your life like when it gets out of balance?
_____
_____

9. How do advertisements and commercials play on how we feel about ourselves?
_____
_____
_____

Pair up with a partner and share what you wrote with each other.

List what you have in common with your partner.
_____
_____
_____

List your unique differences.
_____
_____
_____

Share what you learned with the entire class.

Peace Be With You
WORKBOOK

PHASE III   59
Pure of Heart

What Is "Life in Fast Forward?"

"Life in Fast Forward" is the term used by the authors to describe our accelerated pace of life. There are numerous signs that our world is speeding up and is set to get faster and faster. Change seems to come more and more rapidly as technological advances and other innovations occur in shorter periods of time—not centuries, decades, or even years—but rather in minutes or less. Technology has exponentially increased the speed of calculations from decades to minutes and communication from months to seconds. As a result, this life in "fast forward" becomes normative and pushes us—or we push ourselves—to the brink of exhaustion.

This common state of overdrive makes it easy to become irritable, agitated, less tolerant, impatient, mean, nasty, rude, angry, frustrated, and so on. All of the latter are signs, signals, or symptoms of being in behavioral overdrive—"taxed to the max." Why are we so driven? Where are we going? What's the rush? Is the rush (high) from the rush? Marketing campaigns have certainly worked this angle to appeal to and capitalize on our rushing around. For instance, in 1997 the Coca Cola Company came out with a brand of soda called Surge with the slogan "Feed the Rush!" What are the implications surrounding this accelerated pace of life? What is the academic cost?

If there is any doubt the pace of our world continues to accelerate, here are some interesting thoughts by two authors on this topic. British author Peter Russell (2003) in an article titled "Acceleration: The Quickening Pace" discusses acceleration from a historical perspective. Although change occurs much faster today than it did during medieval times (for example, architecture and agriculture did not change much over the period of a century), during this era change occurred much faster than it did during prehistoric times (Stone Age tools remained unchanged for thousands of years).

In a fascinating book titled, *Faster: The Acceleration of Just About Everything*, author James Gleick (1999) aptly demonstrates with numerous "quick" historical highlights of our accelerated pace. Although published well over a decade ago, it is interesting to note how much accelerated change has occurred since.

A cultural condition termed "hurry sickness" has been defined by doctors and sociologists as a person who is a victim of time, who does not waste a moment and is always flirting with lateness.

Much of our contemporary terminology unambiguously points to acceleration, such as QuickTabs, QuickZoom, QuickFill and Quicken. Other terms include multitasking, streaming, streamline, milli, nano and a pico, which is one-trillionth of a unit. Television news broadcasts use the term "sound bite" to describe a quickening of speech. In 1968, a typical presidential candidate sound bite was over 40 seconds. In 1996 the average presidential sound bite was under 10 seconds. Television commercials typically are 30 seconds; however, more recently TV commercials have been cut down to less than 10 seconds.

There are fast food restaurants, instant breakfast drinks, pre-cooked and pre-packaged meals, as well as powerbars. Any of the latter can be eaten in the car while driving in the express lane.

Considerable advancements have been made from the original typewriters to electric typewriters to word processing—from words per minute to characters per second, to electronic documents. Our phones have advanced from rotary dialing to touch tone to speed dialing to cellular phones that have multiple uses including text messaging, emailing, online surfing, and an explosion of social networking options.

The first elevator was invented by Elisha Otis in the early 1850's and traveled eight inches per second. The TFC 101 Tower in Taipei, Taiwan, one of the tallest buildings in the world at 508 meters, holds the Guinness Book of World Records for elevator speed of 17 meters per second. Passengers can be whisked from the first floor to the top of the TFC 101 Tower in 30 seconds.

What is the social and relational cost? What is the cost to the human spirit? When you pass someone and ask how he or she is doing, notice that the reply is most likely a one- or two-word description. You might hear things like, "great," "fine," "okay," "never better," etc. If the person does take the time to ask how you are in response, it is usually with a quick one word question: "You?" Asking the question, "How are you?" takes more time.

Notice if the person pauses long enough to hear your response or whether you just see the back of the person's head as he or she passes you. You may even hear (or say yourself) numerous references to how busy we are—"I am really busy, how about you?" or the more hurried version, "Busy, you?" or the even more hurried version, "Busy!" meaning "too busy to talk with you." More versions of the same include: "Can't tell if I am coming or going," "not enough hours in the day," "hectic," "crazy," "up to my eyeballs," "so much to do so little time," "complete chaos," "24/7," "get me off this treadmill," "same old busyness," "no time to breathe," "I don't even have time to use the restroom." If the last two are true, that person is in deep trouble!

We don't allow ourselves the time to offer each other any sort of meaningful dialogue because we are "too busy." Busyness keeps us from connecting with others, causing separation in our relationships and deterioration in EI and SI development. This condition of being in overdrive affects how we treat ourselves and others resulting in a profound rippling effect—usually not a positive one.

In the book, *Violence in Our Schools: Halls of Hope Halls of Fear*, author Tamara Orr interviews a number of experts on the topic of school violence. One of the experts, Leo Sandy, associate professor of education at Plymouth State College in New Hampshire shares his views regarding some causal factors surrounding school violence.

Sandy asserts that our society is "adultifying" children; children are being "pushed" into adulthood much too quickly. As a result, key developmental stages seem to be replaced with an early acquisition of high levels of sophistication,

but lack the maturity and coping mechanisms to handle it. Sandy states:

> This culture is so accelerated—faster fast food, speedier cell phones, faster computers, quicker planes and trains—and in the process, people don't have the time to develop relationships. They are always moving faster and faster, but kids need time. They need old-fashioned stuff, like family activities and meals together, you know? Huma-contact! If we have no time for children's needs, they will become alienated and enraged. The world must slow down and spend more time on reflection and analysis. (as cited in Orr, 2003, pp. 87-88)

The accelerated pace of our world is a set up for impulsivity, poor decision making, and peer abuse (i.e., bullying behavior: E > I = IB; see Figure 5, p. 78). Unfortunately, getting caught up in this pace can and often does result in a desensitization and depersonalization of the human condition, resulting in a lack of consideration for self and others. This creates an unwelcoming, sometimes even hostile school climate, causing many students to feel unimportant and devalued.

The world is not going to decelerate for us. The challenge is not how to keep up, but rather how not to get caught up in this accelerated pace. Not many people are going to clue us in about our stress level or manage our stress for us. Stress is personal and subjective and we must take an active role in managing it. Just as we take an active role in monitoring our physical health, we need to frequently evaluate our inner world if we are to achieve mental, emotional, social, and spiritual health. What is at risk if we take time to slow down? What is at risk and what is the price we pay if we don't?

Phase III supports a shift from the imbalances created by an accelerated pace to a more balanced state of well-being (I + E = AB; see Figure 5, p. 78). In order for youth to make good decisions, be more compassionate with others and create a community of reverence, they must be afforded an opportunity to develop skills that teach them how to pause and reflect before acting. Students must learn that peace is an inside job!

Technology and Cyberbullying

No doubt we can all agree technology has many benefits, and we are stymied whenever we are without it. No doubt we also can agree that technology has a serious downside when it is misused to cause harm in the form of cyberbullying. The recent media attention around bullicides due to cyberbullying is horrifying and the stories heartbreaking. This book would be remiss if we did not spend at least some time addressing cyberbullying as one form of bullying. There is no perfect set of best practices in this area; technology is constantly in flux, multiplying the wide-reaching arsenal for cruelty.

Because there are no real boundaries around technology and often no concrete way to enforce policies established regarding cyberbullying, approaches to address the problem are forced to be reactive. Not only are schools struggling with how to prevent and respond to incidences of cyberbullying, case law is outdated and court cases have been unclear and contradictory at best (Davis, 2011).

Also, as this problem is a 24/7 phenomenon, schools have no control when cyberbullying takes place off campus, even though the problem can permeate the school climate. The other big issue emerging is the difficulty with parent cooperation on matters of bullying and cyberbullying. Some principals report that parents often down play the seriousness of the issue (Davis, 2011).

Peace Be With You is designed to be relevant to address all forms of bullying, traditional or technology related. Every school, however, should have thoughtful policies in place for both traditional bullying and cyberbullying that clearly outline what will happen before the incident occurs. A corrective track is strongly recommended, but that is not the focus of this program. Remember that all bullying situations, no matter what form, can be wonderful opportunities for learning and formation.

Have students take 10-15 minutes to fill out Worksheet 2 on p. 60, do a pair and share (2-3 minutes each), and then share with the entire class for another 10-15 minutes. If class time is not available, have students complete the worksheet at home and discuss what was learned in class the next day.

Pay close attention to the specific positive action steps students can take to stop cyberbullying and what students are committed to personally doing to help stop the problem. Student responses most likely will be highly creative. Ask them for permission to share their ideas with the school administration or the bullying prevention.

Worksheet 2

Technology & Cyberbullying

What is helpful about technology?

_____

_____

What are some ways technology can be hurtful? (*Hint*: cyberbullying)

_____

_____

List five positive ways cyberbullying can be stopped among students:

1.
2.
3.
4.
5.

What positive actions can you take to stop cyberbullying?

_____

_____

List three people you will team up with to end cyberbullying:

1.
2.
3.

60   **PHASE III**
Pure of Heart

Peace Be With You
WORKBOOK

Facilitator Script
Living in "Fast Forward"

TIME	PREPARATION & PROCESS	LOGISTICS

Session Preparation

0:00
- Cue CD player or iPod to Track 2.
- Student Workbook, pp. 58-59

CD, iPod, or MP3 player needed

Process

Say: *"Class, listen carefully to this audio track and write down any reflections to what you hear."* (Play Track 2, 5:17 minutes)

****

"Good job listening."

Have students open their workbooks to p. 58 when Track 2 is completed.

6:00 *"Write your responses to the questions in your workbook on pp. 58-59. You have 15 minutes."*

"When you are finished close your workbook and sit quietly."

****

When all students have completed with their worksheet, have them stand and wiggle their whole body for 10 seconds.

21:00 *"Pair up with your partner and decide who is going to be the listener and who is going to be the speaker."*

"Listeners raise your hands."

"Speakers raise your hands."

22:00 *"Speakers you have 3 minutes to share your answers with your partner. I will let you know when to switch."*

25:00 *"Stop. Now the Speakers become the listeners and the listeners the speakers. Begin."*

28:00 *"Stop. Everyone stand and stretch to the right and now to the left."*

29:00 *"Do step three and share what you have in common with your partner. You will have 1 minute each. I will tell you when to switch. Begin."*

30:00 *"Stop. Switch."*

31:00 *"Stop. Now do step four and share what unique differences there are between you and your partner. You will have one minute each. I will tell you when to switch. Begin."*

Teacher Note: Ask "what, why, when, where and how" questions with entire class.

32:00 *"Stop. Switch."*

33:00 *"Stop."*

34:00 *"Pairs share what you have learned with the entire class."*

40:00 *"What have you learned today about yourself?"*

45:00 *"What have you learned about each other?"*

Activity Two

Understanding Stress

(Track 3)

PURPOSE
To help students understand what stress is and how it effects the body, mind, and spirit

LEARNING OBJECTIVES
- Students will identify physical, mental, emotional, social, and spiritual signs of distress and imbalance.
- Students will explore the negative and positive consequences of stress.
- Students will recognize how current relationships can contribute to imbalance or support choices for a balanced life.
- Students will understand the correlation between unmanaged stress and low self-esteem.
- Students will understand the correlation between managed stress as a self-esteem builder.
- Students will recognize inadequate diet, dehydration, and eating too quickly are stress-related and can also contribute to stress.

CORRESPONDING STUDENT WORKBOOK PAGES 62-65
- Student Worksheets   2
- Stress Less Theatre

Worksheet 1

Understanding Stress

1. Write what the word "stress" means to you.
_____
_____
_____

2. How is stress beneficial?
_____
_____
_____

3. Where does stress show up in your body?
_____
_____
_____

4. Why do some people get headaches? What messages might headaches give us?
_____
_____
_____

5. What are some natural ways to relieve a headache instead of taking a drug?
_____
_____
_____

6. What does healthy eating and staying hydrated have to do with our mood, attitude, and overall health?
_____
_____
_____

Continue this exercise on the next page.

62   **PHASE III**
Pure of Heart   *Peace Be With You*
                                                   WORKBOOK

Worksheet 1

Understanding Stress
(continued)

7. What are some physical consequences of too much stress?
_____
_____

Mental or emotional consequences?
_____
_____

Social consequences?
_____
_____

Relational consequences?
_____
_____

Spiritual consequences?
_____
_____

Pair up with a partner and share what you wrote with each other.
What do you share in common with your partner?
_____
_____

What are the unique differences between you and your partner?
_____
_____

Share what you learned with the class.

Peace Be With You
WORKBOOK   **PHASE III**   63
                                            Pure of Heart

Definition of Stress

Stress can be defined simply as anything that has the potential to cause a stress reaction of mental or physical tension in the body (Greenberg, 2002; Wilson, 2001). Use the "guitar string" as an analogy for stress in the Peace2U Stress Less Series audio script in Appendix A to describe how low stress and high stress result in less efficiency and poor performance. With managed stress, we are more likely to get to peak performance in everything we do: academics, extracurricular activities, relationships, etc. (see Figure 7).

Physical Implications of Stress

Stress reactions can include increased heart rate, elevated blood pressure, increased respiration, increased perspiration, a decrease in saliva, and an increase in muscle tension. The body and the accompanying symptoms of stress do not distinguish between the rationale behind the stress. A stress reaction in the body for a person losing one's job may be similar to that of a person getting a job promotion. However, several factors play a role in the effects of the stressor, such as, how a person perceives the stressor, the duration of the stressor, what support a person has around the stressor, a person's lifestyle choices—healthy vs. unhealthy—during the stressor (Greenberg, 2002; Wilson, 2001).

The body's endocrine system is one of the most important systems related to stress. It includes all the glands that secrete hormones. When there is a stressor, this system becomes activated, preparing the body to fight or run. This is called "fight or flight syndrome." One of the stress hormones secreted by the adrenal gland is cortisol. Chronic stress causes a flooding of this stress hormone which can seriously lower the immune system, making a person susceptible to colds, flu, and diseases. Unmanaged stress can also cause general fatigue and make it difficult to recover from stress-related ailments (Greenberg, 2002; Wilson, 2001).

If we take time to manage our stress through exercise, proper rest, relaxation, proper diet, and hydration, we can replenish this adrenal supply, keeping our immune system boosted and feeling refreshed. In order to accomplish a balanced life, it is important to take the time to do so. If we rush or squeeze in time to recharge with all the other stuff we "have to do," we are more than likely cheating ourselves out of full replenishment. Taking time to take care of ourselves takes thoughtful organizational planning.

When students are asked how many have experienced headaches, there is rarely a hand that doesn't go up. When asked, "What do you usually think about when you have a headache, other than, this hurts and I want it to go away?" The usual answer is at least ten different brand names of painkillers.

This becomes a wonderful opening for a discussion on the psychology of advertisements and commercials. Students need to become conscious of the insidious and overt motivations behind commercials and how they (the students) are targets of some very intense manipulation.

Worksheet 2

Understanding Stress

1. Write about a time in your life when you felt a lot of stress. What happened that caused the stress?
_____
_____

2. How did you treat yourself and others when you were under stress?
_____
_____

3. What did you do to try to manage your stress? Did it help?
_____
_____

4. List three new healthy ways to reduce stress that you can add to your "Stress Less Tool Kit":
   1.
   2.
   3.

5. Why is coping with life situations in a healthy way so important?
_____
_____

Pair up with a partner and share what you wrote with each other.
What do you share in common with your partner?
_____
_____

What are the unique differences between you and your partner?
_____
_____

Share what you learned with the entire class.

64   **PHASE III**
     Pure of Heart   *Peace Be With You*
                                        WORKBOOK

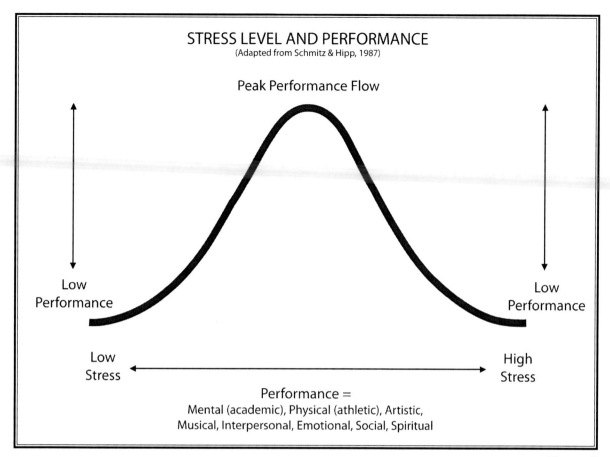

STRESS LEVEL AND PERFORMANCE
(Adapted from Schmitz & Hipp, 1987)

Peak Performance Flow

Low Performance

Low Performance

Low Stress

High Stress

Performance =
Mental (academic), Physical (athletic), Artistic,
Musical, Interpersonal, Emotional, Social, Spiritual

Figure 7

The ultimate goal is to get students thinking about other options before they think of "popping a pill" as their first and only option.

Mental and Emotional Implications of Stress

Earlier we established that bullying causes serious psychological distress:

> School bullying has been linked to individual problems such as depression, suicidal ideation, mental disorders, eating disorders, decreased self-esteem, sleeping problems, bedwetting, headaches, stomachaches, alcohol or tobacco use. (Dake et al., 2004, p. 373)

The stress reduction activities in this book can help these conditions, but are not intended to replace psychological treatment. Students exhibiting any of these symptoms should be referred for professional help.

In general, it is pretty easy for students and adults to feel overwhelmed. We all try to cram more into our day than is sometimes reasonable. The result is an even greater escalation in stress and anxiety, making us feel "taxed to the max." The fight or flight syndrome can easily be triggered as a "false alarm" because of the intensity of how driven we are to keep up with an accelerated cultural pace. As a result, we can become forgetful, have difficulty concentrating, become less tolerant, easily frustrated, highly irritable, and suffer from chronic anxiety or depression. When we cram more than 25 pounds into a 25-pound box, the structure holding the contents becomes unstable. The seams could break or tear ("I am coming apart at the seams"), and consequences are inevitable, because the "bottom could fall out." The box is very difficult, if not impossible, to close ("I can't keep a lid on it"), making it very easy for the contents to spill out ("I feel so overwhelmed"), possibly contaminating others.

Many of us have unrealistic expectations of what we believe we "should" accomplish in a given day. When these expectations are not met, there is a tendency for self-deprecation to creep in. This debasing, in whatever form it takes, will also increase levels of anxiety and stress, often resulting in a self-imposed vicious circle. With high levels of mental and emotional stress, our level of attention is low and can set us up for mistakes or "accidents" due to fatigue, lack of concentration and/or general carelessness. These "accidents" can be of minor or major consequence to us and others; the greater the mistake, the greater the consequence, resulting in a greater degree of stress and anxiety.

Social Implications of Stress

We have also established that there are social consequences to bullying. Again to reiterate, these consequences include:

> fighting, weapon carrying, vandalism, stealing, and having trouble with the police. It has also been linked with interpersonal issues such as lack of social acceptance and difficulty in making friends....School adjustment (following rules, good performance on schoolwork) and school bonding (satisfaction at school, taking school seriously) were also found to be less likely to occur in students who were engaged in school bullying behaviors. (Dake et al., 2004, p. 373)

We are highly adaptive as Homo sapiens, but we may never totally adapt due to the global changes occurring on a daily basis. When we are cranky or irritable and snap at others, this is a warning signal about our level of stress. Unfortunately, snapping at others only exacerbates our and their level of stress. There seems to be a social norm that requires us all to board this high speed train or risk being ostracized in some way.

A popular response to being asked how we are doing most likely includes the word "busy" or another word or phrase with similar meaning. If we do not develop the strength and skills to get off the train, we risk losing our health, loving relationships, and even worse, ourselves. This "busy-ness" can keep us split off from who we truly are and our beliefs, morals, goals, dreams, passions, and vision.

The social norm is to push youth to excel in multiple activities beyond academic expectations. Many parents have their primary grade school children on the "pro-track" with often intense and grueling athletic or other ancillary programming. This well meaning attempt to give our children a "head start" in life forces them to grow up too fast too soon. Pressuring children to take on enormous amounts of stress before they are emotionally ready can often lead to dissatisfaction.

When the stakes are high, the fun factor is usually low. Feeling overwhelmed because the cost of an activity outweighs the benefits, may cause some children to "give up." What ensues is a "push/resist" dynamic in which parents push and then feel frustrated when their child resists. The outcome is excessive stress for the family. Although having a well-rounded child can be healthy, it can be difficult to keep and maintain these daunting schedules even with a daily planner.

The word "leisure" seems to have been eliminated from our vocabulary. It is a rarity today to find a family that takes time to do nothing. "What would we do if we did nothing?" An old adage comes to mind that is worded with a scrupulous twist: "The more I do the less I am" and "The less I do the more I am." Another maxim asks us to consider the question: "Are you a human doing or are you a human being?" Taking leisure time can be one way to replenish or recharge our batteries. I suggest we start a campaign to resurrect leisure time for all individuals and families.

Relational Implications of Stress

Stress is a significant contributor to how we behave toward and interact with each other. If our stress goes unmanaged, we are more likely to act negatively not only toward ourselves, but toward others as well. Our relationships suffer because we often do what is expedient and not always what is prudent, thus causing stressful conflicts due to misunderstandings. Cyberbullying is a case in point.

The relational consequences to unmanaged stress have a serious rippling effect that negatively impacts others both directly and indirectly. If we mistreat another out of our unmanaged stress, we invite and encourage the return of equal or greater mistreatment to ourselves. We also invite and encourage those affected by our initiated treatment to carry out this, or another form of mistreatment, to others. The maxims, anger begets anger or violence begets violence, can easily be replaced with behaviors such as bullying, disrespect, intolerance, etc. It seems as though "The Golden Rule" has been lost or diminished along the way. This program is about making this rule glaringly apparent, by creating a culture of dignity and respect.

Spiritual Implications of Stress

Overwhelming stress or unmanaged stress has numerous spiritual implications as well. This fast pace dulls our senses and hardens our heart, sometimes literally. If we are split off from our heart or passion for life, we are merely existing and not aspiring to be all that we are intended to be. This disconnect with ourselves can cause us to lose sight of our sense of purpose and vision. If we mistreat another out of unmanaged stress, we miscommunicate even good intentions, which can lead to misunderstandings and mixed messages that further divide us from ourselves and others. If our stress reactions cause inner divisions as well as relational divisions, how is it possible to inspire others to be all they are intended to be? There seems to be an inverse relationship

with speed and basic life virtues. Mahatma Gandhi said, "There is more to life than increasing its speed." As the pace of the world accelerates, disrespect, intolerance, impatience, and bullying seem all too common, while virtues such as honesty, trustworthiness, kindness, and compassion appear to be less common.

In Phase I we explored how attitudes cause a rippling effect in our environment with those around us. Attitude has something to do with how students perceive and handle stress as well. An internal rippling effect occurs based on the attitude one adopts toward the various stressors in one's life. We could study a dozen people, all of whom have experienced the same stressor, and observe that each of them copes in different ways and has different reactions, depending on personal perspectives and attitudes surrounding the stressor. Jerrold S. Greenberg (2002) defines this as cognitive appraisal: each person's interpretation of a stressor.

A negative attitude about the stressor could actually exacerbate stress, potentially causing serious distress for a person. A positive attitude, on the other hand, can help keep stress manageable, minimizing negative effects and potentially turning the stressor into an opportunity and a blessing. Winston Churchill said that there are two kinds of people, those that find the difficulty in every opportunity and those that find the opportunity in every difficulty.

Environment also plays a significant role in impacting stress. Crowds, traffic, cluttered space, lack of space, noxious noises, noxious lights, air pollution, crime, and other such effects are all associated with large cities and are factors contributing to increased stress.

The people students hang out with in their environment can also be considered a factor. Students are more likely to engage in behavior and adopt a similar attitude to the "friends" with whom they surround themselves. Students who surround themselves with peers who have a negative attitude and make bad choices are likely to do the same. Students only find encouragement in a circle of support with adults and peers who have a positive attitude and make positive choices. If the classroom contagion is calm, relaxing, and peaceful, this can only be conducive to positive and effective learning.

Activities One and Two, along with student worksheets and Track 3, will help students answer the question: "What is stress?" Allow for a separate class period for "Stress Less Theatre." Students and adults have lots of fun showing off their talent in this creative theater production. Of course, there is learning that takes place, too! In an additional period, four "relaxation tips" are taught that can be used to create a calm, relaxing and peaceful classroom environment. Each relaxation tip has a corresponding worksheet in the workbook.

These exercises are counterbalancing techniques—helpful tools to add to students' personal tool box of life—gently guiding students toward well-adaptive behaviors that enable them to manage stress in healthy ways. The more often the relaxation tips can be put into practice, the more likely they will be integrated and used by students beyond the classroom experience.

Facilitator Script
Understanding Stress

TIME	PREPARATION & PROCESS	LOGISTICS
0:00	**Session Preparation** • Cue CD player or iPod to Track 3. • Student Workbook, pp. 62-63.	**CD, iPod, or MP3 player needed**
	Process **Say:** *"Class, listen carefully to this audio track and write down your reflections of what you hear."* (Play Track 3, 2:11 minutes) **	
3:00	*"You have 10 minutes to write your responses to the questions on Worksheet 1 in your workbooks on pages 62-63."*	**Have students complete pp. 62-63 in Student Workbook when Track 3 is completed.**
13:00	*Note.* There are two pages to Student Worksheet 1 *"When you are finished, close your book and sit quietly."* *"Begin."* *"Pair up with a partner and decide who is going to be the listener and who is going to be the speaker."* *"Listeners, raise your hands. Speakers, raise your hands."*	
14:00	*"Speakers, you have 2 minutes to share your answers with your partner. I will let you know when to switch."*	**Assign partners to expedite time.**
16:00	*"Stop. Now the speakers become the listeners and the listeners the speakers. Begin."*	
18:00	*"Stop. Everyone stand and stretch to the right and now to the left."*	
19:00	*"Share what you have in common with your partner. You will have 2 minutes each. I will tell you when to switch. Begin."*	
21:00	*"Stop. Switch."*	
23:00	*"Share what unique differences there are between you and your partner. You will have one minute each. I will tell you when to switch. Begin."*	
24:00	*"Stop. Switch."*	
25:00	*"Stop."*	**Ask, "what, why, when, where, and how" questions with entire class.**
26:00	*"Pairs, share what you have learned with the entire class."*	
	Note. Do Student Worksheet 2 next or during another class period.	

Activity Two

37:00   *"You have 10 minutes to write your responses to the questions in your workbook on page 64."*

"When you are finished, close your book and sit quietly."

"Begin."

"Pair up with a new partner and decide who is going to be the listener and who is going to be the speaker."

"Listeners, raise your hands."

38:00   *"Speakers, raise your hands."*

"Speakers, you have 2 minutes to share your answers with your partner. I will let you know when to switch."

40:00   *"Stop. Now the speakers become the listeners and the listeners the speakers. Begin."*

42:00   *"Stop. Switch."*

43:00   *"Share what you have in common with your partner. You will have 1 minute each. I will tell you when to switch. Begin."*

44:00   *"Stop. Switch."*

45:00   *"Share what unique differences there are between you and your partner. You will have one minute each. I will tell you when to switch. Begin."*

46:00   *"Stop. Switch."*

47:00   *"Stop."*

48:00   *"Pairs share what you have learned with the entire class."*

49:00   *"What have you learned today about yourself?"*

"What have you learned about each other?"

When transitioning from Worksheet 1 to 2 have students stand and wiggle their whole body for 10 seconds or your own option to create movement.

Stress Less Theatre Production

Create groups of 4-6 students. Groups will choose or be assigned the following two options on p. 65 in the Student Workbook. Students perform their creative work in front of the class.

Option One:
In small groups, students can create a skit, pantomime, or rap song that demonstrates what stress means to them. Have them include ways stress can affect us in body, mind, and spirit as well as healthy ways we can manage our stress. Students have 15 minutes.

Option Two:
Create a parody of what advertisements or commercials are "really saying." Have them include ways advertisements and commercials can affect us in body, mind, and spirit as well as insightful ways we can see the truth behind these commercial messages. Students have 15 minutes.

Notes
- Teachers can bring in magazine ads to share with students for creative ideas.
- Review student skits prior to performance for content and appropriateness.
- Use student-generated content brought up during each of the performances as a springboard for discussion.
- Ask students about their level of "performance anxiety" and what they did to overcome it or what they did to stay focused during their performance.
- Help students translate these concepts to their everyday lives.

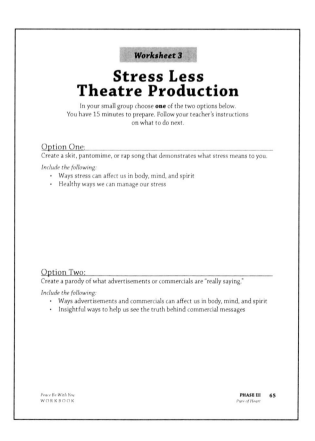

Activity Three

"The Gift"

(Track 4)

PURPOSE

To introduce concepts of self-care, emphasizing the importance of remaining free from harmful substances and creating a circle of support

LEARNING OBJECTIVES

*   Students will focus on the holiness and self-care of mind, body, and spirit.
*   Students will explore how harmful substances prevent whole person growth and success.
*   Students will explore how bullying prevents whole person growth and success.
*   Students will begin to create a circle of support to encourage prosocial behaviors.
*   Students will create common ground to reinforce positive peer influence.

CORRESPONDING STUDENT WORKBOOK PAGE 67

*   Student Worksheet   1

Worksheet 1

"The Gift"

1. Write about how you take care of yourself in body, mind, and spirit.

_____

2. What are some ways you could take better care of yourself in these areas?

_____

3. Why do alcohol, tobacco, or other drugs keep us from being the person we are meant to be?

_____

4. List three people that will support you in staying drug free:

    1.

    2.

    3.

5. How does bullying behavior keep the Bully, Target, and Active or Passive Bystanders from being all they are meant to be?

_____

Pair up with a partner and share what you wrote with each other.

6. What do you share in common with your partner?

_____

7. What are the unique differences between you and your partner?

_____

Share what you learned with the entire class.

Peace Be With You
WORKBOOK

PHASE III 67
Pure of Heart

Cognitive Learning

Cognitive learning is the acquisition of knowledge and skills through mental or cognitive processes (i.e., the procedures used to manipulate information in our heads). Cognitive learning occurs as a result of listening, watching, touching, or experiencing sensory information. Cognitive processes include creating mental representations of physical objects and events and other forms of information processing (Ormrod, 1999). The activities and visual exercises that follow are opportunities for students to build internal assets (inner fortitude) and strengthen cognitive abilities. The exercises can enhance learning and have multiple applications that translate to other subjects (e.g., the ability to "see" math problems or sentence structures prior to writing them down on paper).

The process of mentally imagining an end result prior to the actual experience is a natural and mysterious human marvel, whether we are consciously aware of doing it or not. Mental imaging, short for "imagination" is a multisensory process, leading to positive, negative, or neutral outcomes. If one positively imagines completing a task prior to engaging in the actual task, a successful outcome is likely. If, however, mental imaging focuses on failing the impending task, there is increased likelihood of creating a condition that produces failure, or a likelihood of being less effective and efficient at the actual task.

For example, a golfer could use mental imaging prior to hitting a golf ball to "feel" the ball as it hits the sweet spot of the club, "see" the loft and trajectory to the hole, and "hear" the sound of the ball as it drops into the cup. Norman Vincent Peale (1996) describes imaging as a kind of mental engineering that works best when supported by a strong religious faith. With practice and increased awareness, mental imaging can enhance our ability to create positive choices and outcomes throughout our lives.

One way to become attuned to cognitive learning is to have at least some basic understanding of multiple intelligences (MI) and how each of these intelligences processes information and learns. According to Armstrong (2009), there are nine multiple intelligences, including Visual/Spatial, Verbal/Linguistic, Logical-mathematical, Bodily-kinesthetic, Musical, Interpersonal, Intrapersonal, Naturalistic, and Existential. While this vast body of knowledge is beyond the purposes of this book, teachers and counselors are strongly encouraged to remain updated in the current literature or attend professional development training on this fascinating topic. An abundance of information is available on MI, as expanded and emerging theories and research continue to evolve (Armstrong, 1993, 1999, 2009; Gardner, 1993, 1999, 2006).

For the purposes of this book, three simple yet important common learning styles—Visual, Auditory, and Kinesthetic—will be addressed in brief. Visual learners do well forming or "seeing" mental pictures or images. Their strength lies in taking notes from the board and following other visual cues and symbols. When speaking, they are likely to use words that refer to the visual sense: "I can see that....Looks to me like....Did you see that? What did it look like?"

Auditory learners process information, such as classroom instruction, through their ears. They learn best by hearing what is said and seem to need to vocalize or "echo back" what they hear, hearing the information a second time in their own voice. When speaking, they are more likely to use words that refer to the auditory sense: "I hear you....Sounds to me like.... Did you hear that? What did she say?"

Kinesthetic learners are students who learn best through physical, tactile, or "hands-on" projects or activities. Kinesthetic learners prefer "doing," and may not enjoy sitting for more than 5-10 minutes. When speaking they are more likely to use words that refer to a combination of touch and visual senses, describing the size, shape, texture, and color of an object.

We most likely can find aspects of ourselves in all three learning styles. Each of us, however, has a predominant learning style; the others are considered secondary. Helping students identify primary and secondary learning styles is essential to personal success, now and for the future as adult learners. Mental events are central to human learning, no matter what a person's learning style or MI. Teaching students to identify their multiple intelligences and providing increased opportunities to strengthen learning styles will go a long way in helping them accelerate and integrate cognitive learning.

Negative Social Impact on Cognitive Learning

There are an overwhelming number of negative social implications for cognitive and emotional development; it is a wonder how students have any free attention to learn. Circumstances affecting cognitive development include child abuse and neglect, domestic violence, substance abuse (self and/or relative), gang behavior, gun violence, being at war, peer abuse, overuse of technology, and media violence. All are beyond the scope of this book; however, brief focus on media violence is warranted, because of its insidious and widespread influence.

Media has a strong influence on adults and youth. Media influences can have a profound effect on cognitive and emotional development. Important cognitive abilities can become impaired by the overuse of visual and auditory media, mainly television and movies. The young brain can become atrophied through the overuse and overreliance of this media, causing passive involvement in brain functioning.

Goleman (2006) describes this overindulgence as "mental puppetry." This passivity begins early as it is estimated that by the time children reach the age of 2, they are watching television for a minimum of 2-3 hours a day (Goleman, 2006; KidsHealth 2011). No matter how educational the programming, this is excessive and can only dull creativity and cognitive development, setting a disturbing precedent for future development.

According to the A.C. Nielsen Company, the average American watches more than 4 hours of TV each day (Herr, 2007). The average child will watch 8,000 murders on TV before finishing elementary school and by age 18 will have seen 200,000 acts of violence on TV, including 40,000 murders (Herr, 2007).

Although there is much debate among researchers on both sides of the coin, there are scores of scientific studies over several decades that make a positive correlation between youth viewing TV, movies, and other forms of media with violent and aggressive content resulting in actual violent and aggressive behavior (see Bandura et al., 1961, 1963a, 1963b; Boyatzis et al., 1995; Drabman & Hanratty, 1974, 1976; Huston-Stein & Friedrich, 1972).

John Nelson of the American Medical Association indicates that 2,888 out of 3,000 studies show that TV violence is a casual factor for actual violent behaviors, making this a serious public health problem (Herr, 2007). In addition to children behaving in aggressive or harmful ways toward others, further research on media influences also indicates that youth may become less sensitive to the pain and suffering of others and more fearful of the world around (National TV Violence Study, 1996; Paik & Comstock, 1994). The latter and the former are precursors to the bullying dynamic.

Along with the vicarious everyday exposure to violent and aggressive images, video gamers are active and willing participants of "self-induced" violent and aggressive images, often for countless hours every day. According to the A.C. Nielsen Company, the average American is tuned into an additional four hours a day on other forms of visual media such as video games (video gaming systems, cellphone gaming, or online video games) and Internet computer surfing (Reinberg, 2010). A study by Anderson & Dill (2000) suggests violent video games may be more harmful than violent television and movies because they are interactive, very engrossing, and require the player to identify with the aggressor.

In a report by the American Medical Association (AMA, 2007) video gaming has physical, behavioral, and psychosocial effects on children. Physical effects include an increased risk of epileptic seizures, musculoskeletal disorders of the upper extremities, and an increased metabolic rate (Emes, 1997; Kang et al., 2003). Behavioral effects include increased aggression. The latter is concluded by the AMA (2007) and other literature replete with substantial evidence of the same conclusion (Anderson, 2004; Anderson & Bushman, 2001; Gentile & Stone, 2005; Huesmann & Taylor, 2006).

With regard to psychosocial effects, the AMA (2007) indicates that although there is currently no DSM-IV diagnosis for pathological symptoms pertaining to gaming, the pathologies associated with gaming are closely related to a gambling addiction. Symptoms can include excessive time usage and social dysfunction or disruption that appear in patterns similar to other addictive disorders (Dejoie, 2001; Tejeiro & Moran, 2002), such as dependence-like behaviors, including preoccupation and family or school disruption, as well as an overall decrease in prosocial behaviors (AMA 2007).

Whether violent images are imposed vicariously through the media, are "self-induced," or are a combination of both, youth are ingesting an excessive amount of violence and aggression through their eyes, ears, and other senses. This is bound to have an adverse effect on the human psyche and can be projected toward others in the form of bullying and other forms of aggression. Anderson and colleagues (2003) sum it up by stating:

> Research on violent television and films, video games, and music reveals unequivocal evidence that media violence increases the likelihood of aggression and violent behavior in both immediate and long-term contexts. (p. 8)

No matter how egregious a stronghold the media seems to have on youth, we must be proactive in counterbalancing its effects. Although there are no quick fixes to remedy this, it is imperative that educators and counselors work with and support parents on monitoring their children's time and use of all forms of media. As educators and counselors we can do our part by following through with the exercises and activities throughout this book.

In particular, the following pages in this phase are meant to be helpful, counterbalancing strategies. The relaxation tips, visual exercises, affirmations, meditations, PeaceScape exercises, and other activities will support a prayerful and mindful focus on a healthy inner life for our students.

Facilitator Script
"The Gift"

TIME	PREPARATION & PROCESS	LOGISTICS
0:00	**Session Preparation** • Cue CD player or iPod to Track 4. • Student Workbook, p. 67 **Process** **Say:** *"Class, listen carefully to this audio track and write down your reflections of what you hear."* (Play Track 4, 4:39 minutes) ***	CD, iPod, or MP3 player needed Create a calm, low key classroom atmosphere. If possible dim the lights or allow for natural outside light only.
5:00	*"You have 10 minutes to write your responses to the questions in your workbook on page 67."* *"When you are finished, close your book and sit quietly."*	Have students complete p. 67 in the Student Workbook when Track 4 is completed.
15.00	*"Pair up with a partner and decide who is going to be the listener and who is going to be the speaker."* *"Listeners, raise your hands."* *"Speakers, raise your hands."*	When all students are completed with their Student Worksheet have them stand and wiggle their whole body for 10 seconds or your own option to create movement.
16:00	*"Speakers, you have 3 minutes to share your answers with your partner. I will let you know when to switch."*	
19:00	*"Stop. Now the speakers become the listeners and the listeners the speakers. Begin."*	
22:00	*"Stop. Everyone stand and stretch to the right and now to the left."*	
23:00	*"Answer Question 6 and share what you have in common with your partner. You will have 1 minute each. I will tell you when to switch. Begin."*	
24:00	*"Stop. Switch."*	
25:00	*"Stop. Now answer Question 7 and share what unique differences there are between you and your partner. You will have one minute each. I will tell you when to switch. Begin."*	Teacher Note: Ask "what, why, when, where and how" questions with entire class.
26:00	*"Stop. Switch."*	
27:00	*"Stop. Pairs, share what you have learned with the entire class."*	
30:00	*"What have you learned today about yourself?"*	
35:00	*"What have you learned about each other?"*	

Activity Four

Visual Exercises

(Track 4)

PURPOSE

To strengthen cognitive learning through creative visual exercises that boost focus and concentration for an increase in self-confidence in academic and extracurricular performance

LEARNING OBJECTIVES

- Students will activate imagination through a combination of kinesthetic and visual exercises.
- Students will participate in visual exercises to strengthen cognitive learning.
- Students will practice a balanced posture for increased self-confidence.
- Students will increase focus and concentration.
- Students will physically and mentally prepare for peer pressure.
- Students will learn how to quiet themselves before class or other activities.
- Students will activate imagination by visualizing their ideal school.
- Students will strengthen a belief in what is possible for themselves and their school.
- Students will strengthen their Christ-consciousness.

CORRESPONDING STUDENT WORKBOOK PAGES 68-69

- Student Worksheets   2

Worksheet 2

My Ideal School

In your small group:
- Choose a *Facilitator* to ask your group the questions below.
- Choose a *Time Keeper* to keep time allowing for 1 minute per question.
- Choose a *Recorder* to write down the highlights of what is said during discussion.
- Choose a *Reporter* to report the group's answers to the class.

Discuss the following questions with your small group:

During the "ideal school" visual exercise:

1. What did you see happening at your ideal school?
_____

2. How are you being treated?
_____

3. How are you treating others?
_____

4. How is everyone treating each other?
_____

5. How important do you feel in your ideal school? Valued? Respected?
_____

6. What is your Safety Check number at your ideal school?
_____

68   **PHASE III**
Pure of Heart   *Peace Be With You*
                                   WORKBOOK

Worksheet 3

Finding Christ

In your small group:
- Keep the same *Facilitator* to ask your group the questions below.
- Keep the same *Time Keeper* to make sure everybody gets 1 minute to share.
- The *Recorder* and *Reporter* can relax this round!

During the visual exercise:

1. What is your ideal school like now that Christ has filled your heart? (Look like? Feel like? Sound like?)
_____

2. How do you see yourself treating others from a Christ-filled place?
_____

3. Can your classmates sense the love God has for you?
_____

4. Do you feel important, valued, respected by our loving God?
_____

5. What is your Safety Check number right now?
_____

6. What did Christ say to you about why you are here on this planet and what He is calling you to do?
_____

7. What else happened that you would like to share?
_____

Peace Be With You
WORKBOOK   **PHASE III**   69
                                   Pure of Heart

Visual Exercise 1

TIME	PREPARATION & PROCESS	LOGISTICS
0:00	**Session Preparation** • None • Student Workbook, p. 68	CD, iPod, or MP3 player needed.

Process

Say: *"Stand up."*

"Place your feet about shoulder width apart and point your toes straight ahead."

"Hands at your sides and shoulders back."

1:00

"Now imagine that there is a string on the top of your head."

"Pull the string to help make you as tall as you can be."

"Good!"

"Find a spot on the wall and focus your eyes on it."

2:00 *"Good!"*

"Take a deep breath and close your eyes."

"Now imagine there are roots like the roots of a tree coming out of the bottom of your feet."

"No one can walk up to an oak tree and topple it over."

"Feel the strength of this pose and the confidence that comes with it."

3:00 *"Take a deep breath into this pose."*

"Good!"

"When balanced, you are less vulnerable to negative peer pressure and high risk influences, such as alcohol, tobacco, and other drugs and bullying behavior."

4:00 *"Take a deep breath. Remember the strength you feel in this balanced posture. The health of your body, mind, and spirit depends on your staying balanced by taking good care of yourself."*

"Now from this place of strength imagine this school is your ideal school—the school of your dreams—where everyone is loved, supported, and celebrated."

5:00   *"What do you see happening at your ideal school?"*

"Notice how you are being treated."

"Notice how you are treating others."

"Notice how everyone is treating each other."

"Notice what you see happening when you or someone else does something right."

6:00   *"Notice what you see happening when you or someone else does something wrong."*

"Notice how you feel being at your ideal school."

"Notice how students feel about being with each other."

"Notice how important you feel. How valued. How respected."

"What's your Safety Check number?"

7:00   *"Notice if this is how Christ wants us to treat each other."*

"Notice how you feel about getting up in the morning to go to your ideal school."

"Notice how you feel about leaving your ideal school at the end of the day."

"You can open your eyes now. Look around the room and admire everyone's peaceful strength!"

"Good job everyone!"

8:00   *"Get into your small groups and follow the directions in your workbooks on page 68. Your group has 10 minutes for this activity."*

18:00   *"Reporters share with the class the highlights of your group discussion. Ask for help if you need it. Let's start with Group 1."* Continue with groups 2, 3, 4, etc.

30:00   *Note.* Teacher writes group responses on the board or flipchart. Post student responses visually around the room for reference. You can post one a week or have a bulletin board designated to post all the responses collected.

Facilitator Script
Visual Exercise 2

TIME	PREPARATION & PROCESS

Session Preparation
0:00
- Students remain at their seats in groups.
- Take the visual exercise to a deeper level.
- Use a soft, calming voice.
- Student Workbook, p. 69.

Process
Say: *"Take a slow deep belly breath."*

"Close your eyes and imagine you see someone approaching from a distance."

1:00 *"As the person gets closer, you know you are safe and it is time to meet this person."*

"As He gets closer and closer you realize it is Christ who is approaching you.

"You get closer and closer until you are eye to eye with Jesus."

"Notice the love and compassion in His eyes."

"As you look in each others eyes, Jesus reaches out and places His hands on your head to give you a blessing."

2:00 *"Feel Christ's blessing fill your heart with His love and peace."*

"He leans over and whispers in your ear why you are on this planet."

"Notice what He says to you about why you are here and what He is calling you to do."

"See your loving self surrounded by other loving hearts in the classroom."

3:00 *"Take in a slow deep breath in and exhale slowly and completely."*

"Open your eyes and come back to the room."

"Remain silent. Take one minute to reflect on what you just experienced."

"Turn to page 69 in your Student Workbook and discuss your answers to the questions on Worksheet 3 with your small groups. You have 10 minutes."

5:00 *"Stop."*

"What did you learn about yourself from this exercise?"

"What did you learn about Christ's love for each of you?"

"How can we keep the love of Christ in our classroom and in our school?"

Relaxation Tips

(Track 5)

PURPOSE

To increase awareness of and acquire practical stress management skill sets to enhance physical, mental, emotional, social, and spiritual well-being

LEARNING OBJECTIVES

- Students will add stress management skill sets to their personal "tool box."
- Students will learn a quantitative measurement to determine levels of personal stress.
- Students will understand how to use this quantitative measurement to manage stress.
- Students will increase awareness of inefficient shallow stress breathing.
- Students will contrast with effective breathing techniques to reduce stress and increase efficiency.
- Students will increase awareness of physical tension as an indicator of stressors held in the body.
- Students will learn how to contrast physical tension with physical relaxation.

CORRESPONDING STUDENT WORKBOOK PAGES 71-74

- Student Worksheets   4

Relaxation Tip # 1 Stress Check

A "stress check"—an internal asset building appraisal—is a very practical technique for managing stress. This simple self-assessment utilizes a continuum from 0 to 10, with 0 being the least stress (low stress) and 10 being the most stress (high stress) to help students subjectively determine a number that best represents their current stress level.

As the stress check measurement is cultivated, it is likely to develop into an "internal ally," an internalized aid for recognizing personal stress levels. With practice, students are able to recognize and gauge personal stress in the moment, optimally making it second nature. Using the stress check before and after each relaxation exercise reinforces this cognitive processing technique for enhanced integration.

A stress check works best if conducted as a pre- and post-measurement to the relaxation exercises. The initial stress check (pre-test measurement) acts as the baseline for the relaxation exercise. Having students redo the stress check (post-test measurement) following the relaxation exercise gives them immediate feedback to cognitively assess the contrast between two internal states—subtle or pronounced—depending on the students' experience during the relaxation experience.

For instance, prior to the relaxation exercise, a student may determine that his or her current stress level on the continuum is a 7 (pre-measurement). Following the relaxation exercise, redo the stress check (post-measurement) as a contrast to the initial stress level identified. If the student determines he or she is a 4 on the post stress check measurement, he or she has reduced his or her stress level by 3 points.

Although this measurement is subjective, it is important feedback for students because the overall experience is a feeling of satisfaction (reward), signalling that they do, in fact, have the ability to reduce their own stress level.

Pre-Post Stress Measurement Equation

Pre-Relaxation Measurement – Post-Relaxation Measurement = Stress Reduction Score

Pre-Relaxation Exercise Measurement	7
Post-Relaxation Exercise Measurement	- 4
Stress Reduction Score	3

Stress Check Purpose

Students discover a quick and simple way to subjectively measure their stress level. As a self-assessment, the stress check can be done in the moment anywhere and at any time of day. Doing the pre- and post-stress check measurement exercise helps students take an active role in recognizing and reducing their own personal stress. The pre- and post-stress check can help students measure their success in reducing stress, a reward reinforcement that is an incentive to continue the process. The exercise teaches students to pause and encourages them

---

to do an internal assessment and possibly make an adjustment in behavior. The exercise is a cognitive processing technique to engage the brain with existing body tension.

The stress check is an applicable quantitative measurement for intrapersonal awareness and creating a safe school climate. Throughout the day, a student can apply a stress check self-assessment and identify his or her current level of stress. With this awareness, behavioral brakes can be applied, if necessary, giving the student more productive options (i.e., not "acting out" of the increased stress or off-balanced emotions).

For instance, if one wakes and identifies that his or her stress level is high, for whatever reason, the person has at least two choices: (1) the person can choose to ignore the high stress level and possibly have a negative rippling effect (act out a negative attitude) on others or (2) one can utilize some of the techniques provided in this track to assist in reducing his or her stress level. A reduction in stress will help shift attitude to one more peaceful and positive, increasing the odds that the person will have a positive rippling effect on others.

A stress check can also be helpful for recognizing low stress. If a student is having trouble getting motivated to do a task or project, he or she might actually need to increase his or her stress level. Deadlines, goals, target dates, even exercise can all be catalysts to light a fire and increase motivation.

For instance, if one wakes and identifies that his or her stress level is low (0-3), for whatever reason, the person could do some movement, exercise, or deep breathing to increase stress by increasing serotonin and endorphin levels to a more optimal level, possibly a 4-6, depending on the person, for peak performance.

In Track 3: "Understanding Stress," the bell curve illustrates low and high stress as performance killers. Striving to be totally "stress free" is a faulty notion because if we could accomplish this, we would not be able to hold ourselves upright; we would more closely resemble an amoeba. We do need a certain amount of stress in order to reach optimal performance levels. Mental focus and concentration, as well as the fluidity of physical movement are challenged during elevated stress. Determining what level of stress is necessary for optimal performance is subjective and takes practice. Recognizing that a certain amount of stress is necessary for peak performance requires life experience in situations that involve increased stress.

Awareness and practice of this simple technique helps students get clearer about stress as nuisance or stress as ally, working toward mastery of this internal asset building approach.

STRESS CHECK

0 1 2 3 4 5 **6 7 8 9 10**

Low Stress   **High Stress**

Relaxation Tip #2 Breath Check

Breath is vital to our existence. This fact is not earth shattering news for students. We can help them gain some perspective, however, by asking them the following questions:

- Who thinks breathing is an important thing to do? (Enjoy a good laugh together after this rhetorical question!)
- How long can we go without food? (The teen boys usually say they can go without food for only about two minutes.)
- How long can we go without water?
- How long can we go without breathing?

No matter how the students answer the first questions, their response to the last question is a much shorter amount of time. We can survive for just a short time without breathing. But just breathing enough to survive is not the point. The way we breathe is important—even critical—to our mental, emotional, and physical well-being.

Increased stress is often accompanied by anxiety, fear, and/or worry. A natural consequence to increased stress or distress is to breathe high or shallow into the upper chest. High or shallow breathing deprives oxygen to the brain which activates a warning signal in the most primitive part of the brain called the amygdala. If actual danger is present, this signal is vital for our survival and triggers the fight or flight response. Restricted or erratic breathing, which is high or shallow, accompanied by a hurried pace that feels like "life in fast forward" and can induce an increase in anxiety, fear, and worry even though an actual threat may not be present. In the extreme, these panic attacks can be very debilitating and affect a percentage of people.

If grandfather clocks are placed in the same room long enough, they will all begin to oscillate at the same cadence. The same holds true for a classroom of youth who at various times will collectively breathe in a shallow manner. This may occur prior to an exam, student presentations of a class project, after an incident on the playground, or something happening globally in the school environment that creates this "condition." The teacher can shift this class contagion by having the class pause from academic work to breathe low in an effort to decrease a level of collective anxiety that exists.

By psychologically—most likely unconsciously—creating crisis conditions even in the absence of threat, a physiological false positive is aroused. By simply breathing into the upper chest, the physiological fight or flight response is triggered in the body in the same way it is activated in an actual life threatening condition. These responses include increased muscle tension, sweaty palms, dry mouth, rapid pulse, elevated heart rate, and the release of a surge of adrenalin and dopamine, natural neurotransmitters which are fight or flight chemicals.

The implications of this false positive are significant. A lack of awareness of the source of personal stress accompanied by a lack of skills in managing this stress can unconsciously and unnecessarily cause an elevation in anxiety (high stress), causing a decrease in performance in all aspects of a person's life.

Worksheet 2

Relaxation Tip # 2

Breath Check

List three things that happen in the body when you take shallow breaths because of stress:

1. _____
_____
2. _____
_____
3. _____
_____

List three things you experience when you take slow deep breaths:

1. _____
_____
2. _____
_____
3. _____
_____
_____

"Smile, breathe, and go slowly."
THICH NHAT HANH

Conscious and intentional breathing is simply breathing low into the diaphragm or low abdomen. This low breathing—often called "belly breaths"—helps students increase serotonin levels and other calming chemicals to obtain a more relaxed state of being.

Breath and Spirituality

Theologian and storyteller John Shea has a wonderful story where he asks the question: What is the most important part of our body? Invite students to answer this question letting them know that all their answers are correct. The most common answers will be the soul, the heart, the mind. Thank them for their input.

Share with them that the most important part of their body for today is their nose! After the laughter has subsided, ask them why the nose might be the most important part of their body. Share that all answers are correct. The most important response will be "without breathing, we will die."

Then share Scripture verse, Genesis 2:7, "The Lord God formed man out of the clay of the ground and blew into his nostrils the breath of life, and so man became a living being."

This Scripture recalls the sacred touch of God's mouth to man's nostrils. Invite the students to sit up straight with their feet firmly on the ground. Have them close their eyes and breathe deeply through the nose. Now have them imagine God's mouth is blowing air into their nostrils filling their lungs with His breath. As they exhale, have them imagine they are breathing out God's love around the classroom, the school, the community, and the world.

Relaxation Tip #3 Tension Check

Everyone experiences tension in the body at various times throughout the day. During times of increased stress or distress these "tension spots" become more pronounced. Although highly subjective, tension spots are commonly reported to show up in such areas of the body

as the head, jaw, neck, shoulders, and low back. Becoming more attuned to the body by listening to our personal "stress cues" or "stress indicators" makes these tension spots important messengers, increasing awareness and helping us progress toward optimal performance.

If I am overly tight or tense (high stress), I will likely experience a decrease in performance. If I am overly loose (low stress), my performance may decrease as well. By tracking or listening to my tension spots I can also communicate with them to let go or get moving! If we ignore our tension spots or medicate them so they "go away," we are killing the messenger, a critical indicator that can help us gain insight and awareness about our body and performance.

We can train the body to become more aware of these tension spots by intentionally tensing and releasing body parts. Tensing a body part in an exaggerated way brings a focused attention to the body part. This focused attention helps the student recognize the sensations involved with tensing and releasing a specific body part. Holding tension with a body part for 10-20 seconds and then releasing or "letting go" the

---

Worksheet 3

Relaxation Tip # 3

Tension Check

List where your tension spots are located when you are stressed out:

1. _____

2. _____

3. _____

4. _____

5. _____

Communicate with your tension spots reminding them to let go....to loosen the grip.

"Tension is who you think you should be.
Relaxation is who you are."
CHINESE PROVERB

Peace Be With You
WORKBOOK

PHASE III 73
Pure of Heart

---

tension helps juxtapose the two physical states. This dramatic contrast gives students a discernible difference which they can consciously and unconsciously "record" for increased body awareness.

The "Tense and Release" exercises help students become more aware of physical stress. With practice, students notice more of where they have a tendency to hold physical stress—personal tension spots. These exercises are an important precursor to the Progressive Relaxation process on Track 8.

Relaxation Tip #4 Balance Check

In this exercise, the body can be used as a metaphor to demonstrate how our lives can get out of balance with increased stress. Allow students to feel the imbalance and juxtapose this with a more balanced pose. This will create awareness through "muscle memory." The balanced position is called the Mountain Pose in Yoga. Students can use this pose to align the body and "communicate" balance between the right and left hemispheres of the brain.

Emphasize during this metaphor that when our lives are out of balance, we are much more susceptible to illness, negative peer pressure, and poor academic and extracurricular performance. When balanced, we are more immune to illness and more likely to use good judgment.

Worksheet 4

Relaxation Tip # 4

Balance Check

- Stand tall with your feet shoulder width apart and toes pointing straight ahead.
- Place your arms and hands at your side. Feel the balance. This is base position.
- Lift one foot and then your entire leg to contrast balance and imbalance.
- Come back to base position.

List three things you will do to help yourself stay balanced:

1.
_____
_____

2.
_____
_____

3.
_____
_____

"Be aware of wonder. Live a balanced life—learn some and think some and draw and paint and sing and dance and play and work every day some."
ROBERT FULGHUM

74   **PHASE III**
Pure of Heart

Peace Be With You
WORKBOOK

Facilitator Script
Stress Check

TIME	PREPARATION & PROCESS	LOGISTICS
0:00	**Session Preparation**	**CD, iPod, or MP3 player needed**

Session Preparation
- Cue CD player or iPod to Track 5.
- Draw Stress Check continuum on board or use image on previous page.
- Student Workbook, p. 71.

Process

Say: *"Class, listen carefully to this audio track and write down your reflections of what you hear."* (Play Track 5, 6:02 minutes)

****

6:00 *"Class, turn to page 71 in your workbook to find the Stress Check."*

"Zero represents the lowest stress you've ever experienced and 10 represents the highest stress you've ever experienced."

Note. Only have students pick a Stress Check number if you plan to do the Short Meditation.

"Pick a number between 0 and 10 on this scale that best represents what your stress level is right now."

"Raise your hand when you have picked a number."

"Thank you!"

7:00 *"Do not share your number. Remember your number, because we will redo the Stress Check after one of the other exercises coming up."*

Note. Continue with Breath Check.

Breath Check

TIME	PREPARATION & PROCESS	LOGISTICS
0:00	**Session Preparation**	Post one or all of the following quotes as visuals in your classroom:

<table>
<tr><td></td><td>• None
• Student Workbook, p. 72</td><td></td></tr>
</table>

Process

"*When we are stressed out and feel anxious or worried we often breathe way up here.*" (With an open hand, motion across your upper chest.)

"*This is called high or shallow breathing. This kind of breathing releases what are called fight or flight chemicals that signal to the brain that we are in some danger.*"

"*Fight or flight is very important if there were actually a real danger present. If we were threatened by an animal, person, or a situation that could cause us harm, fight or flight is activated.*"

"*Fight or flight helps us run faster, jump higher, or do whatever we need to do to survive.*"

1:00 "*Most of the time we are very safe. When we breathe high or shallow because of stress it can trick our brain into believing there is danger and trigger fight or flight even though no danger is present. This creates even more stress!*"

"*This means that we can actually cause ourselves to feel stressed out, anxious, and worried when we really don't need to.*"

"*One of the things we can do to help reduce the stress is to practice proper breathing.*"

"*This is a slow, intentional breath that will help slow us down.*"

2:00 "*We call these belly breaths.*"

"*Place a hand on your belly and breathe in with me slow and low.*" As you say this, place one or two of your open hands on your low abdomen. "*Hold it....Hold it....Hold it....and exhale slowly and completely.*"

"*Take in another belly breath. Notice your hand rise with the inhalation. Now exhale noticing your hand fall as you breathe out.*"

LOGISTICS column:

"*Smile, breathe and go slowly.*"
-THICH NHAT HANH

"*Focusing on the act of breathing clears the mind of all daily distractions and clears our energy enabling us to better connect with the Spirit within.*"
-AUTHOR UNKNOWN

"*For breath is life, and if you breathe well you will live long on earth.*"
-SANSKRIT PROVERB

"If your hands do not rise and fall with your breath, it may mean that you are breathing high or shallow into the upper chest."

"Breathing low takes some practice, but I noticed that you all did very well with this."

3:00   *"Good!"*

4:00   *"Turn to page 72 in your workbook and take one minute to list your experiences to the Breath Check exercise."*

Note. Continue with Tension Check.

Tension Check

TIME	PREPARATION & PROCESS	LOGISTICS

0:00   **Session Preparation**

- None
- Student Workbook, p. 73

Students can stand or be seated for this activity.

Process

Say: *"When stressed we hold tension in different places in the body—like the jaw, shoulders, and low back."*

Post the following quotes as visuals in your classroom:

"If we ignore this tension, it can hurt our body and hurt our performance on test and in other activities."

"It's important to learn how to relax the body to help improve our performance on test, activities, and be more open to God."

"Tension is who you think you should be. Relaxation is who you are."
     -CHINESE PROVERB

"Let's train our body to know the difference between tension and relaxation."

"Hold your two hands straight out in front of you without bothering your neighbor." (Demonstrate as you say this.)

"If your teeth are clenched and your fists are clenched, your lifespan is probably clenched."
     -ADABELLA RADICI

1:00   *"Now make two fists and feel the tension in your hands."*

"Really exaggerate and hold the tension in your hands."

"Make a mental note: This is tension in my hands."

"Look at your fist. See and feel the tension."

"What do you notice as you look at your hands?"

Possible Responses: Hands and fingers are discolored. Feel a tingling sensation in hands. Hands get sweaty.

"Continue to look at your fists. Now, very slowly and gently open both hands—like a flower unfolding—notice the releasing sensation. Notice how your hands feel as you let go of the tension."

"Wiggle your fingers (hold two hands up palms out wiggling 10 fingers) *to exaggerate the release and freedom from the tension."*

2:00   *"Now say to yourself, 'This is relaxation!'"*

"What do you notice in your hands now?"

Possible Responses: Aaahhh! Better! Not so tight! More comfortable.

"This letting go sensation is relaxation! That's all relaxation is—it's just letting go!—loosening the grip!"

"Let's do another tension release exercise."

"Shrug your shoulders." Demonstrate as you say this.

3:00   *"Hold this tension in your neck and shoulders making a mental note that this is tension I am holding in my neck and shoulders."*

"Hold the shrug a little longer noticing the tension."

"What do you notice in your neck and shoulders?"

Possible Responses: Feel a tingling sensation. Feels uncomfortable.

"Now slowly and gently drop your shoulders to their normal base position and notice the releasing sensation. Observe how your neck and shoulders feel as you let go of the tension."

"Make a mental note: This is relaxation!"

"Gently roll your head from side to side allowing yourself to feel the freedom from the release of tension." Demonstrate as you say this.

4:00   *"Good job!"*

Optional. Have students tense the entire body from head to toe and then release. Discuss how this option compares with exercises one and two.

Note. Continue with Balance Check.

Balance Check

TIME	PREPARATION & PROCESS	LOGISTICS

Session Preparation

0:00
- Ensure students are physically safe while participating in this activity to help them safely understand the concept of balance vs. imbalance.
- Create an environment conducive to playfulness and learning.
- Make sure there is ample space between students.
- Determine if this activity will work in your classroom or another suitable space.
- Student Workbook, p. 74

Process

Say: *"Balance is like having both feet firmly planted on the ground while standing straight and tall."*

Note. If you have any students who cannot stand or for whom balancing may be a safety concern, include them in this exercise from a seated position. This will model inclusiveness to the class.

"Balance is also sitting up straight and tall with feet firmly planted on the floor."

Note. If able, facilitator demonstrates the balanced postures in both standing and seated positions.

2:00
"This is balance! (while demonstrating). *We call this 'base position,' which is both feet planted firmly, standing as straight as possible or for those that need to remain seated sitting up straight and tall with feet firmly planted on the ground."*

Note. Have students get into and practice base position.

3:00
"Allow yourself to quietly feel the strength and confidence of this posture." (Pause for a moment to allow students to experience base position. Suggest to students the option of closing their eyes to eliminate distractions and to connect fully.)

"Whenever you want to feel strength and confidence go to your base position."

"Stress is like lifting one foot off the floor."

(To students seated): *"Stress is like tilting your head to one side or the other."*

Note. If able, facilitator demonstrates the imbalance in both the standing and seated positions.

LOGISTICS

Arrange the classroom for an open space or for another space free of any hazardous obstacles.

If you are moving the class to another location allow for transition time.

4:00   *"Notice how lifting your foot is different from base position."*

"What do you notice?" Echo their responses.

Possible Responses: More stress on the leg holding up the other. Body shifts to the right or the left. Head feels heavier. Feel off balance.

5:00   *"Come back to base position."*

"How long can we realistically maintain one foot off the floor or keep our head tilted to one side?" (You will get a variety of responses).

6:00   *"If we had to keep our foot off the floor or our head tilted for a long period of time (a sustained stressful event), what would we do to adapt to this situation?"*

Possible responses: Hold on to something or someone. Lean to one side to physically adjust. Live with the discomfort/pain or try to get back to base position.

"Whatever the adjustment, there are many problems that could occur."

"What might some of these problems be?"

Possible responses: Relying on an object or person for support. Physical problems in parts of the body may show up. Turning to alcohol, tobacco, or other drugs to medicate the pain. Having to work harder to get back to base position, because of the accumulated stress.

8:00   *"What is the price we pay for ignoring our signs of stress?"*

Possible response: Things get worse, not better.

"Lift one foot/leg even higher off the floor and notice the difference between this and base position."

"Those of you that are seated tilt your head to one side along with your body and notice the difference between this and your base position."

"Increasing stress is like having to lift your foot higher off the ground or your body begins to move with the head."

10:00   *Note.* Allow students to safely struggle with the imbalance while you discuss this point for greater impact.

"Notice the difference between balance and being off balance."

"Come back to base position."

"This may not seem hard at first, but if we had to hold this position for a period of time it only gets harder."

"How is this like real life stress?" Echo their responses.

"We can't be out of balance very long before we start paying a price."

"The bigger the stress and the longer it lasts, the greater the price we pay."

12:00   *"This is why it is so important that we take care of ourselves everyday and do our best to maintain a balanced life!"*

"While you were off balance, would it be harder or easier for someone or something to push you over all the way?"

Expected Response: Very easy.

"Would it be harder or easier to push you over in base position?"

Expected Response: Harder.

13:00   *"When a person is off balance, what are some negative influences that might seep in?"*

Possible responses: Abuse of alcohol, tobacco, other drugs, peer pressure, more susceptible to colds, flu, infections, disease.

"In what physical position are we more prepared to deal with these outside influences?"

Expected response: Base position.

"Why?" Echo their responses.

14:00   *"When we are balanced in mind, body, and spirit, we are less susceptible to outside influences that can be harmful to us."*

"What does 'inoculation' mean?"
(If students do not know, have them look it up in the dictionary.)

"How can maintaining balance inoculate us from these outside influences?"

Possible responses: Boost the immune system, happier, less negative conflict, lower blood pressure, etc.

15:00   *"If you are feeling out of sorts on any given day, get into base position for a minute or so, to help yourself find balance."*

Activity Six

Short Meditation

(Track 6)

PURPOSE

To introduce students to a short meditation to increase awareness of how to access a peaceful place within to be more open and connected to God

LEARNING OBJECTIVES

- Students will practice relaxation and accessing a peaceful place within the self.
- Students will practice a quantitative Stress Check measurement.
- Students will practice increasing focus and attention.
- Students will practice activating their imagination by drawing a PeaceScape.
- Students will naturally be more compassionate with each other when in a relaxed state.

CORRESPONDING STUDENT WORKBOOK PAGE 75

- Journal Entry   1

Short Meditation
Journal your experience from the short meditation.

Journal Entry

Peace Be With You
WORKBOOK

PHASE III   75
Pure of Heart

Facilitator Script

Short Meditation

TIME	PREPARATION & PROCESS	LOGISTICS
0:00	**Session Preparation** • Cue CD player or iPod to Track 6. • Teacher is encouraged to listen to Track 6 prior to students. • Settle students before beginning to play Track 6. • Room lights should be dimmed or turned off if there is enough natural light. • Student Workbook, Journal Entry p. 75	**CD, iPod, or MP3 player needed**
	Process **Say:** *"Class. There are two important rules for this exercise:* • *Rule # 1: No talking.* • *Rule # 2: Do Not Disturb Your Neighbor."* *"Raise your hand if you agree to these rules."* *"Thank You."* *"Sit comfortably in your seats during this exercise."* *"Do not write during this exercise. Just relax and listen carefully to the audio track."*	
2:00	*"When the track is over sit quietly without talking, until I give you the next direction."* (Play Track 6, 12:27 minutes) ***	
15:00	*"Welcome back. Without talking, stand up. Stretch to the left. Stretch to the right."* (Demonstrate this or some other movement)	**Play gentle music of your choice as background.**

Activity Seven
Post-Meditation Stress Check
(Track 6)

PURPOSE
To reinforce successful meditation outcomes using a simple contrasting quantitative measurement

LEARNING OBJECTIVES
- Students will learn a practical quantitative measurement.
- Students will enhance critical thinking skills by contrasting pre and post Stress Check measurement.
- Students will build confidence by experiencing a successful outcome.

CORRESPONDING STUDENT WORKBOOK PAGE 76
- Student Worksheets   1

Worksheet 1

Redoing Your Stress Check
Pick a number that best represents your current stress level.

Stress Check number before the meditation   _____

Stress Check number after the meditation   _____
(Subtract the top number from the bottom number).

Current Stress Check number   _____

Give yourself a pat on the back for taking the time to "Stress Less!"

STRESS CHECK

0 1 2 3 4 5 6 7 8 9 10

Low Stress   **High Stress**

Post-Meditation Stress Check

TIME	PREPARATION & PROCESS	LOGISTICS

Session Preparation

0:00
- Post-Meditation Stress Check Measurement
- Have students redo the Stress Check following the meditation

Process

Say: *"Turn to page 76 in your workbook. Redo your Stress Check, picking a new number between 0 and 10 that best represents what your stress level is right now after the meditation."*

"Raise your hand when you have a new number."

"Thank you."

1:00 *"Now take the first number you came up with before the meditation and subtract it from your number after the meditation."*

"If I started the exercise at 7 and after the meditation I'm a 3, how many points did my stress level come down?"

Expected Response: Four.

2:00 *"Correct."*

"Raise your hand if you are able to subtract your first Stress Check number from your Stress Check number after the meditation?"

"Good!"

"How many points did you reduce your stress?"

3:00 Note. Listen for responses. Students will have a variety of numbers to share. Any one point is worth celebrating.

"Great! There is no right or wrong answer. These are your personal Stress Check numbers. Everyone did super at this exercise and with practice you will get better and better!"

PeaceScape
(Track 6)

PURPOSE
To encourage self expression, imagination, and positive images through art

LEARNING OBJECTIVES
- Students will draw their experience with the Short Relaxation.
- Students will creatively express positive images.
- Students will counterbalance negative images.

CORRESPONDING STUDENT WORKBOOK PAGES 77-78
- PeaceScape Drawing
- Student Worksheets   1

MATERIALS NEEDED
- CD player, iPod, or MP3 player
- Gentle background music of your choice
- White drawing paper or typing paper
- Colored pencils, crayons, or markers

PeaceScape Drawing

Worksheet 2

PeaceScape Sharing

Pair up with a partner.
Decide who will be the listener and who will be the speaker.
Switch when instructed to do so by your teacher.

Speaker: Show your PeaceScape to your partner.
Listener: Admire your partner's PeaceScape.
Speaker: Tell your partner about your PeaceScape. Share with your partner:

1. Why you used the colors you did in your PeaceScape?

2. What meaning do shapes or symbols hold in your PeaceScape?

3. If you drew human figures in your PeaceScape, who are they? Why did you put them in your PeaceScape?

4. During the meditation, who was surrounding you? Supporting you? Celebrating you?

5. How did they celebrate you?

6. What importance does a supportive circle of family and friends hold in your life?

7. Who supports you most in being the best person you can be?

8. How can you and your partner support each other?

9. Thank your partner for sharing.

10. Partners share what they learned with the class.

What Is a PeaceScape?

The term "PeaceScape" originated from the authors' belief that youth have the ability to actively create (imagine from the inside) peaceful images. The multitude of violent images that plague our youth can make us feel helpless and overwhelmed as we see the effects listed in the referenced studies. How can we possibly counteract such a barrage? How do we sensitize students to the pain of others? How do we help students feel safe in an unsafe world? How do we teach students that violence and disrespect are not the ways to resolve conflicts or get what one wants in life?

By engaging students in PeaceScape exercises, we can take a proactive step even if it is a small one—toward reinforcing nonviolent images. A PeaceScape is a way to counteract toxic, violent media input by activating and embracing nonviolent images. During relaxation and visual exercises, students often find a peaceful "place" and are open to visualizing safe, gentle, and serene mental images. Phase III provides opportunities for students to experience relaxation along with visual exercises in Tracks 6 and 8. Following these tracks, teachers are encouraged to use an art medium with students for them to create a PeaceScape.

Following a relaxation visualization exercise, students are encouraged to simply draw positive peaceful images from what they visualized during the exercise or from their current peaceful state. If a student is uncomfortable doing this through art form, journaling about the experience is another option. Although the objective of PeaceScape is to help students create a visual, writing is also an effective medium.

Either application will assist students in reinforcing and further integrating a vision for peace:

a safe and reverent school. Page 77 in the Student Workbook provides a space for students to draw or journal. PeaceScapes can be shared and hung in the classroom or halls. Have students complete the interactive pair and share, student worksheet on page 78 in their workbook.

Youth are in the early stages of developing the mental and emotional coping mechanisms necessary to internally censor these toxic messages and images. Much research exists on toxic media messages demonstrating convincing evidence that indicate these continual assaults on youth have very serious physical, mental, emotional, and spiritual implications.

Introducing youth to the idea of visualization is imperative for activating imagination, creativity, and critical thinking. Although visualization is natural, much of it occurs unconsciously. This phase helps youth become more conscious of the power of visualization. By helping students become more aware of how to visualize, we can increase opportunities to activate their imagination. Activities such as drawing, playing music, face-to-face communication, and reading actively stimulate brain function, increasing creativity and critical thinking. We must impress upon students the infinite power of the mind. Through visualization, also called imagery, we go beyond the limitations we often impose on our potential. We are only limited by our own imagination!

We must exercise our imagination just as we would exercise our bodies to train for an athletic contest. If we do not work our muscles, they become atrophied. The same holds true for our imagination. If we do not work our imaginations, they too will become atrophied. Visual exercises can help students with focus and concentration, as well as creating and accomplishing goals.

PeaceScape

TIME	PREPARATION & PROCESS	LOGISTICS
0:00	**Session Preparation** • Teachers are encouraged to create their own PeaceScape ahead of time following their own independent listening of Track 6 on the Peace2U Stress Less Series Audio CD (download). • Room lights are conducive to creative drawing. • Student Workbook, PeaceScape Drawing p. 77 and Worksheet 2 on p. 78.	CD, iPod, or MP3 player needed **White drawing paper or typing paper, colored pencils, crayons, or markers.** **Play gentle music of your choice.**

Process

"Turn to page 77 in your workbook and draw a picture of your peaceful meditation experience. Take 10 minutes to create your PeaceScape."

"This is a silent exercise."

****

10:0   *Note.* Teacher is to walk around the room noticing and admiring students' work.

"Time's up. All of you have created beautiful PeaceScapes!"

11:00   *"Stand up. Hold your creative work waist high. Now walk around the room admiring each others PeaceScapes."* (Teacher is encouraged to hold up his or her PeaceScape and walk around with students.)

"Stop. Now get into your pairs and follow directions on page 78 in your workbooks."

14:00   *"You have 3 minutes each. I will tell you when to switch."*

17:00   *"Stop. Switch. Speakers become listeners and listeners become speakers."*

18:00   *"Stop."*

"I will display your PeaceScapes (around the room, in the hall, other location) for us all to admire and appreciate for the next (week, month, etc.)."

Activity Nine

Put-Down Messages

(Track 7)

PURPOSE

To identify put-down messages from others and self-defeating messages in an effort to inoculate students from the damaging effects of these messages by replacing them with written expression and positive self-talk

LEARNING OBJECTIVES
- Students will write defeating messages other students have said about them.
- Students will identify and write personal self-defeating messages.
- Students will learn how to inoculate themselves from toxic messages.

CORRESPONDING STUDENT WORKBOOK PAGE 79
- Student Worksheets   1

Shift Formula

(Track 7)

PURPOSE

To boost self-image by making a shift from defeating self-talk to positive self-talk

LEARNING OBJECTIVES
- Students will learn how to deflect put-downs targeted at them and shift to positive messages.
- Students will learn how to shift from negative self-talk to positive self-talk.
- Students will understand how self-talk—positive and negative—affects thinking, feeling, and behavior.
- Students will contrast positive and negative self-talk.

CORRESPONDING STUDENT WORKBOOK PAGES 80-81
- Student Worksheets   2

Put-Down Messages & Shift Formula

TIME	PREPARATION & PROCESS	LOGISTICS
0:00	**Session Preparation** • Cue CD player or iPod to Track 7. • Student Workbook, pp. 79-81.	CD, iPod, or MP3 player needed
	Process **Say:** *"Class, listen carefully to this audio track and write down your reflections of what you hear."* (Hit the pause button after the first 1:36 minutes of Track 7)	
	***	
2:00	*"Stand up."* *"With your feet on the floor, try to touch the ceiling with your right hand. Stretch up with your right hand. Now your left hand. Stretch up with your left hand."* *"Good. Be seated."*	
3:00	*"Turn to page 79 in your workbook. You have 3 minutes to do this worksheet on put-downs. You may begin."* *"Stop."* *"What do you feel as you notice the negative messages said about you and negative messages you say about yourself?"* Possible Responses: Not good. Sad. Mad. They don't feel good. I don't like them. I wish I could get rid of them. *"Raise your hand if you'd like to get rid of these negative messages."*	Have students complete p. 79 in the Student Workbook after the first 1:36 minutes have played from Track 7.
8:00	Expected Response: All hands raised. *"Turn to page 80 in your workbook and look at how the Shift Formula is used to help you get rid of negative messages."*	
9:00	*"Write down the put-down messages on page 81 in the Obliterator column and replace them with Welcoming Messages to the right."* *"I want 5 people to stand one at a time and share their Shift Formula with us."* Note. Facilitator picks 5 students randomly to model the Shift Formula. *"Thank you!"*	Pages 80-81 Student Workbook: Worksheet 2, Shift Formula

"Look over the faulty messages you wrote down on page 81 one last time."

"Tear out page 81 in your workbook."

"Let go of all your negative messages with one of these fun and safe ways. As you do, say to yourself or out loud, 'I'm letting go of all my negative messages now!' You can:
- *Make an airplane and fly it around the room and into the waste-basket.*
- *Rip up the paper and toss it into the air and then pick up the pieces and toss them in the wastebasket.*
- *Wad up the paper and toss into the wastebasket."*

Note. Allow 2 minutes for this letting go exercise and clean up.

The Shift Formula was inspired by the Prayer of St. Francis of Assisi, which can be found on p. 30 of the student workbook.

Place options on a Smart Board, flip chart, poster board or any other way you desire

---

Shift Formula

Recognize the negative words or phrases you hear playing in your head.

Obliterate the unwanted messages using an "Obliterator Word" you will remember such as *Delete, Clear, Let go, Erase, Shake, Give up* or make up your own "Obliterator Word."

Replace the unwanted message choosing a "Welcoming Word" you will remember such as *Repeat, Hear, Know, Replace, Make, Receive* or make up your own "Welcoming Word."

Repeat the desired message over and over until you believe the message.

Here are some examples:

Obliterator Words............Shift to............Welcoming Words			
Delete	*doubts*	Repeat	*"I am confident."*
Clear	*"I'm not good enough."*	Hear	*"I am good enough."*
Let go	*"I'm not lovable."*	Know	*"I am lovable."*
Erase	*"I can't do it."*	Replace	*"I can do it."*
Shake	*bad decisions*	Make	*good decisions*
Give up	*put-downs*	Receive	*put-ups*

Use the next page to fill in your "Obliterator" and "Welcoming Words."

Worksheet 2

Shift Formula

Recognize the negative words or phrases you hear playing in your head.

Obliterate the unwanted messages using an "Obliterator Word" you will remember such as *Delete, Clear, Let go, Erase, Shake, Give up* or make up your own "Obliterator Word."

Replace the unwanted message choosing a "Welcoming Word" you will remember such as *Repeat, Hear, Know, Replace, Make, Receive* or make up your own "Welcoming Word."

Repeat the desired message over and over until you believe the message.

Use the "Obliterator" and "Welcoming Word" that works for you:

Obliterator Words............Shift to............Welcoming Words			
Delete	_____	Repeat	_____
Clear	_____	Hear	_____
Let go	_____	Know	_____
Erase	_____	Replace	_____
Shake	_____	Make	_____
Give up	_____	Receive	_____

Use this formula often to change negative thoughts into positive thoughts!

Crafting a Positive Affirmation

(Track 7)

PURPOSE

To help students integrate a sustainable shift from cognitions that interfere with academic and extracurricular success

LEARNING OBJECTIVES

- Students will learn how to craft a positive affirmation statement.
- Students will learn how to craft a positive affirmation statement that is relevant to them.
- Students will learn how to craft a positive affirmation statement that creates a lasting shift in consciousness.

CORRESPONDING STUDENT WORKBOOK PAGES 84-85

- Student Worksheets   2

Worksheet 1

Crafting a Positive Affirmation

Follow these six guidelines for crafting a positive affirmation.

1. Write a positive affirmation. Keep it short and simple. Check out the examples on the next page if needed.

2. Use positive words of encouragement.

3. Write the affirmation in two ways, first using "I" and then using "you."

4. Include a positive emotion.

5. Phrase the affirmation as fact.

6. Say, write, or sing your affirmation frequently.

_____

_____

_____

_____

_____

_____

_____

_____

_____

Positive Affirmation Examples

I am safe and at peace in my body.
You are safe and at peace in your body.

I am special and celebrate my uniqueness.
You are special and celebrate your uniqueness.

I am positive in my attitude.
You are positive in your attitude.

I am good enough.
You are good enough.

I am confident and capable of making good decisions.
You are confident and capable of making good decisions.

I accept the feelings I have in any given moment as my inner truth.
You accept the feelings you have in any given moment as your inner truth.

I speak up for myself.
You speak up for yourself.

I am surrounded by loving-kindness.
You are surrounded by loving-kindness.

I am treating problems as opportunities to grow in wisdom and love.
You are treating problems as opportunities to grow in wisdom and love.

I am worthy of all the good in my life.
You are worthy of all the good in your life.

I am imaginative and creative.
You are imaginative and creative.

I am confident my future is bright and promising.
You are confident your future is bright and promising.

I celebrate my accomplishments.
You celebrate your accomplishments.

I am patient and tolerant of differences in others.
You are patient and tolerant of differences in others.

I surround myself with people who support me in making healthy choices.
You surround yourself with people who support you in making healthy choices.

I am loved and accepted as I am.
You are loved and accepted as you are.

I am capable of being a great thinker.
You are capable of being a great thinker.

I am grateful for my life.
You are grateful for your life.

I am strong in my faith.
You are strong in your faith.

Affirmations

On a regular daily basis, there is a "little nagging voice" in the back of our minds that has something negative to say about ourselves, something, or someone. This negative voice is just that, negative! These repeated messages are like taped recordings being played over and over again in our heads, and they are difficult to turn off.

At an early age, we were most likely told either verbally or nonverbally, that we couldn't or shouldn't do certain things, such as climb on the furniture, stick objects in our noses or ears, touch hot stoves, eat worms, hit siblings, jump on or off beds, play in or near streets, etc. All parents have a responsibility to protect their children from these safety concerns. Even if parents respond in a loving and nurturing way, the child naturally perceives any approach as a rebuff to his or her natural curiosity.

Because there are normal, healthy, and boundless amounts of curiosity in children, parents spend considerable time correcting (protecting) their children. Children need to internalize these limits to discern safe from unsafe and right from wrong. At the same time, they are internalizing a form of rejection. A child's little brain is only capable of "decoding" parental controls in two ways: (1) To decide there is something wrong with me or (2) to decide there is something wrong with these big people in my life. It is possible that a child could perceive some things the first way and other things the second way.

If we hear something and perceive something about ourselves often enough, we tend to believe it, making "it" difficult to overcome. Some of these messages have to be positive in order for us to survive and thrive. Because of this parental "right steering," however, there is a tendency to reinforce these "negative messages" in our heads throughout our lives. The messages may even become "safe" because they are familiar.

What we habitually say to ourselves has a very profound impact on our self-image, self-esteem, self-confidence, relationships, academic and extracurricular performance, overall well-being, and eventual success. Negative self-talk communicates specific messages to our subconscious mind, which in turn triggers physiological responses to match the images and thoughts we have of our self to make them happen. Unfortunately, it is estimated that 70% or more of self-talk is negative (Gleick, 1999). Negative self-talk can wreak havoc on how we think about our self and others, feel about our self and others, and behave toward our self and others. It also increases fear, self-doubt, and other "negative emotions," which increase stress, reduce confidence (self-defeating behaviors), decrease motivation, and drain our energy.

As an educator, you probably have heard students say things like, "I can't do that....I'll never be able to do that...They're better than me at that....Why can't I do that?" It is normal and natural for us to have doubts, even as adults, when we try something new. What matters is what we say to ourselves when doubts creep in. Do we just quit and cave into the message of doubt? Do we wrestle with the message for a while and eventually cave in because the message is stronger than we are? Or do we say words of support and encouragement to help subside the messages of doubt? We've probably done all of the above.

Remember *The Little Engine That Could*? There have been numerous versions of this classic story, but it is believed to have originated by an unknown author in 1906, in a book titled, *Thinking One Can*. The story reappeared in 1910 in the Kindergarten Review as *The Pony Engine*, written by Mary C. Jacobs (1877-1970).

Although the story has been told and retold many times for more than a hundred years, the central theme remains the same. A little blue engine is willing, when other larger engines built to haul large loads refused, to try hauling a long train up and over a mountain to its destination. In order to accomplish the task, she repeats the mantra: "I think I can. I think I can. I think I can." When she reaches the summit of the mountain and begins to descend, she exclaims, "I thought I could. I thought I could. I thought I could!" Her optimism helps her overcome a seemingly impossible task.

The little blue engine had to have very serious and overwhelming doubts that she could carry this kind of load up and over a mountain. Her optimistic and encouraging words (self-talk) align her positive thinking with positive feelings, which propel her courageous behavior (small action steps) toward the desired result and completed state—overcoming difficult odds to arrive at the destination. By repeating the same words or mantra, she is able to counteract her doubt and communicate with the subconscious that this feat, though difficult, is doable.

This mantra is similar to a positive affirmation statement. By repeating this statement over and over, we can encourage our brain to see or visualize the task progressing from current reality (where the task begins) to accomplishing the desired result (completing the task). By repeating the positive self-esteem affirmation, "I think I can. I think I can. I think I can," the little blue engine activated positive images which communicated a powerful message to her little engine brain that, in turn, triggered a physiological reaction that became her "fuel" (motivation) to propel her up and over the mountain.

What Is a Positive Affirmation?

A positive affirmation is a short, positive, self-affirming declaration that describes a desired result or completed state. Affirmations are encouraging words or self-talk, purposeful, and repeated sayings to the self that are helpful, optimistic, accepting, loving, and reassuring. Affirmations are statements you would use to put-up a family member or a friend. By barraging yourself with these "mental bumper stickers" and by taking small steps toward the desired result, this practice will slowly erase the old mindset and craft a new outlook.

Positive affirmations are a type of auto-suggestion or self-hypnosis whereby a person trains the unconscious mind into believing something (a desired result) and brings about a shift from negative thinking and behavior to positive thinking and behavior. The affirmation may not be true now, but it is something one wants to be true in the future. For example, an affirmation may be: "I am my ideal weight." If not currently true, the person is informing his or her subconscious that this is where he or she wants to be, which encourages the self to align thinking and behavior accordingly.

By reminding ourselves to celebrate our abilities, talents, accomplishments, and strengths on a daily basis, we positively reinforce healthy and optimistic thinking about our self and others and optimistic actions toward our self and others. This increases positive emotions, which will decrease stress and increase confidence, motivation, and energy. Through the use of this track, students can learn the "secret" of how to get a boost in these areas by developing and practicing positive affirmations.

The three main purposes of an affirmation statement are:

1. To challenge, counteract, and override negative self-talk
2. To communicate a more optimistic view of the self to the subconscious mind.
3. To eventually come to believe the positive affirmation and accomplish the desired result.

Sometimes students do not fully understand how we are interdependent with each other. This is one of the prime reasons for having students do the "Buddy Up" exercise. When introducing "Buddy Up" you can share the following optional story. Using humor is engaging and can convey important truths. Before we can love God and neighbor fully, we must love ourselves, which comes with the responsibility of self-love, self-care, and self-empowerment.

Interconnectedness, interdependency, and unity are lead words into the traditional words of oneness, "many parts, yet one Body," and the dogma: Body of Christ. The Mystical Body of Christ as written in 1 Corinthians 12:12, and Romans 12:4, emphasizes that we are many different parts, yet we affect the one body of which we are a part. From Phase II, students clearly understand the negative rippling effect bullying has on the group. With meditation, we need to help them understand that their inner work of reducing stress and caring for self likewise have rippling effects. Self-care will lead to positive rippling effects within as well as with all those with whom they surround themselves.

Guidelines for Crafting a Positive Affirmation

1.
Personalize the Affirmation Using the Words "I" and "You"

When researching the affirmations track for the *Peace2U Stress Less Series* Audio CD, the author found Louise Hay's *Self-Esteem Affirmations* CD to be extremely helpful. In her CD, Louise uses a process called the "I/You method." Track 7 on *Peace2U* contains 20 affirmations using this method.

When a child hears a negative statement from an adult, he or she has little choice but to internalize the statement. When the child hears or "intuits" that he or she is doing something wrong or being "bad," the child internalize these statements in the first person: "I am unlovable, I am bad, I am not wanted, I am dirty, I am messy, I am undeserving, I am a burden," etc. In the third person, the child internalizes "you are unlovable, you are bad, you are unwanted, you are dirty, you are messy, you are undeserving, you are a burden," etc. In order for a positive affirmation to fully counteract the negative internalized message, the positive affirmation has to come from both the "I" and the "You" (the first and third person).

2.
Keep the Affirmation Short, Simple, and in the Present Tense

By keeping the affirmation short, it is easy to remember. By keeping it simple, it is less convoluted and more believable. An affirmation in the present tense is stated in a way that already accomplishes the desired result. For example, rather than a statement like, "When I get good grades I will be smart," my affirmation could be "I am smart. You are smart."

3.
Use Words of Encouragement

Make sure that all the words used in the affirmation are positive. Rather than "I will do well on the test even if I am nervous," say "I am confident and calm about taking this test. You are confident and calm about taking this test."

4.
Include a Positive Emotion

Negative messages are usually paired with intense negative emotions. In order to successfully counteract these negative messages, use a positive emotion or phrase that triggers a positive emotion. This strengthens the affirmation. For example, "My goals matter and excite me."

5.
Phrase Affirmations as Fact

Phrase an affirmation as though it is happening even if you have not achieved it yet. The subconscious believes mental messages and works to make them a reality. For example rather than "I can become happy," say "I am happy....You are happy."

6.
Say, Write, or Sing
the Affirmation Frequently

Repeating the affirmation daily enhances self-confidence, acts as a reminder, and stimulates the subconscious to make the affirmation a reality. Say the affirmation to yourself silently and out loud in the mirror while making good eye contact. Also, say the affirmation out loud to others. This raises the emotional intensity and acts as a commitment to those that have heard it. Writing the affirmation helps integrate it by adding the visual sensory input. You can also post the affirmation on a Post-it note and place it in a helpful location. Advertisements use jingles to help us remember products and to increase brand loyalty. Create a fun affirmation jingle that you can sing to yourself or out loud.

Positive Affirmation Examples

I am safe and at peace in my body.
You are safe and at peace in your body.

I am special and celebrate my uniqueness.
You are special and celebrate your uniqueness.

I am confident and capable of making good decisions.
You are confident and capable of making good decisions.

I am positive in my attitude.
You are positive in your attitude.

I am good enough.
You are good enough.

I accept the feelings I have in any given moment as my inner truth.
You accept the feelings you have in any given moment as your inner truth.

I speak up for myself.
You speak up for yourself.

I am surrounded by loving-kindness.
You are surrounded by loving-kindness.

I am treating problems as opportunities to grow in wisdom and love.
You are treating problems as opportunities to grow in wisdom and love.

I am worthy of all the good in my life.
You are worthy of all the good in your life.

I am imaginative and creative.
You are imaginative and creative.

I am confident my future is bright and promising.
You are confident your future is bright and promising.

I celebrate my accomplishments.
You celebrate your accomplishments.

I am patient and tolerant of differences in others.
You are patient and tolerant of differences in others.

I surround myself with people who support me in making healthy choices.
You surround yourself with people who support you in making healthy choices.

I am loved and accepted as I am.
You are loved and accepted as you are.

I am capable of being a great thinker.
You are capable of being a great thinker.

I am grateful for my life.
You are grateful for your life.

I am strong in my faith.
You are strong in your faith (DiLallo, 2001).

Crafting a Positive Affirmation

TIME	PREPARATION & PROCESS	LOGISTICS
0:00	**Session Preparation** • Have CD player or iPod cued to Track 7. • Student Workbook, pp. 84-85	CD, iPod, or MP3 player needed
	Process **Say:** *"Class, listen carefully to the affirmation statements on the audio track. Do not write anything for this part of the track."* (Press play and play the remainder of Track 7, 11:10 minutes) **	
12:00	*"Stand up."* *"Stretch to your right. Stretch to your left. Stretch forward. Stretch backward."* *"Good. Be seated."*	Have students complete p. 84 in the Student Workbook when Track 7 is over.
13:00	*"Turn to page 84 in your workbook on Crafting a Positive Affirmation and begin writing an affirmation for yourself."* *"The affirmations your heard on the audio track are in your workbooks on page 85 for you to refer to as examples."* *"I will be coming around to help and answer questions."* *"You have 10 minutes to craft your own affirmation."*	Affirmation examples are on page 85 in the Student Workbook.
23:00	*"Stop."* *"I want 10 people to stand and share their affirmation statement with us."* *Note.* Facilitator picks 10 students randomly to share their affirmation statement with the class. *"Thank you!"* *"Good work everyone!"*	
33:00	*"Copy your affirmation on a Post-it note and stick it on a place where you will be sure to remind yourself to look at it and say it often."*	

Activity Eleven
Strength Bombardment
(Track 7)

PURPOSE
To help students see Christ within by actively and inclusively noticing each others' gifts and talents to promote a Christ-centered environment

LEARNING OBJECTIVES
- Students will practice seeing Christ within others by speaking their truth about others' gifts and talents.
- Students will feel affirmed, supported, and celebrated by their classmates.
- Students will practice reverence by honoring each student.
- Students will practice listening and receiving supportive feedback.
- Students will practice writing supportive feedback.

CORRESPONDING STUDENT WORKBOOK PAGE 86
- Student Worksheets   1

Buddy Up!
(Track 7)

PURPOSE
To partner students with classmates they are least likely to affirm, generating greater community compassion to more deeply promote a Christ-centered environment

LEARNING OBJECTIVES
- Students will step out of their comfort zones by actively bridging divisions.
- Students will practice seeing Christ within classmates they usually dismiss or exclude.
- Students will practice reverence through inclusion and by honoring each student.
- Students will practice listening and receiving supportive feedback from classmates they are unaccustomed to receiving support from.
- Students will practice writing supportive feedback from classmates they are unaccustomed to supporting.

CORRESPONDING STUDENT WORKBOOK PAGE 87
- Student Worksheets   1

Strength Bombardment & Buddy Up!

TIME	PREPARATION & PROCESS	LOGISTICS
0:00	**Session Preparation** Arrange seats in a circle.	Total time is based on 30 students at 20 seconds each. Time will vary with class size. Include 20 seconds for each facilitator.

Process

Say: *"Class, it's really easy to put others and even ourselves down, but it is hurtful and damaging as we have learned."*

"I want it to be safe for us to build each other up by supporting and celebrating each other."

"One way we can help build each other up is through put-ups."

1:00 *"When we put each other up, we feel better about ourselves and we build respect and trust with others, which makes it safer for everyone."*

"We're also practicing positive leadership."

"Just like anything else, to improve in school, sports, music, dance, etc., we have to work at it by practicing over and over what it is we want to get better at."

"We are going to practice putting each other up today, so we can get better and better at it."

2:00 *"Go around spending 20 seconds with everyone in the circle, telling them what we admire and appreciate about them, gifts and talents we see, how they inspire us, the positive leader we see in them, and so on."*

"I'll be time keeper and will say 'Stop' at the end of the 20 seconds and 'Begin' to start with the next person in the circle."

3:00 *"Let's start to my left with (Student Name). Begin."*

Note. Continue around the circle until every student has had their 20 seconds.

****

"Good job! I feel good and encouraged by this put-up practice and want to see and hear more of it outside of our circle."

13:00 *"Turn to page 86 in you workbooks and write for one minute all the put-ups your heard about yourself during your 20 seconds."*

"I would encourage you to place the put-ups you've just written down in your leadership folder or in a place where you can refer to them often."

"Look around the room. Pick a person you would least likely give put-ups to."

14:00 *"Go to that person and sit next to him or her."*

"This is your buddy for Buddy Up!"

"For the next week, starting today you are responsible for putting up your buddy at least once a day for one week."

"You can share a put-up with your buddy by saying the put-up, writing the put-up, or posting the put-up on our new 'Buddy Up Board.'"

"Write down the put-up you hear or the put-up action in your leader folder."

Teachers are encouraged to create a space in the classroom for a "Buddy Up Board."

"Clap once. Clap twice. Clap three times!"

15:00 *"Great job! I notice everyone working hard to treat each other like a 10 and to create a safe and respectful school."*

Worksheet 2

Strength Bombardment

List five things you heard your classmates say to put you up:

1.
2.
3.
4.
5.

How did this make you feel to hear these things from your classmates?

_____
_____
_____

How did it feel to give your classmates put-ups?

_____
_____
_____

When you heard these things did it move your Safety Check number closer to a 10? Why?

_____
_____
_____

List three things you will do to help keep put-ups going in your class and in your school.

1.
2.
3.

Worksheet 3

Buddy Up!

My buddy's name is: _____

Five things I learned about my Buddy Up! buddy are:

1.
2.
3.
4.
5.

Three things my Buddy Up! buddy learned about me are:

1.
2.
3.

Write about what you learned about yourself because you participated in Buddy Up!

_____
_____
_____
_____
_____
_____
_____

Activity Twelve

Long Meditation

(Track 8)

PURPOSE
To provide an extended meditation to more deeply access a peaceful place within to be fully open to God's presence

LEARNING OBJECTIVES
- Students will practice an "inner retreat" meditation to access a peaceful place within themselves.
- Students will practice a quantitative Stress Check measurement.
- Students will practice increasing focus and attention.
- Students will practice activating their imagination.
- Students will naturally be more compassionate with each other when in a relaxed and peaceful state.

CORRESPONDING STUDENT WORKBOOK PAGE 88
- Journal Entry   1

Progressive Relaxation

Edmund Jacobson is considered the founder of progressive relaxation with his published book by the same name in 1929, following 20 years of research. He was able to demonstrate the connection between muscle tension and various disorders in the body (ulcers, insomnia, and hypertension) including anxiety. Jacobson proved tension affected the central nervous system functioning causing such disorders, while the contrary state of relaxation was the remedy. He argued that since anxiety is accompanied by muscular tension, one can reduce anxiety by learning how to relax the muscular tension. The technique involves systematically tensing and then relaxing specific muscle groups throughout the body. The desired result of this process is to put oneself in a state of total relaxation.

In order to achieve a relaxed state, progressive relaxation exercise commonly focuses on 16 areas: hands, biceps, triceps, shoulders, neck, mouth, tongue, eyes, breathing, back, buttocks, thighs, stomach, calves, feet, and toes.

Progressive Relaxation Exercises

1. Hands
The fists are tensed; relaxed. The fingers are extended; relaxed.

2. Biceps
The biceps are tensed (make a muscle—but shake your hands to make sure you are not tensing them into a fist); relaxed (drop your arm to the chair).

3. Triceps
The triceps are tensed (try to bend your arms the wrong way); relaxed (drop them).

4. Shoulders
Pull them back (careful with this one); relax them. Push the shoulders forward (hunch); relax.

5. Neck (lateral)
With the shoulders straight and relaxed, the head is turned slowly to the right, as far as you can; relax. Turn to the left; relax.

6. Neck (forward)
Dig your chin into your chest; relax. (Bringing the head back is not recommended because you could break your neck.) Turn your head slowly to the right, as far as you can; relax. Turn to the left; relax.

7. Mouth
The mouth is opened as far as possible; relaxed. The lips are brought together or pursed as tightly as possible; relaxed.

8. Tongue (extended and retracted)
With mouth open, extend the tongue as far as possible; relax (let it sit in the bottom of your mouth). Bring it back in your throat as far as possible; relax.

9. Tongue (roof and floor)
Dig your tongue into the roof of your mouth; relax. Dig it into the bottom of your mouth; relax.

10. Eyes
Open them as wide as possible (furrow your brow); relax. Close your eyes tightly (squint); relax. Make sure you completely relax the eyes, forehead, and nose after each tensing.

11. Breathing
Take as deep a breath as possible and then take a little more; let it out and breathe normally for 15 seconds. Let all the breath in your lungs out and then a little more; inhale and breathe normally for 15 seconds.

12. Back
With shoulders resting on the back of the chair, push your body forward so that your back is arched; relax. Be very careful with this one or don't do it at all.

13. Buttocks
Tense the buttocks tightly and raise pelvis slightly off chair; relax. Dig buttocks into chair; relax.

14. Thighs
Extend legs and raise them about 6 inches off the floor or the foot rest, but don't tense the stomach; relax. Dig your feet (heels) into the floor or foot rest; relax.

15. Stomach
Pull in the stomach as far as possible; relax completely. Push out the stomach or tense it as if you were preparing for a punch in the gut; relax.

16. Calves and feet
Point the toes (without raising the legs); relax. Point the feet up as far as possible (beware of cramps—if you get them or feel them coming on, shake them loose); relax.

17. Toes
With legs relaxed, dig your toes into the floor; relax. Bend the toes up as far as possible; relax.

Track 8 will guide you and your class through a progressive relaxation exercise. Although the audio exercise will not look exactly like the focus areas above, it will utilize many of the same muscle groups. Students can actually tense the body part mentioned during the exercise or just notice the tension that exists in the body part and release this tension. Both options will accomplish the desired effect.

Long Meditation

TIME	PREPARATION & PROCESS	LOGISTICS
0:00	**Session Preparation** • Cue CD player or iPod to Track 8. • Listen to Track 8 prior to exercise. • If acceptable, permit students to lie down on carpeted floor and bring in a head pillow for this exercise. • Room lights dimmed or off if there is enough natural light. • Settle students and begin playing Track 8. • Student Workbook, Journal Entry p. 88.	**Students sit quietly at their desks. Students are encouraged to lie down on the floor, but can opt to remain seated.**

Process

Say: *"Class. There are two important rules for this exercise:*
Rule # 1: No talking.
Rule # 2: Do Not Disturb Your Neighbor."

"Raise your hand if you agree to these rules."

"Thank You."

"The track you are about to hear is similar, but longer than the first meditation."

"Sit comfortably in your seats or you can find a place on the floor to lie down."

1:00 *"Do not write during this exercise. Just relax and listen carefully to the audio track."*

"When the track is over sit quietly without talking, until I give you the next direction." (Play Track 8, 28:54 minutes)

****

30:00 *"Welcome back. Without talking, stand up. Stretch to the left. Stretch to the right."* (Demonstrate this or some other movement.) **Play gentle music of your choice in the background.**

"Good job everyone. I see and feel God's Peace in all of you."

"You have two options now. Option #1 is to draw a PeaceScape from this meditation practice or Option #2 is to journal about your meditation experience in your Leadership Folder."

"Those of you choosing to draw a PeaceScape, take out paper and colored pencils and begin drawing."

"Those of you choosing to write, take out your workbooks and begin writing on page 88."

45:00 *"Do these activities in silence. You have until the end of the period."*

Teacher and Counselor Reflection

The authors are confident teacher attitude plays a major role in classroom behavior and classroom management. This will be reflected in managing your time, nurturing yourself, and finding collegial and spiritual support for your vocation. We would like to call your attention to two resources that might be of help as you continue your successful faith journey to nurture and sustain yourself and your vocation:

Sustaining the Spirit: Calling, Commitments & Vocational Challenges
by Catherine Cronin Coratta & Michael Carotta, 2005, Twenty-Third Publications

The Work of Your Life: Sustaining the Spirit to Teach, Lead & Serve
by Catherine Cronin Coratta, 2003, Harcourt Religion Publications

Do acknowledge your hard work and dedication, not only with the program, but with all that you do in service of the Church. Undoubtedly, a great deal of transformation has occurred in your classroom and possibly even within you. The hand of God has touched many. Hopefully, He has touched you as well. Your personhood, presence, and professionalism are a true gift for your students and to the school you serve. Honor yourself as you soak in the title of peacemaker and take in God's blessing as the Beatitude says: "Blessed are the peacemakers, you shall be called children of God."

With that being said, we extend to you a personal invitation to take time for yourself by recalling your journey with your students through Phases I, II, and III. Spend some quiet time in reflection and to journal significant moments during the process. Take time to still yourself. Take some deep cleansing breaths. The oxygen in our atmosphere has been cleansed over millions of years. This same oxygen has been taken into the lungs of all humanity throughout time. Imagine one of the molecules of air that was once in the lungs of Jesus is now in your lungs filling you up with His love and peace. We are all connected through His glorious creation of Mother Earth! Sense His connection and listen to His gentle voice, as He calls you by the name only He knows for you!

Peace be with you!

Appendix A
Peace2U Stress Less Series Audio CD Track Scripts

Track 1:   Introduction Script (2:11)

Here's what you'll find on the tracks coming up:

On the next track—Track 2—I share some thoughts about living in today's world and how it is a set-up for stress in our lives.

On Track 3, I'll help you understand what the word "stress" means.

On Track 4, you can listen to a short story titled, "The Gift."

On Track 5, you'll find some helpful tips on preparing yourself and your environment for relaxation. In order for you to get the most out of the meditations on this CD, listen to track 5 at least once, then refer back to it whenever you want, to help you improve on the relaxation skills.

Track 6 is a relaxation meditation for those of us on the go. It's designed for those times when we are not able to fit the full meditation on Track 8 into our schedules.

On Track 7, affirmations are provided to build your confidence and help you feel good about yourself.

On Track 8, you will find the longer relaxation meditation and guided imagery, which is lots of fun. If you allow yourself to experience this track on a daily basis or even several times a week, I know your confidence and concentration level will increase. As a result you may find you're not struggling as much to get your grades up or to maintain the grades you want. Your relationships at home and school may improve. You may also find your performance improving in extracurricular activities, such as, sports, speech and debate, or band.

Track 2: Living in "Fast Forward" (5:19)

Technology was originated to save time and money, therefore, creating more leisure time for us. It certainly has many advantages. For instance, the creation of this CD could not have happened without the availability of technology. There is a downside, though, to technology at which experts have only just begun to look.

Our culture operates on billionths of a second. We are constantly being pushed to do more and more, at an overwhelming pace. Our bodies and brains are not really set up to handle the speed at which information and life situations are pushed on us. We are constantly rushing to classes, meetings, and practices. Having a relaxed meal with family rarely happens anymore. We are skipping meals or hurrying to a fast food restaurant for something on the "fly."

This pace is so easy to get caught up in that we are not always aware of the toll it takes on the body, mind, and spirit. The stress caused by this accelerated pace of life makes us very susceptible to poor health, poor decision-making, angry outbursts, poor academic performance, relationship problems, poor athletic performance, and so on. It's easy to get out of balance!

When our unmanaged stress becomes too severe or extreme, our bodies physically force us to slow down. This may show up in the form of some physical ailments including: headaches, pain in the lower back, neck, shoulders or jaw. We may also experience difficulty breathing, stomach problems or sleeping problems. Even more seriously, stress may show up as a disease, be it short term or terminal. Whatever ailment shows up in the body is a message telling us about our lifestyle and ourselves. What message is your body sending you?

Life in "Fast-Forward" sets us up to accept only rapid results and quick fixes. Our society thrives on immediate gratification! We want to feel good fast. We get frustrated easily and don't want to take the time needed to learn a new skill, a musical instrument or read a book.

If we don't give ourselves time to build inner strength, the "Fast Forward" pace makes us very susceptible to negative peer influences, and we may have trouble resisting temptations such as consuming alcohol, tobacco, or other drugs and giving into sexual advances. Any one of these quick fixes will give us a false sense of confidence or happiness. This is similar to a stone that looks like gold, but is really "fools" gold. It's not worth anything to anyone. When we take the necessary time to take care of ourselves and put balance in our lives, we will find true happiness and realize our full potential. This is the "real gold!"

We are constantly bombarded with advertisements and commercials that play on our insecurities, making us believe we cannot fully be ourselves unless we are wearing certain designer clothes or driving a certain make of car. This "billboard" attitude that "looks are every thing" and "more is better," is plastered everywhere throughout our lives. People make career decisions based on how much money the job will pay, instead of seeking work for personal satisfaction. All of these beliefs and attitudes cause us to feel stress and never feel satisfied or pleased with ourselves. Professionals are seeing more and more depression and even suicidal thoughts or attempts among young people because of this kind of pressure. This CD is one way for you to take the pressure off yourself. It should in no way be used to replace medical or professional psychological help.

Surround yourself on a daily basis with peers and adults who treat you well in their words and actions. Choose people to be in your life who will encourage you to be your best and accept you as you are. Do something to change your "Fast Forward" pace! I encourage you to slow down in a natural and healthy way. If we don't take care of ourselves by managing our stress and keeping balance with body, mind, and spirit, we are split from the true nature of who we are, and the potential of who we can become. By managing our stress we are calmer... more centered... and more confident.

Track 3:   Understanding Stress (2:12)

Stress is a normal and natural part of life. It's not something we can avoid. We can try to escape stress, but this will only make us more stressed out! Just like the natural reflex of pulling our hand away from a hot stove, stress is a warning signal. When we are doing too much, stress tells us to slow down. Stress can also help us get motivated when we aren't doing enough or need to stay focused in a certain direction.

Stress is our body's response to what is going on around us and within us. For example, if we have a big test coming up or a paper due, we may experience physical stresses like headaches, sweaty palms, restlessness, or irregular heart beats. We may also experience psychological stresses like worry, anxiety, "down" feelings, or unrealistic fears. Stressful situations in our lives cause a chemical response in our bodies. This "stress response" can be mild, such as feeling happy about getting an A on a test or very intense, such as panic if we're threatened or attacked.

Stress is like the tension on a guitar string, it needs to be tight enough to play great music, but not so tight that it breaks. Just like the guitar string, a certain level of stress and tension can be good, but we need to keep it tuned to the right pitch for our body and mind to use it effectively. If we know we can't get rid of our stress, what can we do to manage it? Listen ahead to find out.

On the next track, I want to give you a chance to practice guided imagery, to prepare you for the meditations. In the story, "The Gift," you will find a fun way to try this out.

Track 4:   "The Gift" (4:39)

Imagine yourself as a small child and your parents have a gift for you. They tell you, "When you are old enough, we will give you the coolest car, any car you want, at any price, in your favorite color The only condition to receiving this gift is that you can never, ever, get another car. In fact, this car will be so unique and so rare, that you will not be able to replace its parts and no paint could match the special color." Your parents go on to say, "We will teach you everything we know about taking care of your car every day and how to drive it safely. Relatives, teachers, coaches, and mentors will be helpful for you too."

Feel the excitement around what your parents just told you! Notice where the sensation of excitement shows up in your body. Maybe your face is making an excited expression about the news of your gift. Maybe you feel excitement in your stomach, which can feel like it's filled with butterflies or you may experience a falling sensation. Notice the temperature of your body. Is your body hot? Is it cold? Is it hot in certain places and cold in others? Listen to your body.

Allow yourself to get a mental picture or image of what your gift looks like. See your car and its sleek design. Notice its size. Notice its shape. Notice how far it sits off the ground. Notice the size of the tires. Notice the magnificent color of your car. How shiny, how bright, how true the color is.

Let yourself ease into the driver's seat of your car. Notice the new smell of your new car. Feel the texture of the interior and how well the driver seat supports you. Place your hands on the steering wheel. Notice the sensation in your hands and how easy it is to grip. Place the key in the ignition. Turn the key. The engine starts. Feel the smile on your face, as you to listen to the engine's perfect pitch. You marvel at this sound, because you have never heard anything quite like it. Enjoy this moment! Knowing this is the only car you could ever own in your lifetime, how do you see yourself taking care of this gift? My guess is that you would wash and wax your car often, because you want it to look great all the time. You would have the oil changed and the engine tuned up, because you want it running perfectly. You would be very protective of your car in places where it could possibly get scratched or dented. You wouldn't let anyone else drive your car. You certainly wouldn't let passengers smoke or drink in your car for fear that this would permanently damage the interior. You would give your car a lot of attention and show it off when ever you could.

What metaphor does the car hold in this story? That's right! The car is our body...our mind...and our spirit. We are only given this precious gift once and it is up to us, with whatever help we need, to take care of this gift in the best possible way. So make good decisions and be really good to yourself!

Practicing the exercises in this CD is a gift that you can give yourself every day. It's an opportunity for you to slow down in a natural and healthy way—a chance for you to keep balance in your life and let your God-given talents and abilities unfold in you. I challenge you to be a non-conformist, even a rebel! Don't let society drive you! Take time for yourself every day.

The next track will give you some helpful tips on preparing yourself and your environment for the relaxation meditations.

Track 5:   Relaxation Tips and Techniques (6:02)

As we get set to do our relaxation meditation, let's check our stress level. On a scale of 0-10, 10 being the most stress possible, 0 being the least, rank yourself on this continuum, with the level of stress you are experiencing right now. Remember this number; because I will have you do another "stress check" after the relaxation meditation is over. Your second "stress check" should be a smaller number than your first. This scale will help you measure how many points on the "stress continuum" you have reduced your stress level. Do the stress check before and after you listen to tracks 6 and 8. By practicing the stress check you'll learn how to manage your stress better. With practice you'll discover how successful you are at reducing your stress level with very little effort.

Now, let's teach the body the difference between tension and relaxation. Place your hands out in front of you and gradually make two fists. Make your fists tighter...tighter. As you hold your fists, be aware of the tension in your hands. Tightening our fists is very similar to the way stress shows up in our body. Being aware of tension in our body is the first important step in helping us to relax. Now, gradually open both fists, feeling the release. Be aware of this letting go sensation as relaxation.

Try the same kind of tension/release experiment by shrugging your shoulders, moving the shoulders up toward the ears. Hold this tension in your neck and shoulders...hold it...hold it. Now, very slowly and gently, let your shoulders drop to their normal position. You should notice an even more dramatic tension and release here.

In Track 8, we go through a progressive relaxation exercise. During this exercise, I mention a body part and suggests that you relax that body part. There are two ways you can do this. One way is by actually tensing the body part, like the experiments I just had you do with your hands and shoulders. The other way is to simply be aware of the tension in that part of your body and releasing it. Try both ways and see which way helps you get to a more relaxed state.

Also in Track 8, I suggest some mental pictures or images, which take you to a very serene and familiar place, guiding you deeper into the relaxation. Really let yourself enjoy this!

When beginning your relaxation, take charge of your environment. Your surroundings should be free from distractions: no bright lights, noises, pesky brothers or sisters. Remove anything that would take away from your experience. When you settle in for your relaxation it is best to lie on your back, without crossing body parts or sit in a comfortable chair with your feet flat on the floor and hands resting on your thighs.

During the relaxation process pay attention to your breathing. When we are experiencing stress, many of us take shallow breaths that only go as far as our upper chest. This robs the brain of oxygen it needs, which causes the body to feel panic, anxiety, or agitation. By breathing shallow or high, we needlessly create more stress! We need to teach ourselves to breathe deeper...lower...more in the area of the diaphragm or lower abdomen.

On Tracks 6 and 8, I have you focus on your breath, to help you get to a deeper state of relaxation. When breathing, remember to inhale slowly and completely. Hold this inhalation breath for about eight seconds, and then exhale slowly and completely for about the same amount of time. Breathe this way for several rotations. Following these cleansing breaths, let your abdomen rise and fall naturally, continuing to breathe low, throughout the relaxation exercise. How we breathe is so important. Low, deep breaths before a test, speech, recital, or athletic contest, help us to feel more relaxed, confident, and mentally alert! Allow yourself to become more aware of your breathing in each moment of every day!

From now on, skip ahead on your CD to whatever meditation fits for you on any given day. There is no need to go through the discussion tracks again, unless you want to refer to them as a reminder to help you improve your relaxation practice. Try to do Track 6, Track 7 or Track 8 every day, at least several times during the week. You will really notice a difference in how you feel about yourself.

Relax; enjoy the rest of the CD and Peace Be With You!!!

Track 6:   Short Meditation (12:27)

Start this relaxation meditation with a stress check. Allow yourself to sit or lie down, so that you're comfortable. Let the chair or floor support you. Notice your breathing. Take a slow...deep inhalation breath...gently inhaling...holding this inhalation breath as low as you can...hold it. Slowly breathe out...exhaling gently and completely. Again, slowly breathe in...gently. Hold this breath as low as possible...hold it...hold it. Exhale slowly...gently...completely. One more cleansing breath... slowly inhale deeper than the first two breaths. Gently hold this inhalation breath low...hold it... hold it. Slowly exhale...gently and completely. Be mindful of your breath, allowing your belly to rise and fall naturally throughout the relaxation.

Let your mind and body rest for the next few moments. Let the word "peace" come to mind. Allow your mind to be peaceful for this moment. Allow your body to be peaceful for this moment. As you allow yourself to rest, let your mind and body be at peace. Let go of any worries you may have about your day. Let the worries go. Let go of any resentments you may have about going into your day. Let any resentments go. Let go of any other negative feelings that you may have about going into your day. Let any negative feelings go.

This is your time to be quiet and still. Allow your mind to be quiet and still. Any thoughts that come up...notice them. Then let them go. No need to think or plan in this moment. Let your mind be at rest.

Allow your body to be quiet and still. Any tension you feel in your body melts away. No need to hold on to any tension. Notice any tightness in your body. Then let it go. Allow your body to be soft for this moment. Allow yourself to be gentle with your body.

Let your body rest.

Imagine yourself lying on your back in a rubber raft, safely floating down a slow, gentle stream. The raft takes you to a place that only knows peace. The journey down the stream on the raft helps you feel more and more relaxed...more and more at peace. The raft very gently shores up on the soft grassy bank. You know that you need to leave the raft now, because up ahead is the place to which you journeyed. A place where you feel loved and cared for. You walk toward the most beautiful place you could ever imagine. Notice the surroundings...the wonderful smells...the colorful scenery. Notice how peaceful you feel.

You look up ahead and see a group of people who seem to be preparing a celebration. As you walk closer, they turn to greet you. Suddenly you realize these are your family and closest friends. They have been preparing to celebrate you. Allow yourself to breathe in their warm welcome. You are invited to walk into the center of a circle they have created to honor you. As you enter this loving and caring circle, notice how safe you feel. Let yourself breathe in their blessing and total acceptance of you. Allow yourself to feel complete joy...complete peace.

Visualize yourself starting your day now. See the radiant smile on your face. Each person that comes in contact with you today notices how peaceful you are. See how pleased they are to see you...how much they have looked forward to being with you. Every step you take today is a step toward peace. By taking this moment in time to create peace in you, peace is created in the world around you.

Allow yourself to fully enjoy the inner peace you have created, throughout your day. Breathe in as you say to yourself, "I am at peace with myself. Today, I am peace."

Allow yourself to fully enjoy the inner peace you have created throughout your day.

Track 7:   Self-Esteem Affirmations (11:10)

Many of us have had the experience of being put-down. To make sure we're all on the same page, a put-down is defined in Webster's Dictionary as "a humiliating remark or action...to degrade, belittle or squelch."

I've included these affirmations in The Peace Project, because words and actions that put us down are harmful and affect us very deeply. Think about a time when you were put down. How did you feel? My guess is that you felt hurt and angry! You might have also had thoughts of wanting to get even. Put-downs by one person, plus, put-downs by another person to get back, can never equal good feelings or anything positive for anyone. This vicious circle of hurtful words and actions are what cause the spark to ignite the flame of violence.

When we feel put down, we form certain beliefs about ourselves, which suggest, we're "too big... too small...too short...too tall...not smart enough...not fast enough." The overall message we come to believe is, "I'm not good enough." These negative beliefs get played out over and over in our heads; in a similar way that messages are replayed from a tape recorder. Put-downs between people and negative messages in our heads, cause stress and drain our energy.

The affirmations in Track 7, can help us record over these old messages with new positive messages. It's a way for us to counteract our negative thinking and feeling. By affirming ourselves and others, we will be more loving, much more positive and fully alive!

Find a relaxed, comfortable position. Take a few deep cleansing breaths. As you hear the affirmations, say them to yourself. Allow yourself to receive these powerful affirmations by breathing in each positive message.

I am safe and at peace in my body.
You are safe and at peace in your body.

I am special and celebrate my uniqueness.
You are special and celebrate your uniqueness.

I am confident and capable of making good decisions.
You are confident and capable of making good decisions.

I am positive in my attitude.
You are positive in your attitude.

I am good enough.
You are good enough.

I accept the feelings I have in any given moment as my inner truth.
You accept the feelings you have in any given moment as your inner truth.

I speak up for myself.
You speak up for yourself.

I am surrounded by loving-kindness.
You are surrounded by loving-kindness.

I am treating problems as opportunities to grow in wisdom and love.
You are treating problems as opportunities to grow in wisdom and love.

I am worthy of all the good in my life.
You are worthy of all the good in your life.

I am imaginative and creative.
You are imaginative and creative.

I am confident my future is bright and promising.
You are confident your future is bright and promising.

I celebrate my accomplishments.
You celebrate your accomplishments.

I am patient and tolerant of differences in others.
You are patient and tolerant of differences in others.

I surround myself with people who support me in making healthy choices.
You surround yourself with people who support you in making healthy choices.

I am loved and accepted as I am.
You are loved and accepted as you are.

I am capable of being a great thinker.
You are capable of being a great thinker.

I am grateful for my life.
You are grateful for your life.

I am strong in my faith.
You are strong in your faith.

Choose the affirmation you would like to reinforce most and say it to yourself or out loud throughout the day. Feel free to add to this list of affirmations or change the wording to get the most positive message possible. Write the most helpful affirmations on Post-it notes and stick them on your bathroom mirror, the refrigerator, locker, or school desk.

Let the power of these messages stay with you today and always!

Track 8: Long Meditation (28:54)

Set up your environment so that you are free of any distractions for the length of this relaxation meditation. Do a "stress check" to begin this exercise. Lie down flat on your back, in your quiet, comfortable space, without crossing body parts, and place a comfortable pillow under head for support.

Notice your breath. Slowly...breathe low into your belly... gently...deeply. Hold it...hold it...hold it as low as you can. Slowly exhale...gently and completely. Again, slowly breathe in...gently. Hold this breath as low as possible. Hold it...hold it. Exhale slowly...gently...completely. One more cleansing breath. Slowly inhale deeper than the first two breaths. Gently hold this inhalation breath low. Hold it...hold it. Slowly exhale...gently and completely. Be mindful of your breath, allowing your belly to rise and fall naturally throughout the relaxation.

Imagine that inside of you is a volume knob, just like the one you control on your stereo or boom box. In your mind's eye, see yourself reaching inward... placing your fingers on the volume knob... slowly turn the knob to the left...turning...turning the noise down inside of you...all the way down...just for this moment.

You are above time...below time...you are beyond time. There is no time, other than this moment... completely for you. Focus on your feet. Imagine that roots are coming out of the bottom of your feet, like the roots of a large oak tree...deeply planted in the precious earth. The deeper your roots go and the wider they spread out, the more solid, the more balanced, you will be. Just as an oak tree cannot be toppled over, you remain firmly planted in all that is good.

Continue to focus on your feet, letting go of any tension here. Relax the heel, arch, and ball of both feet, the sides, the top of your feet, and each individual toe. Continue the relaxation from both feet, up to the lower legs. Relax your Achilles, soften your calf muscles, relax. Relax your shins, allow your knees to relax, soften behind your knees. Relax the front of your legs, soften the back of your legs. Let your hips, pelvis, and buttocks relax.

From your waist down you feel completely relaxed...warm...peaceful.

Continue this sensation from the waist to your abdomen, then around the waist to your lower back. Let go of the tension. Let your belly be soft. Let your middle chest and solar plexus relax. Soften your upper chest.

Release the tension in your back. Let your low back, middle back, and upper back relax. Soften the entire trunk of your body. Let all of your internal organs relax: your liver...pancreas...kidneys... the small and large intestines. Relax your lungs. Let your heart relax...soften your spine. Imagine you can go in with your hand and touch each vertebrae one at a time, starting with the tail bone. Gently touch each vertebrae, giving your entire spine permission to relax.

Continue this relaxation up the back of your head and scalp. Relax the top of your head. Let your forehead and brow soften. Smooth out any lines in your forehead and brow. Let your eyes be soft. Relax behind your eyes. Relax your nose and sinuses. Let your face soften. Relax your cheeks and jaw. It's okay to let your mouth drop open slightly, taking any tension off the jaw.

Relax your lips and mouth. Inside your mouth, relax your tongue. Let your ears relax and inside your ears. Continue this relaxation to the neck. Let your entire neck relax...the front of the neck, your Adam's apple, throat, and esophagus...the sides and the back of the neck.

Relax your shoulders, removing any burdens you may be carrying. See them evaporate into the air around you. Continue this relaxation down to your upper arms...the elbows. Let your forearms relax. Relax your wrists. Let your hands soften. Allow each of your individual fingers and thumbs to relax.

Your entire body is completely relaxed. You feel relaxed, warm, and at peace in your body.

Now, in your mind's eye see a blank screen in front of you. See a color emerging on the screen. There is no need to work hard at this. Be patient if a color doesn't show up right away. Your color will appear in its own way, in its own time. This is your "peace color." Imagine your "peace color" in the form of a cloud. Allow your magic cloud to very slowly and gently swirl around your body and in your body sensing any remaining tension. Wherever it finds tension in or on your body, your cloud will softly swirl around and in this tension giving the tension permission to go...to release in the air...away from you. Continue to let your magic cloud, in your "peace color" locate any remaining tension...swirling around it...giving the tension permission to go...releasing the tension to the air...away from you...allowing you to go deeper into a very calm and peaceful place.

Take a full breath in and say, "I am," then breathe out and say, "safe and relaxed." Again, breathe in "I am," breathe out, "safe and relaxed."

See yourself on a beautiful serene beach. You are in clothing comfortable for you...in your bare feet. Feel the fine, white, warm sand on your feet, as you stroll along the beach. Feel the warm sun on your back. Feel the gentle wind from the ocean, calming your face, softly blowing your hair back. Smell the sea air. Hear the rhythms of the ocean. Pause along the way to taste the luscious tropical fruit from trees nearby. Feel connected with all that surrounds you. With each step you take you feel more and more relaxed, more and more at peace.

As you continue to stroll along the beach, notice a low tide up ahead. Walk in the low tide and enjoy the warm temperature of the ocean on your feet. Lie down on your back, with your feet facing the ocean and your head toward the shore. You feel safe, calm and relaxed. The low tide gently rolls in underneath you, giving you a chance to let go of any remaining tension, worry, or anxiety. Let it go. As you do, the low tide carries this tension, worry, and anxiety out from underneath you from the top of your head...down...down...down to your feet and far out into the ocean.

As the new low tide comes in it brings many gifts...treasure that you have been looking for. Whatever you need...love, courage, peace, joy, blessing...the ocean will provide. These gifts from the ocean begin to fill you up from the bottom of your feet...up...up...up to the top of your head.

Notice as you continue to release into the ocean what you don't want and accept from the ocean what you do want, the sand has formed around you, holding you safely...securely. Let yourself enjoy this nurturing feeling.

Let yourself feel completely loved and cared for.

When ready, see yourself in your mind's eye standing up to look at the impression your body has made in the earth...keenly aware of what makes up how you think, feel, act...along with your precious spirit. You make a special impression while here on this earth. You are mindful that just as there are no two snowflakes exactly alike, there is no other person exactly like you. You are uniquely you. You exist on this planet for a very special purpose. Let this purpose unfold in you gently...peacefully...lovingly.

As you stroll along the beach in a new direction you are deeply relaxed, feeling more connected to your surroundings...more centered...more balanced. You are at peace with yourself. You feel fully alive!

When you're ready, allow yourself to come back into the room very slowly and gently. Open your eyes. Notice the space around you. Continue to come back slowly. Stretch your hands and arms up above you. Slowly sit up.

In this position touch a part of your body, such as your nose, chin, or earlobe to help your body remember the positive feelings from this exercise. This is called an "anchor." Touching a body part anchors or records the positive relaxation feelings in that body part. If you need to during the day, you can touch this body part whenever you want to recreate the relaxed state again.

You have just been through a very deep and powerful experience. Take as much time as you need to stand up and orient yourself to your environment.

Do the "stress check" to measure how many points you've come down on the scale. Celebrate how well you've done with this exercise.

Be gentle with yourself today. Throughout the entire day see yourself surrounded by your "peace color" and say "I am peace."

Have a wonderful and peaceful day!

Appendix B
Internet Sources

BULLYING INFORMATION

http://www.bullying.org
Dedicated to increasing the awareness of bullying and preventing, resolving, and eliminating bullying in society.

http://www.lifeskillstraining.com/other_prevention.php
Botvin Life Skills Training with a link to their Bullying Prevention in the Classroom series.

http://www.pacerkidsagainstbullying.org
Pacer National Center for Bullying website. Includes Kids Against Bullying Oath, games, activities and information for kids, parents, and professionals.

http://www.bullies2buddies.com
Bullies to Buddies by school psychologist Izzy Kalman whose mission is to end the suffering of victims of teasing and bullying throughout the world. Includes free manuals for kids and adults.

http://www.schoolsafety.us
National School Safety Center with downloadable facts sheet, news journals, and more.

http://www.educationworld.com/a_issues/issues/issues103.shtml
Education World on bullying intervention strategies.

http://www.olweus.org/public/index.page
Hazelden and the Olweus Bullying Prevention Program.

http://www.kidpower.org
KidPower is a non-profit organization dedicated to creating cultures of caring, respect, and safety for all.

http://www.kidsareworthit.com
Website for author Barbara Coloroso.

http://www.stopbullyingnow.hrsa.gov/kids/
The Stop Bullying Now Campaign website has a section for kids with fun activities and adults with information about bullying and cyberbullying as well as information about State Laws.

http://www.cartoonnetwork.com/tv_shows/promotion_landing_page/stopbullying/index.html
The Cartoon Network campaign on "Stop Bullying Speak Up."

http://www.cnn.com/SPECIALS/2010/bullying/
Anderson Cooper 360 CNN television series on bullying.

http://www.education.com/topic/school-bullying-teasing/
Informative site on bullying at school and online from education.com.

http://www.bullypolice.org
Bully Police USA is a watchdog organization advocating for bullied children and reporting on state anti-bullying laws.

RELATIONAL AGGRESSION

http://en.wikipedia.org/wiki/Relational_aggression
Definition of relational aggression from Wikipedia.

http://www.relationalaggression.com
Defines ten specific aspects of relational aggression.

http://www.spsk12.net/departments/specialed/Relational%20Aggression.htm
Roles, what schools can do, tips for parents and resources.

http://www.namesdohurt.com
Fun and games that educate, lingo, resources including a PSA.

http://wings.buffalo.edu/psychology/labs/SocialDevLab/Ostrov_&_Godleski_in%20press_ToLDx.pdf
Research paper titled, "Relational Aggression, Victimization and Language" from the University at Buffalo, The State University of New York, Buffalo, New York.

http://www.opheliaproject.org
The Ophelia Project serves youth and adults who are affected by relational and other non-physical forms of aggression by providing them with a unique combination of tools, strategies, and solutions.

http://www.daughters-sisters.org
Teen Talking Circles emphasizing healthy relationship development.

http://www.smartgirl.org
SmartGirl is an online community of thousands of girls who anonymously share their opinions, hopes, concerns, and dreams with each other.

CYBERBULLYING

http://www.cyberbullying.org
Examples, what can be done, and multiple links.

http://www.cyberbullying.us
Identifies the causes and consequences of online harassment.

http://www.stopcyberbullying.org
Defines what cyberbullying is, how it works, prevention, taking action, and the law.

http://www.youtube.com/watch?v=YxKYU3SIDhI
YouTube video about the painful effects of cyberbullying.

http://abcnews.go.com/TheLaw/story?id=6297275&page=1
Usually cyberbullying involves only minors; however, a case is currently in trial on a mother who played a MySpace hoax on a minor female teen neighbor which led to her suicide.

http://stopbullyingnow.hrsa.gov/adults/cyber-bullying.aspx
Cyberbullying information from Stopbullyingnow.

http://www.wcs.k12.va.us/users/honaker/cyberbullying-for-teachers.pdf
Article from the Center for Safe and Responsible Internet Use, "An Educator's Guide to Cyberbullying and Cyberthreats"

http://www.asdk12.org/MiddleLink/AVB/bully_topics
Downloadable educators guide to cyberbullying.

http://www.cyberbullyhelp.com/Cyber%20Bullying%20Guide%20for%20Parents.pdf
A cyberbullying quick reference guide for parents.

http://www.cyberbullying.us/cyberbullying_warning_signs.pdf
Cyberbullying warning signs.

http://www.cyberbullying.us/cyberbullying_emotional_consequences.pdf
Cyberbullying emotional and psychological consequences.

http://www.connectsafely.org
A forum for parents, teens, and others on safe socializing on the fixed and mobile web.

EMOTIONAL INTELLIGENCE

http://eqi.org
Emotional intelligence site with links to a definition, history, listening skills, teen suicide, cutting behavior, an extensive feeling words list and more.

http://www.danielgoleman.info/blog
Dan Goleman's blog site.

http://www.eiconsortium.org
Consortium for Research on Emotional Intelligence in Organizations.

SOCIAL EMOTIONAL LEARNING

http://www.casel.org/home.php
Home site for Collaborative for Academic, Social, and Emotional Learning.

http://www.casel.org/basics/faqs.php
Link to the most frequently asked questions about SEL.

http://www.schoolclimate.org
National School Climate Center promotes positive and sustained school climate: a safe, supportive environment that nurtures social and emotional, ethical, and academic skills.

http://responsiveclassroom.org
The Responsive Classroom is an approach to elementary teaching that emphasizes social, emotional, and academic growth in a strong and safe school community.

http://www.devstu.org
Developmental Studies Center (DSC) is a nonprofit organization dedicated to children's academic, ethical, and social development.

http://www.esrnational.org
Educators for Social Responsibility (ESR) helps educators create safe, caring, respectful, and productive learning environments.

http://www.wingsforkids.org
An organization dedicated to social emotional earning in after-school programs. Includes information, skills, video, and more.

http://www.wingsforkids.org/files/HotWINGS-feedback.pdf
Giving effective feedback.

MULTIPLE INTELLIGENCES

http://educationalvoyage.com/multiintell.html
An educational voyage portal on a variety of topics including multiple intelligences.

http://surfaquarium.com/MI
This site is filled with information on profiles, inventories, brain links, multiple intelligences (MI) and instruction, MI lesson template, a discussion group, and many MI links.

http://thomasarmstrong.com
Website of Dr. Thomas Armstrong.

http://projects.coe.uga.edu/epltt/index.php?title=Multiple_Intelligences_and_Learning_Styles
This website is a great resource on MI with many useful links. It includes a Multiple Intelligences Profile to print out after answering a series of questions that pertain to eight of the nine intelligences.

POSITIVE SCHOOL CLIMATE

http://www.nobully.com
A mission to make school a place where every student feels included by their peers and accepted for who they are.

http://www.youthfrontiers.org
Programs to improve school climate and strengthen student character.

http://www.ancomm.com
Anonymous online messaging service to promote student and school safety.

http://www.edu.gov.mb.ca/k12/specedu/fas/pdf/3.pdf
Creating a Positive School Climate

http://www.schoolclimate.org/climate/
National School Climate Center

http://nscc.csee.net/effective/school_climate_research_summary.pdf
School Climate Research Summary from the Center for Social Emotional Education.

http://www.nais.org/publications/ismagazinearticle.cfm?ItemNumber=150284
"Evaluating and Improving School Climate: Creating a Climate for Learning" from the National Association of Independent Schools. Includes ten essential dimensions of school climate.

INTERNET SAFETY

http://www.isafe.org
Online safety education.

http://netbullies.com
Website of cyberlawyer Parry Aftab.

http://www.wiredkids.org
Wired Kids, Inc. is a U.S. charity dedicated to protecting all Internet users, especially children, from cybercrime and abuse. Includes educational resources.

http://www.safekids.com
A family guide to making the Internet and technology fun, safe, and productive.

http://getnetwise.com
Internet safety information with how-to video tutorials.

http://www.justice.gov/criminal/cybercrime/rules/kidinternet.htm
Site by the U.S. Department of Justice's Computer Crime and Intellectual Property Section. It provides adults, children, and teens with information on how to use the Internet safely and responsibly.

http://www.netsmartz.org
An informational site from the National Center For Missing and Exploited Children which includes children's animated online videos about Internet safety.

http://www.mcgruff.org
Children's games, videos about Internet safety, and more.

http://www.teenangels.org
About teens trained to conduct programs in schools on responsible Internet usage to other teens, children, parents, and teachers.

http://www.connectsafely.org
A forum for parents, teens, and others to discuss safe socializing on the fixed and mobile web.

http://www.katiesplace.org
Named after Katie Tarbox, this site is for young victims of Internet sexual exploitation.

http://www.chatdanger.com
Chatdanger was created to inform young people about the potential dangers and ways of keeping safe in interactive areas online, such as chatrooms, instant messenger, online games and email, and also via mobile phones.

http://www.kidscomjr.com/games/safety/safety.html
Games and tips for Internet safety and good manners.

http://catalog.ncyi.org/products/classroom_counselors/1250283871
Cybersmart Game (Grades 3-7), covers Internet safety, bullies, scams, viruses, and identity theft as they pertain to computers, cell phones, MP4 players, Blackberries, and other wireless devices.

http://www.teenchatdecoder.com
Help with decoding text message abbreviations.

http://www.noslang.com
Internet Slang Dictionary & Translator.

http://www.netsmartz411.org
Ask an expert if you get stumped trying to translate electronic communications. A program of the National Center for Missing & Exploited Children.

DIGITAL CITIZENSHIP

http://www.ciconline.org/Resource/digital-ethics
Cable in the Classroom curriculum that teaches ethical, courteous, and productive behavior while using digital media. Included are resources on plagiarism, copyright, and using digital media productively.

http://www.medialit.org
Provides educational resources to develop skills needed to live fully in the 21st century media culture.

http://www.cybersmartcurriculum.org/home
The CyberSmart! Curriculum is non-sequential and is easily integrated, in part or in full. Organized in five units, each teaches an important facet of Internet use and consists of 65 original standards-based lesson plans with activity sheets.

http://www.cybercitizenship.org/index.html
Provides approaches for teaching children about "cyber ethics." Includes multiple links for adults and children to gain a better understanding of the Internet.

http://www.digitalcitizenship.net
Nine themes of digital citizenship and other resources.

http://www.digitalcitizenship.net/uploads/1stLL.pdf
A downloadable curriculum on appropriate technology use for Grades K-12.

http://www.digitalcitizenshiped.com
The digital Citizenship and creative content program is a free instructional program for Grades 8-10.

http://www.digizen.org
Information advice and resources for using social networking services with young people. Also provides information and advice on recognizing and tackling cyberbullying.

STRESS

http://www.stress.org
The American Institute of Stress (AIS) is a nonprofit organization committed to helping advance knowledge of the role of stress in health and disease.

http://www.dstress.com
A site devoted to stress management and information to enhance health and wellness and productivity.

http://responsiveclassroom.org/newsletter/20_4nl_3.html
Interesting article titled; "Gremlins: A Tool for Managing Everyday Anxiety" by fifth grade teacher Leslie Schwartz Leff, who applies this strategy with her class.

http://www.readysetrelax.org
Hosts multiple resources on meditation and relaxation

http://www.teachhealth.com
Easy to understand presentation on how the body and brain responds to stress.

http://www.mindtools.com/smpage.html
A "how to" site on understanding stress and its effects, and stress management techniques.

http://www.stresscure.com
General stress information and strategies for coping with stress.

http://hyperstress.com
The Institute for Stress Management & Performance Improvement.

http://www.selfgrowth.com/stress.html
Links to 60 articles on managing stress and stress-related websites.

http://www.meditationcenter.com
Provides straightforward meditation instruction, including a variety of techniques including sections on links and resources.

http://www.holisticonline.com/stress/stress_home.htm
A stress management information center with general knowledge on stress and multiple ways to cope with it.

http://www.guidedimageryinc.com
Stress and the benefits of imagery are examined.

http://ehs.okstate.edu/links/stress.htm
Oklahoma State University online library of stress management links.

http://www.stressmanagingtips.com
How to manage stress effectively. Includes simple tips and techniques.

http://www.focusas.com/Stress.html
Comprehensive information, resources, and support for teen and family issues including stress with multiple links.

MISCELLANEOUS

http://www.ipj-ppj.org
The Institute for Peace and Justice (IPJ) is an independent, interfaith, not-for-profit organization that creates resources, provides learning experiences, and advocates publicly for alternatives to violence and injustice at the individual, family, community, institutional, and global levels.

http://www.kickitin.com
Website of motivational speaker Fran Kick, his books on motivating students, leadership, and other resources.

http://www.gurianinstitute.com
Michael Gurian, renowned author and speaker, on how boys and girls learn differently.

http://search-institute.org
Search Institute is an independent non-profit organization whose mission is to provide leadership, knowledge, and resources to promote healthy children, youth, and communities.

http://www.teachmeteamwork.com/teachmeteamwork/files/Teambuilding_on_a_Shoestring_sml.pdf
Team Activities on a Shoestring, a free e-book by Tom Heck. Contains 8 teambuilding games

http://www.ciraontario.com/ehr/page/resources
Excellent resource for interactive games.

http://www.tolerance.org
A wonderful resource filled with classroom activities on Teaching Tolerance, information about bullying and "Mix It Up At Lunch." This organization will mail educators their magazine for FREE!

Appendix C
Bibliography

Adamshick, P. Z. (2010). The lived experience of girl-to-girl aggression in marginalized girls. *Quality Health Research, 20*(4), 541-555.

Aftab, P. (2006). *Wired safety.* Retrieved June 2010, from http://wiredsafety.net

Ahmad, Y., & Smith, P. K. (2004). Bullying in schools and the issue of same sex differences. In J. Archer (Ed.), *Male violence* (pp. 70-83). London: Routledge.

Ahmed, E., & Braithwaite, V. (2004). What, me ashamed? Shame management and school bullying. *Journal of Research in Crime and Deliquency, 41*(3), 269-294.

American Medical Association. (2007). *Report 12 of the Council on Science and Public Health (A-07) Full Text.* Retrieved from http://www.ama-assn.org/ama/no-index/about-ama/17694.shtml

Anderson, C. A. (2004). An update on the effects of playing violent video games. *Journal of Adolescence, 27,* 41-52.

Anderson, C. A., Berkowitz, L., Donnerstein, E., Huesmann, L. R., Johnson, J. D., Linz, D., & Malamuth, N. M. (2003). The influence of media violence on youth. *Psychological Science in the Public Interest, 4,* 81-110.

Anderson, C. A., & Bushman, B. J. (2001). Effects of violent video games on aggressive behavior, aggressive cognition, aggressive affect, physiological arousal, and prosocial behavior: A meta-analytic review of the scientific literature. *Psychological Science, 12,* 353-359.

Anderson, C. A., & Dill, K. E. (2000). Video games and aggressive thoughts, feelings, and behavior in the laboratory and in life. *Journal of Personality and Social Psychology, 78*(4), 772-790.

Armstrong, T. (1993). *7 kinds of smart: Identifying and developing your many intelligences.* New York: Plume.

Armstrong, T. (1999). *7 kinds of smart: Identifying and developing your multiple intelligences, revised and updated with information on 2 new kinds of smart.* New York: Plume.

Armstrong, T. (2009). *Multiple intelligences in the classroom* (3rd ed.). Alexandria, VA: Association for Supervision and Curriculum Development.

Atlas, R. S., & Pepler, D. J. (1998). Observations of bullying in the classroom. *Journal of Educational Research, 92,* 86–99.

Bandura, A., Ross, D., & Ross, S. (1961). Transmission of aggression through imitation of aggressive models. *Journal of Abnormal and Social Psychology, 63,* 575–582.

Bandura, A., Ross, D., & Ross, S. (1963). Imitation of film-mediated aggressive models. *Journal of Abnormal and Social Psychology, 66,* 3–11.

Bandura, A., Ross, D., & Ross, S. (1963). Vicarious reinforcement and imitative learning. *Journal of Abnormal and Social Psychology, 67,* 601–607.

Batsche, G. M., & Knoff, H. M. (1994). Bullies and their victims: Understanding a pervasive problem in the schools. *School Psychology Review, 23,* 165-174.

Beatty, A. (2006). *Studying media effects on children and youth: Improving methods and measures. Workshop summary*. Washington, DC: National Academies Press.

Bernstein, J. Y., & Watson, M. W. (1997). Children who are targets of bullying: A victim pattern. *Journal of Interpersonal Violence, 12*, 483-498.

Bitney, J., & Title, B. (1997). *No-bullying program: Preventing bullying/victim violence at school. Programs director manual*. Central City, MN: Hazelden and Johnson Institute.

Bjorkqvist, K., Osterman, K., & Kaukiainen, A. (1992). The development of direct and indirect aggressive strategies in males and females. In K. Bjorkqvist & P. Niemela (Eds.), *Of mice and women: Aspects of female aggression* (pp. 51-64). San Diego, CA: Academic Press.

Bjorkqvist, K., Osterman, K., & Lagerspetz, K. M. J. (1994). Sex differences in covert aggression among adults. *Aggressive Behavior, 20*, 27-33.

Bjorkqvist, K., Osterman, K., & Hjelt-Back, M. (1994). Aggression among university employees. *Aggressive Behavior, 20*, 173–184.

Bosworth, K., Espelage, D. L., & Simon, T. R. (1999). Factors associated with bullying behavior in middle school students. *Journal of Early Adolescence, 19, 341 362.*

Boulton, M., & Underwood, K. (1992). Bully/victim problems among middle school children. *Developmental Psychology, 25*, 320-330.

Boulton, M. J., Trueman, M., & Flemington, I. (2002). Associations between secondary school pupils' definitions of bullying, attitudes towards bullying, and tendencies to engage in bullying: Age and sex differences. *Educational Studies, 28*, 353–370.

Boyatzis, C. J., Matillo, G. M., & Nesbitt, K. M. (1995). Effects of the 'Mighty Morphin Power Rangers' on children's aggression with peers. *Child Study Journal, 25*(1), 45-55.

Brizendine, L. (2006). *The female brain*. New York: Morgan Road Books.

Broidy, L., Cauffman, E., Espelage, D., Mazerolle, P., & Piquero, A. (2003). Sex differences in empathy and its relations to juvenile offending. *Violence and Victims, 18*, 503-516.

Burns, S., Maycock, B., Cross, D., & Brown, G. (2008). The power of peers: Why some students bully others to conform. *Quality Health Research, 18*(12), 1704-1716.

Bushman, B., & Baumeister, R. (1998). Threatened egotism, narcissism, self-esteem, and direct and displaced aggression: Does self-love or self hate lead to violence? *Journal of Personality and Social Psychology, 75*, 219–229.

Campbell, A. (1993). *Men, women, and aggression*. New York: Basic Books.

Campbell, S. B., Spieker, S., Vandergrift, N., Belsky, J., Burchinal, M., & The NICHD Early Child Care Research Network. (2010). Predictors and sequelae of trajectories of physical aggression in school-age boys and girls. *Development and Psychopathology, 22*, 133–150.

Catholic Church. (2010). *Catechism of the Catholic Church*. Retrieved from http://www.vatican.va/archive/ccc_css/archive/catechism/ccc_toc.htm

Center for the Study and Prevention of Violence. (2010a). *Blueprints for violence prevention*. Retrieved from http://www.colorado.edu/cspv/blueprints/modelprograms/BPP.html

Center for the Study and Prevention of Violence. (2010b). *Matrix of programs*. Retrieved from http://www.colorado.edu/cspv/blueprints/matrixfiles/matrix.pdf

Cillessen, A. H. N., & Mayeux, L. (2004). From censure to reinforcement: Developmental changes in the association between aggression and social status. *Child Development, 75*, 147–163.

Coloroso, B. (2003). *The bully, the bullied, and the bystander: From preschool to high school, how parents and teachers can help break the cycle of violence*. New York: Harper Resource.

Committee for Children. (2001). *Steps to Respect curriculum*. Retrieved from http://www.cfchildren.org/programs/str/overview/

Council on Science and Public Health, American Medical Association. (2007). *Emotional and behavioral effects of video games and internet overuse* (CSAPH Report 12-A-07). Retrieved from http://www.ama-assn.org/ama/no-index/about-ama/17694.shtml

Cowie, H. (2000). Bystanding or standing by: Gender issues in coping with bullying in English schools. *Aggressive Behavior, 26*, 85-97.

Craig, W. M., & Pepler, D. J. (1995). Peer processes in bullying and victimization: An observational study. *Exceptionality Education in Canada, 5*, 81-95.

Craig, W. M., Pepler, D. J., & Atlas, R. S. (2000). Observations of bullying on the playground and in the classroom. *School Psychology International, 21*, 22-36.

Crick, N. R., & Bigbee, M. A. (1998). Relational and overt forms of peer victimization: A multi-informant approach. *Journal of Consulting and Clinical Psychology, 66*, 237-347.

Crick, N. R., Casas, J. F., & Nelson, D. A. (2002). Toward a more comprehensive understanding of peer maltreatment: Studies of relational victimization. *Current Directions in Psychological Science, 11*(3), 98-101.

Crick, N. R., & Grotpeter, J. K. (1995). Relational aggression, gender, and social-psychological adjustment. *Child Development, 66*, 710-722.

Crick, N. R., & Grotpeter J. K. (1996). Children's treatment by peers: Victims of relational and overt aggression. *Development and Psychopathology, 8*, 367-380.

Crick, N. R., Nelson, D. A., Morales, J. R., Cullertonsen, C., Casas, J. F., & Hickman, S. (2001). Relational victimization in childhood and adolescence: I hurt you through the grapevine. In J. Juvonen & S. Graham (Eds.), *School-based peer harassment: The plight of the vulnerable and victimized* (pp. 196-211). New York: Guilford Press.

Crick, N. R., Werner, N. E., Casas, J. F., O'Brien, K. M., Nelson, D. A., & Grotpeter, J. K. (1999). Childhood agression and gender: A new look at an old problem. In D. Bernstein (Eds.), *Nebraska symposium on motivation* (pp. 75-141). Lincoln: University of Nebraska Press.

Crothers, L., Field, J., & Kolbert, J. (2005). Navigating power, control, and being nice: Aggression in female adolescent friendships. *Journal of Counseling and Development, 83*, 349-354.

Dake, J. A., Price, J. H., Telljohann, S. K., & Funk, J. B. (2004). Principals' perceptions and practices of school bullying prevention activities. *Health Education & Behavior, 31*(3), 372-387.

Davis, M. R. (2011). *Digital directions: Teacher professional development sourcebook*. Retrieved from http://www.edweek.org/dd/articles/2011/02/09/02cyberbullying.h04.html

Dejoie, J. F. (2001). Internet addiction: A different kind of addiction? *Revue Médicale de Liège, 56*, 523-530.

Dellasega, C., & Nixon, C. (2003). *Girl wars: Twelve strategies that will end female bullying*. New York: Fireside.

Demaray, M. K., & Malecki, C. K. (2006). A review of the use of social support in anti-bullying programs. *Journal of School Violence, 5*, 51-70.

DeVoe, J. F., & Kaffenberger, S. (2005). *Student reports of bullying: Results from the 2001 School Crime Supplement to the National Crime Victimization Survey* (NCES 2005–310). U.S. Department of Education, National Center for Education Statistics. Washington, DC: U.S. Government Printing Office.

DiLallo, F. A. (2001). *The peace project: A relaxation meditation for young adults* (CD). Toledo, OH: Author.

Drabman, R. S., & Hanratty-Thomas, M. (1974). Does media violence increase children's toleration of real-life aggression? *Developmental Psychology, 10*, 418–421.

Drabman, R. S., & Hanratty-Thomas, M. (1976). Does watching violence on television cause apathy? *Pediatrics, 57*, 329–331.

Eagly, A. H., & Steffen, V. J. (1986). Gender and aggressive behavior: A meta-analytic review of the social psychological literature. *Psychological Bulletin, 100*, 309–330.

Eisenberg, N., & Mussen, P. H. (1989). *The roots of prosocial behavior in children*. New York: Cambridge University Press.

Emes, C. E. (1997). Is Mr. Pac Man eating our children? A review of the effect of video games on children. *Canadian Journal of Psychiatry, 42*, 409-414.

Espelage, D. L., & Holt, M. K. (2001). Bullying and victimization during early adolescence: Peer influences and psychosocial correlates. *Journal of Emotional Abuse, 2*, 123-142.

Espelage, D., & Swearer, S. (2004). *Bullying in American schools: A social-ecological perspective on prevention and intervention*. Mahwah, NJ: Lawrence Erlbaum.

Evangelical Lutheran Church of America. (2010). *Bullying: The congregation's responsibility to address bullying*. Retrieved from http://www.elca.org/Our-Faith-In-Action/Life-Transitions/Youth-issues/Bullying.aspx

Farrington, D. P. (1993). Understanding and preventing bullying. In M. Tonry & N. Morris (Eds.), *Crime and justice* (Vol. 17, pp. 381-458). Chicago: University of Chicago Press.

Faulkner, M. (2009). Taking a stand against cyberbullying. *Living Ethics, 78*. Retrieved from http://www.ethics.org.au/living-ethics/taking-stand-against-cyberbullying

Feder, J., Levant, R. F., & Dean, J. (2007). Boys and violence: A gender-informed analysis. *Professional Psychology: Research and Practice, 38*, 385-391.

Feinberg, T. (2003). Bullying prevention and intervention. *Principal Leadership, 4*(1), 10-14.

Flannery, D., Vazsonyi, A., Liau, A., Guo, S., Powell, K., Atha, H., …Embry, D. (2003). Initial behavior outcomes for the PeaceBuilders universal school-based violence prevention program. *Developmental Psychology, 39*(2), 292-308.

Freeman, H. S., & Mims, G. A. (2007). Targeting bystanders: Evaluating a violence prevention program for "nonviolent" adolescents. In J. E. Zins, M. J. Elias, & C. A. Maher (Eds.), *Bullying, victimization, and peer harassment: A handbook of prevention and intervention* (pp. 163-177). New York: Haworth Press.

Frey, K. S., Hirschstein, M. K., Edstrom, L. V., & Snell, J. L. (2009). Observed reductions in school bullying, nonbullying aggression, and destructive bystander behavior: A longitudinal evaluation. *Journal of Educational Psychology, 101*(2), 466-481.

Fried, S., & Fried, P. (2003). *Bullies, targets, & witnesses*. New York: M. Evans and Company.

Fritz, R. (1989). *The path of least resistance: Learning to become the creative force in your own life*. New York: Ballantine Books.

Garandeau, C., & Cillessen, A. H. N. (2006). From indirect aggression to invisible aggression: A conceptual view on bullying and peer group manipulation. *Aggression and Violent Behavior, 11*, 612-625.

Gardner, H. (1983). *Frames of mind: The theory of multiple intelligences*. New York: Basic Books.

Gardner, H. (1993). *Multiple intelligences: The theory in practice*. New York: Basic Books.

Gardner, H. (1999). *Reframed: Multiple intelligences for the 21st century*. New York: Basic Books.

Gardner, H. (2006). *Multiple intelligences: New horizons*. New York: Basic Books.

Garrity, C., Jens, K., Porter, W., Sager, N., & Short-Camilli, C. (2004). *Bully-proofing your elementary school: Working with victims and bullies* (3rd ed.). Longmont, CO: Sopris West.

Gentile, D. (2009) Pathological video game use among youth 8 to 18: A national study. *Psychological Science, 20*(5), 594-602.

Gentile, D. A., & Stone, W. (2005). Violent video game effects on children and adolescents: A review of the literature. *Minerva Pediatrica, 57*, 337-358.

Gleick, J. (1999). *Faster: The acceleration of just about everything*. New York: Pantheon.

Goleman, D. (1994). *Emotional intelligence: Why it can matter more than IQ*. Toronto, Ontario: Bantam Book.

Goleman, D. (2006). *Social intelligence: The new science of human relationships*. New York: Bantam Books.

Graham, S., & Juvonen, J. (1998). Self-blame and peer victimization in middle school: An attributional analysis. *Developmental Psychology, 34*, 587–599.

Greenberg, J. S. (2002). *Comprehensive stress management* (7th ed.). Boston: McGraw-Hill.

Greene, M. B. (2006). Bullying in schools: A plea for measure of human rights. *Journal of Social Issues, 62*, 63-79.

Halford, G. S. (1993). *Children's understanding: The development of mental models*. Hillsdale, NJ: Lawrence Erlbaum.

Harmon, J. A., Contrucci, V. J., & Stockton, T. S. (1992). *Gender disparities in special education*. Madison, WI: Bureau for Exceptional Children, Wisconsin Department of Public Instruction.

Hartjen, R. (2004). *The preeminent intelligence: Social IQ*. Retrieved from http://www.educationfutures.org/Social_IQ.htm

Hays, E. (1979). *Prayers for the domestic church: A handbook for worship in the home*. Leavenworth, KS: Forest of Peace.

Hays, E. (1998). *Psalms for zero gravity*. Leavenworth, KS: Forest of Peace.

Health Resources and Services Administration. (2006). *Tip sheets: Best practices in bullying prevention and intervention*. Retrieved from http://stopbullyingnow.hrsa.gov/adults/tip-sheets/tip-sheet-23.aspx

Henington, C., Hughes, J. N., Cavell, T. A., & Thompson, B. (1998). The role of relational aggression in identifying aggressive boys and girls. *Journal of School Psychology, 36*, 457–477.

Herr, N. (2007). *Television & health*. Retrieved from http://www.csun.edu/science/health/docs/tv&health.html

Hodges, E. V. E., & Perry, D. G. (1999). Personal and interpersonal antecedents and consequences of victimization by peers. *Journal of Personality and Social Psychology, 76*, 677-685.

Hoover, J. H., Oliver, R., & Thompson, K. A. (1993). Perceived victimization by school bullies: New research and future directions. *Journal of Humanistic Education and Development, 32*, 76-84.

Huesmann, L. R, & Taylor L. D. (2006). The role of media violence in violent behavior. *Annual Review Public Health, 27,* 393-415.

Huston-Stein, A., & Friedrich, L. K. (1972). Television content and young children's social behavior. In J. M. E. Rubinstein & G. Comstock (Eds.), *Television and social behavior* (Vol. 2, pp. 207-317). Washington, DC: U.S. Government Printing Office.

Hyde, J. S. (1984). How large are gender differences in aggression? A developmental meta-analysis. *Developmental Psychology, 20,* 722– 736.

Jacobson, E. (1976). *You must relax: A practical method of reducing the strains of modern living* (5th ed.). New York: McGraw-Hill.

John Paul II. (1988). *Like us in all things except sin.* Retrieved from www.vatican.va/holy_father/john_paul_ii/ audiences/alpha/data/aud19880203en.html

Juvonen, J., & Graham, S. (Eds.). (2001). *Peer harassment in school: The plight of the vulnerable and victimized.* New York: Guilford Press.

Kandersteg Declaration. (2007). Retrieved from http://www.kanderstegdeclaration.com/original in english 2007

Kang, J. W., Kim, H., Cho, S. H., Lee, M. K., Kim, Y. D., Nan, H. M., & Lee, C. H. (2003). The association of subjective stress, urinary catecholamine concentrations and PC game room use and musculoskeletal disorders of the upper limbs in young male Koreans. *Journal of Korean Medical Science, 18,* 419-424.

Kaukiainen, A., Bjorkqvist, K., Osterman, K., & Lagerspetz, K. M. J. (1996). Social intelligence and empathy as antecedents of different types of aggression. In G. Ferris & T. Grisso (Eds.), *Understanding aggressive behavior in children* (pp. 364-366). New York: New York Academy of the Sciences.

Kaukiainen, A., Bjorkqvist, K., Lagerspetz, K. M. J., Osterman, K., Salmivalli, C., & Rothberg, S. (1999). The relationships between social intelligence, empathy, and three types of aggression. *Aggressive Behavior, 25,* 81-89.

Kelly, M. (2002). *Rediscovering Catholicism.* Cincinnati, OH: Beacon Publications.

Kick, F. (2002). *Kick it in: Developing the self-motivation to take the lead* (Vol. 1). Instruction and Design Concepts.

Kidshealth. (2011). *How TV effects your child.* Retrieved from http://kidshealth.org/parent/positive/family/ tv_affects_child.html

Kim, S., Kim, S. H., & Kamphaus, R. (2010). Is aggression the same for boys and girls? Assessing measurement invariance with confirmatory factor analysis and item response theory. *School Psychology Quarterly, 25,* 45-61.

Knoff, H., (2007). Teasing, taunting, bullying, harassment, and aggression: A school-wide approach to prevention, strategic intervention, and crisis management. In J. Zins, M. Elias, C. Maher (Eds.), *Bullying, victimization, and peer harassment: A handbook of prevention and intervention* (pp. 389-412). New York: Haworth Press.

Kochenderfer, B. J., & Ladd, G. W. (1996). Peer victimization: Cause or consequence of school maladjustment. *Child Development, 67,* 1305-1317.

Kochenderfer-Ladd, B. J., & Ladd, G. W. (2001). Variations in peer victimization: Relations to children's maladjustment. In J. Juvonen & S. Graham (Eds.), *Peer harassment in school: The Plight of the vulnerable and victimized* (pp. 310-331). New York: Guilford Press.

Kowalski, R. M., Limber S. P., & Agatston, P. W. (2008). *Cyber bullying.* Malden, MA: Blackwell Publishing.

Kumpulainen, K., Rasanen, E., Henttonen, I., Almqvist, F., Kresanov, K., Linna, S.L., ...Tamminen, T. (1998). Bullying and psychiatric symptoms among elementary school-age children. *Child Abuse and Neglect, 22,* 705–717.

Kumpulainen, K., Rasanen, E., & Henttonen, I. (1999). Children involved in bullying: Psychological disturbance and the persistence of the involvement. *Child Abuse and Neglect, 23*(12), 1253-1262.

Lapsley, M. (2010). Michael Lapsley (South Africa). *The Forgiveness Project.* Retrieved from http://theforgivenessproject.com/stories/michael-lapsley-south-africa/

McNamara, B. E., & McNamara, F. J. (1997). *Keys to dealing with bullies.* New York: Barron's Educational Series.

Menesini, E., Codecasa, E., Benelli, B., & Cowie, H. (2003). Enhancing children's responsibility to take action against bullying: Evaluation of a befriending intervention in Italian middle schools. *Aggressive Behavior, 29,* 1-14.

Menard, S., Grotpeter, J., Gianola, D., & O'Neal, M. (2007). *Evaluation of Bully-Proofing Your School: Final report.* Retrieved from http://www.ncjrs.gov/pdffiles1/nij/grants/221078.pdf

Messer, J., Goodman, R., Rowe, R., Meltzer, H., & Maughan, B. (2006). Preadolescent conduct problems in girls and boys. *Journal of the American Academy of Child & Adolescent Psychiatry, 45,* 184–191.

Mihalic, S., & Aultman-Bettridge, T. (2004). A guide to school-based prevention programs. In W. T. Turk (Ed.), *School crime and policing.* Englewood Cliffs, NJ: Prentice Hall.

Moretti, M. M., Holland, R., & McKay, S. (2001). Self-other representations and relational and overt aggression in adolescent girls and boys. *Behavioral Sciences and the Law, 19,* 109-126.

Nansel, T. R., Overpeck, M., Pilla, R. S., Ruan, W. J., Simons-Morton, B., & Scheidt, P. (2001). Bullying behaviors among U. S. youth: Prevalence and association with psychosocial adjustment. *Journal of the American Medical Association, 285*(16), 2094-2100.

Nassal, J. (2000). *Premeditated mercy.* Leavenworth, KS: Forest of Peace Publishing.

National Center for Educational Statistics (2009). *Indicators of school crime and safety: 2009, Figure 11-4.* Retrieved from http://nces.ed.gov/programs/crimeindicators/crimeindicators2009/figures/figure_11_4.asp

National Conference of Catholic Bishops, Committee on the Liturgy. (1988). *Catholic household blessings and prayers.* Washington, DC: United States Catholic Conference.

National Crime Prevention Council. (2010). *Cyber bullying.* Retrieved from http://www.ncpc.org/cyberbullying/?searchterm=cyberbullying

National Institute of Justice, Office of Justice Programs. (2007). *Restorative justice.* Retrieved from http://www.ojp.usdoj.gov/nij/topics/courts/restorative-justice/welcome.htm

National Television Violence Study. (1996). *National television violence study* (Vol. 1). Thousand Oaks, CA: Sage.

Natvig, G. K., Albrektsen, G., & Qvarnstrom, U. (2001). School-related stress experience as a risk factor for bullying behavior. *Journal of Youth and Adolescence, 30,* 561-575.

O'Connell, P., Pepler, D., & Craig, W., (1999). Peer involvement in bullying: insights and challenges for intervention. *Journal of Adolescence, 22,* 437-452.

O'Donnell, A. M. (1999). *Cognitive perspectives on peer learning.* Mahwah, NJ: Lawrence Erlbaum Associates.

Office of Juvenile and Delinquency Prevention. (2007). Model programs. Retrieved from http://www.ojjdp.gov/mpg/mpgProgramDetails.aspx?ID=382

Olweus, D. (1978). *Aggression in the schools: Bullies and whipping boys.* Washington, DC: Hemisphere Press.

Olweus, D. (1991). Bully/victim problems among schoolchildren: Basic facts and effects of a school based intervention program. In D. J. Pepler & K. H. Rubin (Eds.), *The development and treatment of childhood aggression* (pp. 441-448). Hillsdale, NJ: Lawrence Erlbaum.

Olweus, D. (1993). *Bullying at school: What we know and what we can do.* Cambridge, MA: Blackwell.

Olweus, D. (1994). Annotation: Bullying at school: Basic facts and effects of a school based intervention program. *Association for Child Psychology and Psychiatry, 35,* 1171-1190.

Olweus, D. (1999). Sweden. In P. K. Smith (Eds.), *The nature of school bullying: a cross-national perspective* (pp. 7-27). New York: Routledge.

Olweus, D. (2001). Peer harassment: A critical analysis and some important issues. In J. Juvonen, & S. Graham (Eds.), *Peer harassment in school: The plight of the vulnerable and victimized* (pp. 3-20). New York: Guilford Press.

Olweus, D. (2003). A profile of bullying at school. *Educational Leadership, 60,* 12-18.

Olweus, D., Limber, S., & Mihalic, S. F. (1999). *Bullying prevention program, Blueprints for violence prevention, Book 9.* Boulder, CO: Center for the Study and Prevention of Violence, Institute of Behavioral Science, University of Colorado.

O'Moore, M., & Kirkham, C. (2001). Self-esteem and its relationship to bullying behavior. *Aggressive Behavior, 27,* 269-283.

Ormrod, J. E. (1999). *Human learning* (3rd ed.). Upper Saddle River, NJ: Prentice-Hall.

Orr, T. (2003). *Violence in our schools: Halls of hope, halls of fear.* New York: F. Watts.

Owens, L., Slee, P., & Shute, R. (2001). Victimization among teenage girls. In J. Juvonen, & S. Graham (Eds.), *Peer harassment in school* (pp. 355– 377). New York: Guilford Press.

Paik, H., & Comstock, G. (1994). The effects of television violence on antisocial behavior: A meta-analysis. *Communication Research, 21,* 516-546.

Paul, J., & Cillessen, A. H. N. (2007). Dynamics of peer victimization in early adolescence: Results from a four-year longitudinal study. In J. Zins, M. Elias, & C. Maher (Eds.), *Bullying, victimization, and peer harassment: A handbook of prevention and intervention* (pp. 25-44). New York: Haworth Press.

Pellegrini, A. D., & Long, J. D. (2002). A longitudinal study of bullying, dominance, and victimization, during the transition from primary through secondary school. *British Journal of Developmental Psychology, 20,* 259–280.

Pelligrini, A. D., & Long, J. (2004). Part of the solution and part of the problem: The role of peers in bullying, dominance, and victimization during the transition from primary school through secondary school. In D. L. Espelage & S. M. Swearer (Eds.), *Bullying in American schools: A social-sociological perspective on prevention and intervention* (pp. 107-117). London: Lawrence Erlbaum.

Perry, D. G., Perry, L. C., & Kennedy, E. (1992). Conflict and the development of antisocial behavior. In C. U. Shantz & W. W. Hartup (Eds.), *Conflict in child and adolescent development* (pp. 301-329). New York: Cambridge University Press.

Putallaz, M., Grimes, C. L., Foster, K. J., Kupersmidt, J. B., Coie, J. D., & Dearing, K. (2007). Overt and relational aggression and vicitimization: Multiple perspectives within the school setting. *Journal of School Psychology, 45,* 523–547.

Rahal, M. (2010). *Focus on: Bullying prevention.* Alexandria, VA: Educational Research Service.

Reinberg, S. (2010, January 20). U.S. kids using media almost 8 hours a day. *Bloomberg Business Week.* Retrieved February 2, 2011, from http://www.businessweek.com/

Rigby, K. (1996). *Bullying in schools and what to do about it.* Melbourne: Australian Council for Educational Research.

Rigby, K. (2000). Effects of peer victimization in schools and perceived social support on adolescent well-being. *Journal of Adolescence, 23*, 57-68.

Rigby, K. (2001) Health consequences of bullying and its prevention in schools. In J. Juvonen & S. Graham (Eds.), *Peer harassment in schools: The plight of the vulnerable and victimized* (pp. 310-331). New York: Guilford Press.

Rigby, K. (2002) Bullying in childhood. In P. K. Smith & C. H. Hart (Eds.), *Blackwell handbook of childhood social development* (pp. 549-568). Malden, MA: Blackwell Publishers.

Rigby, K., & Johnson, B. (2006). Expressed readiness of Australian schoolchildren to act as bytanders in support of children who are being bullied. *Educational Psychology, 26*, 425–440.

Rivers, I., & Smith, P. K. (1994). Types of bullying behavior and their correlates. *Aggressive Behavior, 220*, 359-368.

Roland, E. (1989). A system-oriented strategy against bullying. In E. Roland & E. Munthe (Eds.), *Bullying: An interventional perspective* (pp. 143-151). London: David Fulton

Russell, P. (2003). *Acceleration: The quickening pace*. Retrieved from http://www.peterrussell.com/WUIT/Accel.php

Salmivalli, C. (2001). Group view on victimization: Empirical findings and their implications. In J. Juvonen & S. Graham (Eds.), *Peer harassment in school: The plight of the vulnerable and the victimized* (pp. 398-419). New York: Guilford.

Salmivalli, C. (2010). Bullying and the peer group: A review. *Aggression and Violent Behavior, 15*, 112–120.

Salmivalli, C., Kaukiainen, A., Kaistaniemi, L., & Lagerspetz, K. M. (1999). Self-evaluated self-esteem, peer-evaluated self-esteem, and defensive egotism as predictors of adolescents' participation in bullying situations. *Personality and Social Psychology Bulletin, 25*, 1268-1278.

Salmivalli, C., Lagerspetz, K., Bjuorkqvist, K., Osterman, K., & Kaukianinen, A. (1996). Bullying as a group process: Participants and their relations to social status within the group. *Aggressive Behavior, 22*, 1-15.

Sangwon, K., Seock-Ho, K., & Kamphaus, R. W. (2010). Is aggression the same for boys and girls? Assessing measurement invariance with confirmatory factor analysis and item response theory. *School Psychology Quarterly, 25*, 45-61.

Schaeffer, C. M., Petras, H., Ialongo, N., Masyn, K. E., Hubbard, S., ...Kellam, S. (2006). A comparison of girls' and boys' aggressive–disruptive behavior trajectories across elementary school: Prediction to young adult antisocial outcomes. *Journal of Consulting and Clinical Psychology, 74*, 500–510.

Schmitz, C., & Hipp, E. (1987). *A teacher's guide to fighting invisible tigers*. Minneapolis, MN: Free Spirit.

Schuster, B. (1999). Outsiders at school: The prevalence of bullying and its relation with school status. *Group Process and Intergroup Relations, 2*(2), 175-190.

Simmons, R. (2002). *Odd girl out: The hidden culture of aggression in girls*. New York: Harcourt.

Skiba, R., Poloni-Staudinger, L., Gallini, S., Simmons, A., & Feggins-Azziz, R. (2006). Disparate access: The disproportionality of African American students with disabilities across educational environments. *Exceptional Children, 72*, 411–24.

Slee, P. T. (1995). Peer victimization and its relationship to depression among Australian primary school students. *Personality and Individual Differences, 18*, 57-62.

Slee, P. T., & Rigby, K. (1993). Australian school children's self-appraisal of interpersonal relations: The bullying experience. *Child Psychiatry and Human Development, 23*(4), 273-282.

Solarz, A. (Ed.). (2002). *An annotated bibliography on the implications of interactive media for adolescents*. Washington, DC: American Psychological Association.

Stepanek. M. (2002). *Hope through heartsongs*. New York: Hyperion.

Stockdale, M., Hangaduambo, S., Duys, D., Larson, K., & Sarvela, P. (2002). Rural elementary students', parents', and teachers' perceptions of bullying. *American Journal of Health Behavior, 26*, 266-277.

Stuecker, R. (2010). *Inspiring leadership in teens: Group activities to foster integrity, responsibility, and compassion*. Champaign, IL: Research Press.

Susman, E. J., & Pajer, K. (2004). Biology-behavior integration and antisocial behavior in girls. In M. Putallaz & K. L. Bierman (Eds.), *Aggression, antisocial behavior, and violence among girls* (pp. 23-47). New York: Guilford Press.

Sutton, J., & Keogh, E. (2000). Social competition in school: Relationships with bullying, Machiavellianism, and personality. *British Journal of Educational Psychology, 7*, 443-56.

Swearer, S. M., & Espelage, D. L. (2004). Introduction: A socialecological framework of bullying among youth. In D. L. Espelage & S. M. Swearer (Eds.), *Bullying in American schools: A social-ecological perspective on prevention and intervention* (pp. 1-12). Mahwah, NJ: Lawrence Erlbaum.

Tattum, D., & Tattum, E. (1992). *Social education and personal development*. London: David Fulton.

Taylor, J., Gilligan, C., & Sullivan, A. (1995). *Between voice and silence: Women and girls, race and relationships*. Cambridge, MA: Harvard University Press.

Tejeiro Salguero, R. A., & Moran, R. M. (2002). Measuring problem video game playing in adolescents. *Addiction, 97*, 1601-1606.

Thomas, S. P. (2003). Identifying and intervening with girls at risk for violence. *Journal of School Nursing, 19*(3), 130-139.

Tomada, G., & Schneider, B. H. (1997). Relational aggression, gender, and peer acceptance: Invariance across culture, stability over time, and concordance among informants. *Developmental Psychology, 33*, 601–609.

TuTu, D. (1999). *No future without forgiveness*. New York: Doubleday.

Twenge, J. M., & Campbell, K. (2009). *Living in the age of entitlement: The narcissism epidemic*. New York: Free Press.

United States Catholic Conference. (1968). *Mandate of the Committee on Ecumenical and Interreligious Affairs*. Retrieved from http://www.usccb.org/seia/history.shtml

United States Conference of Catholic Bishops. (2002). *New American Bible*. Washington, DC: Author.

United States Conference of Catholic Bishops. (2006). *United States Catholic catechism for adults*. Washington, DC: Author.

Underwood, M. K. (2003). *Social aggression among girls*. New York: Guildford.

Unnever, J. D., (2005). Bullies, aggressive victims, and victims: Are they distinct groups? *Aggressive Behavior, 31*, 153-171.

U.S. Department of Education. (2001). *Exemplary and promising safe, disciplined, and drug-free schools programs*. Retrieved from http://www2.ed.gov/admins/lead/safety/exemplary01/exemplary01.pdf

Vail, K. (2009). *Bullying: From words to action*. American School. Retrieved from http://asbj.com/TopicsArchive/Bullying/Bullying-From-Words-to-Action.aspx

Vatican II Council. (1966). *Pastoral Constitution on the Church in the modern world.* New York: Guild Press.

Whitted, K.S., & Dupper, D. R. (2005). Best practices for preventing or reducing bullying in schools. *Children & Schools, 27*(3), 167-175.

Willard, N. (2006). *Cyber bullying and cyberthreats: Responding to the challenge of online social cruelty, threats, and distress.* Eugene, OR: Center for Safe and Responsible Internet Use.

Williams, K. D., Cheung, C. K. T., & Choi, W. (2000). CyberOstracism: Effects of being ignored over the Internet. *Journal of Personality and Social Psychology, 79,* 748-762.

Wiseman, R. (2002). *Queen bees & wannabes: Helping your daughter survive cliques, gossip, boyfriends, and other realities of adolescence.* New York: Three Rivers Press.

Wolke, D., Woods, S., Bloomfield, L., & Karstadt, L. (2000). The association between direct and relational bullying and behavior problems among primary school children. *Journal of Child Psychology and Psychiatry, 41,* 989-1002.

Wooden, C. (2010, February 8). Cardinal asks dialogue partners if an ecumenical catechism might work. *Catholic News Service.* Retrieved from http://www.catholicnews.com/data/stories/cns/1000540.htm

Ybarra, M. L., & Mitchell, K. J. (2004). Online aggressor/targets, aggressors and targets: A comparison of associated youth characteristics. *Journal of Child Psychology and Psychiatry, 45,* 1308-1316.

Zins, J., Elias, M., & Maher, C. (Eds.). (2007). *Bullying, victimization, and peer harassment: A handbook of prevention and intervention.* New York: Haworth Press.

Diocese of Toledo
Catholic School Credo

As Catholic School Educators

We believe our Catholic School is not only a school,
but a community of faith;

We believe those entrusted to us are not only students,
but children of God;

We believe we are not only educators,
but Ministers of the Gospel;

We believe the values we teach are not only character development,
but a call to Holiness;

We believe our courses of study are not only academic pursuits,
but a search for Truth;

We believe the purpose of education is not only
for personal gain and the development of society,
but for the Transformation of the world.

About the Authors

Frank A. DiLallo received a B.A. degree in Sociology from Adrian College in 1980 and his M.Ed. in Guidance & Counseling from the University of Toledo in 1982. He holds licensure in Ohio as a Professional Counselor and Independent Chemical Dependency Counselor and is certified as a Prevention Specialist II. Frank has over 30 years of experience and training in prevention, intervention, and treatment of alcohol, tobacco, and other drugs and violence.

Frank has served the Catholic Diocese of Toledo since 1990. Currently, he serves as the Safe & Drug Free Schools Consultant and Diocesan Case Manager for 81 diocesan schools preK-12 and 131 parishes in 19 counties of Northwest Ohio. Founder of Counseling & Training Services, Frank previously maintained a private counseling practice serving the greater Toledo area for over 20 years. He has also conducted countless professional development trainings for educators and counselors on a variety of topics, including bullying. Frank is a frequent public speaker and trainer in both private and public sectors including regional, state, and national conferences.

Raised Lutheran, Frank's faith journey called him to convert to Catholicism. Co-author Thom Powers was one of Frank's sponsors and is a wonderful mentor and friend who truly embodies what it means to be Christ-like. Through his constant loving presence and demonstrations of kindness, Thom reveals for everyone he meets, the grace and healing power of our risen savior Jesus Christ. It was during Frank's conversion experience that he was led to create compassionate approaches to bullying and other forms of peer abuse. Married to his loving and supportive wife, Michelle, he is inspired by family, friends, and colleagues. As the father of three sons and a daughter, Frank has a special interest in seeing all youth be at their best. He enjoys time with family, hiking, and being a lifelong learner. For information on his speaking, trainings, and workshops, please visit http://www.peace2usolutions.com

Thom Powers attended the former St. Mary's College Seminary in Kentucky and St. Maur's School of Theology in Indianapolis, Indiana. Leaving prior to receiving orders in 1969, he entered the workforce, yet never lost touch with religious education. Working production, he picked up the titles of "padre" and "unofficial chaplain" among co-workers. From this experience, Thom realized the deep hunger for richer spirituality among adults, especially for men. Having served as a speaker on the diocesan speaker roster for Sacramental preparation, Thom's specialty has been adult education. Along with his wife, Dianne, Thom spent over 20 years in religious education with an inner-city parish in the Diocese of Toledo. More recently, Thom has been working with pastoral councils and the spiritual dimension of their ministries. He was the first lay president for the Board of Trustees of Our Lady of the Pines Retreat Center in Fremont, Ohio, and is currently serving in an advisory capacity.

It is a rare opportunity when an Italian, named Francis (Frank), asks you to work for peace. This was a personal invitation to become an "instrument of peace." Weaving Scripture, theology, and spirituality into an already dynamic communal process of addressing the bullying dynamic is a powerful tool for teachers and counselors within Catholic schools.

Thom and Dianne have been married 39 years, parents to two married daughters, and have three grandchildren. "Peace be with you."

CPSIA information can be obtained at www.ICGtesting.com
Printed in the USA
LVOW031146150312

273155LV00003B/1/P